CW00458215

FOURSQUARE
The Last Parachutist

George Bearfield

Published by Thought Four Ltd 2021
All rights reserved
ISBN 978-1-5272-8656-6
Copyright © George Bearfield 2021

No part of this book may be reproduced or transmitted in any form or by any means, electronic or mechanical, including photocopying or recording, or by an information storage and retrieval system without permission in writing from the publisher.
Cover design by Nick Trivuncic

Typewriter font is 'Urania Czech' and is licensed from Lukas Krakora

First Published in Great Britain in 2021 by Thought Four Ltd

The Truth Prevails

PROLOGUE

At the start of May 1945, World War Two was reaching its climax and Europe was at a point of transition. With the destruction of Nazi Germany, two nascent superpowers were hurtling towards each other from opposite sides of the continent, their likely meeting place: Prague. Edvard Beneš, the Czechoslovak President - who had laboured tirelessly in exile for his country's sovereignty - was at this time approaching his nation's capital from the east, embedded with the Red Army. But his hope was secretly with the United States, whose forces were massing on his western border. An uprising by his countrymen would give the American forces an excuse to enter Prague before the Soviets and allow Beneš to take political control. But his people were fearful after years of subjugation and would need encouragement to rise up against the remnants of the German Army. On the night of May 4, an RAF airplane containing four Czech soldiers took off from Dijon with a secret instruction from Beneš to provide that encouragement.

1

As the plane arrived at its dropping point ahead of the US 3rd Army's planned path to Prague, the group's leader, Jaroslav Bublík, rested his back against the body of the plane, took a deep breath and felt the rattling drone of its engines shuddering through him. He looked across the cabin at his team. He was only a handful of years older than them, but he had lived a lifetime in those brief years. He had seen imprisonment and war. And he had done his apprenticeship in the intelligence services, party to the most momentous actions his country had seen.

He felt the weight of the gold sovereigns carried tight to his chest and was reminded of the cyanide tablet tucked away at his other breast. He looked across the bulkhead to the hold and the crates that would be parachuted down with them. They contained their radio set, their stores and provisions, and even a tub of renardine to hide their scent from Gestapo dogs after they hit the ground. But buried amongst all of that were the most essential items they carried for their mission: four silenced machine guns. As the call came from the plane's navigator, Bublík climbed to his feet and his movements became choreographed to their long-practised plan.

HOME

'Domov'. It means 'my home' in Czech, and the word formed a distinctive and familiar sight on the door of my grandfather's bungalow. Each letter was hand-carved from a block of wood and painted white, joined together by the continuous flow of their italic script. Like the house the sign adorned, it had been fashioned by hand and with no little skill. My grandfather had come to this anonymous corner of Lincolnshire (on the eastern coast of England) in the mid-1970s as a retired civil servant and decided that he would build himself a house on a plot of land he'd bought right next to the village post office. And so he did. He designed it, dug the foundations, laid the bricks, pitched the roof, and did the electrics. All on his own. The locals thought this stocky foreigner was more than a little crazy to start with as they saw him happily turn up on site day after day, in all weathers. But, as the house steadily, painstakingly took shape, he earned their respect and interest. By the time I came here for the first time, as a child in the late 1970s, the house had been finished for some time and he'd had become part of the fixtures and fittings of this small seaside village.

I stretched out my finger and pressed the doorbell so hard my finger bowed, causing a weedy electrical buzz to sound. After a pause I heard a bustle of sounds at the door and saw a shape fluttering behind its textured glass panel as my grandmother fumbled with the lock. They were expecting me. I'd called my grandfather a few days before. He'd not been that well for several years now. A succession of strokes and heart attacks in the previous years had diminished him in many ways but in doing so had taken the edge from his once ferocious temper. I'd decided that if I was ever going to get answers to the riddles and rumours that had surrounded him and his life history, I would have to do it soon. And not just by innocently asking: "Granddad, what did you do in the war?" That would draw a blunt quip. Either that, or a raised eyebrow and an invisible shrug without looking up from his book. I would have to show that I was serious in my interest. That my grandfather had taken part in some daring and deeply significant actions in the Second World War was an accepted truth in our family. Somehow we collectively understood that he had been a parachutist and had been dropped behind enemy lines, but no one knew exactly how they knew this or anything more specific. It had been intuited over fifty years of halted conversations, knowing looks and the certain knowledge that 'he doesn't like talking about it.' My grandmother would refer to things occasionally, like the Czech exiles they knew after the War, but nothing she said ever seemed to shed any light on what specifically my grandfather had done in his military career, or even where he had been. She was much more interested in speaking about how he

4

charmed her in the very final days of the War; a whirlwind romance that led to a quick marriage, moving abroad and mixing in senior diplomatic circles. There were more specific clues over the years though. One night when I was about ten, I heard the women of the family in the kitchen of my grandfather's house discussing in semi-muted tones how there was a film on the TV that night which was about his cousin – Josef; a Czechoslovak war hero who had been his dearest friend. I was too young to stay up but my brother, who was three years older, somehow managed to. The film had Martin Shaw from the TV cop show "The Professionals" in it, he said the next day. It was about some Czech soldiers who parachuted from England and shot Reinhard Heydrich – a big Nazi officer. Granddad's cousin "wasn't in it much" but he was mentioned by name - my Granddad's name: Bublík – in one scene. Sparse information, but it was more than enough to spark my interest.

After that, I developed a deep fascination with this tale of Czechoslovak heroism and my family's part in it; over the years my interest grew as I did. I picked up sparse knowledge about it from documentaries, or in later years by scouring libraries and bookstores. But in the weeks before my visit I had made it my quest to understand more: devouring all I could find out about the topic, the story of the German occupation of Czechoslovakia, and all about Heydrich. He had many nicknames, none of which painted a pleasant picture: 'the blonde beast'; 'the butcher of Prague'; 'the hangman of Bohemia and Moravia.' Heydrich had formalised the Nazis 'final solution,' chairing the Wannsee conference that agreed the details of the pitiless slaughter of Europe's Jewish populations with the calm and formality of a routine town council meeting. The thought that my grandfather and his cousin had played even a small part in tackling this soulless gangster was an immense source of pride and I wanted to piece the story together. But with his health in steady decline I knew that my time was running out. I'd finally called him about a week before to tell him I'd been doing some research and that I was interested in understanding more about what he and his cousin had done, and where they'd been during the War. There was no quip this time. Just a pause before he spoke:

"Yes...we can talk a little about that."

As I entered the front room, he greeted me with a visible flush of happiness and stood briskly but unsteadily as I clasped his hand and squeezed his dry chunky fingers; his grip still firmer than one would expect of a man of his age. He sank back into his sofa carefully and I lowered myself onto the matching chair adjacent to him.

"How is job going?"

I was working as an engineer just outside Leighton Buzzard in Bedfordshire, on an industrial estate near a small place called Hockliffe.

"I'm thinking about moving on. I'm not sure they really know what to do with me and I've got the experience on my CV now. I might look for a job in London."

He nodded slowly. "What about your doctorate?"

This would usually have been a loaded question. Academia had an allure for him and he had always had some unfulfilled ambitions in that area himself. He had once told me about a trip to the University of London to play their chess team when he worked at the Post Office in London. It was graduation time and he had noted the gravity with which the senior academics had moved around the campus.

"So pompous in their gowns."

But there was a tinge of admiration in this tone and words.

"Czechoslovakia was founded by Professors you know."

I did know. He had told me many times. But he wasn't in such a talkative mood yet today and after a pause I realised his question was still hanging in the air.

"I'd have to give that up. If I left the company the university wouldn't continue to support it."

He looked doubtful. "Are you sure about that one?"

I smiled but didn't immediately answer. He wasn't going to put up a fight.

#

The history of Czechoslovakia is a history that sprung from its Geography. Its centrality in Europe positioned it geographically, culturally and politically between the West and the East. The nineteenth century Prussian statesman Otto Von Bismarck is rumoured to have said, "Who rules Bohemia rules Europe," and this is a mantra that is well understood by the Slavic people of the Czech and Slovak lands. Their experience is one of constant struggle and long periods of domination by their neighbours, with their fate continually decided in larger power struggles. However, by the end of the nineteenth century, the Austro-Hungarian Empire of which the Czechs and Slovaks had been part for over two hundred and fifty years, was coming to an end with the First World War.

Spotting the opportunity that this conflict created, a Czech academic – Tomáš Garrigue Masaryk - and his number two Edvard Beneš, made their move to assert the establishment of Czecho-Slovakia as an independent, sovereign, Slavic state. Developing a strategic blueprint that would have strong echoes in subsequent struggles, they exiled themselves and built strong relations with key foreign countries: Great Britain, France, Russia and the United States. Their central European base allowed them to have a significant impact in gathering intelligence, and they organised independent Czechoslovak forces abroad, culminating in the creation of the Czechoslovak legion – a battalion of troops to fight with the Russians against Austro-Hungary– in 1914.

My great grandfather, Martin Bublík, was a farmer in a small village called Banov, in Moravia - the central portion of the new country - close to its border with Slovakia. He had been drafted into the Great War as a subject of Austro-Hungary, however in a clear indication of his loyalties, he soon deserted from the army, unwilling to fight against his Slavic brothers in Russia. Many others shared his views and the empire dissipated at the close of the War. Masaryk and Beneš' strategy ultimately proved successful and Masaryk was elected President three days after the guns fell silent in 1918. Martin Bublík certainly cheered as loud as any, when this new state of independent Czechs and Slovaks was born with a man from nearby Hodonín at its head.

Masaryk was a rationalist philosopher and a humanist. He was also an early proponent of feminism – taking the maiden name of his American born wife 'Garrigue' as a gesture to this effect. In line with his philosophies and viewpoints, he sought to create a country founded on faith but not a slave to the church; a country built on socialist revolution, but democratic rather than communist and one built on healthy national pride, not bigotry or hatred of others. His vision was to unify the Czech and Slovak people into a new nation, mixing the energy and legacy of national myths of nationhood with more forward-thinking liberal characteristics.

The shared history of the Czech and Slovak people had created a sense of national pride, a natural brotherhood and kinship with each other and Slavs in other nations (the Poles, Yugoslavs and Russians), a healthy disrespect for authority, (particularly that of the Catholic Church, which had exerted control over the Czech and Slovak lands over many years) and a deep-seated love of learning for all, peasant and non-peasant: girl and boy.

So in the period of my grandfather's youth, there was a golden era for the people of Czechoslovakia. The country had emerged from the First World War as a modern liberal democracy and was flourishing. Its inheritances from Austro-Hungary made it one of the most industrialised countries in the world, renowned for its engineering, its glassware, its beer, and its culture.

\#

"What do you want to be then?"

"I don't know…I'll be a 'fat cat'."

He laughed, looking quite satisfied with this answer. "I've been reading about these 'fat cats' he said, rolling the words playfully around his tongue. "Well, you know what you want to do," he said with resignation. "It's all a bit beyond me now."

There was an awkward pause. I turned to see my grandmother setting a cup of tea down with an unsteady hand, leaving it tottering on a low stack of books.

"Can I get your photos out?" I asked quietly. My grandfather nodded and I went to the cupboard at the front window and pulled out a well-worn green folder stuffed full of photos, cards and papers.

#

As a loyal follower of Masaryk and a Czech patriot, Martin Bublík raised his six children in his own image. His youngest son, Jaroslav, was a late variant in his efforts to create model citizens of the new republic. As a boy, Jaroslav was enrolled as an enthusiastic member of the local 'Sokol' club. The Sokols - Czech for 'Falcon' – engaged in gymnastics training, weightlifting and other physical endeavours to build their physical strength and fitness. The objective was to have a sound mind and body but also to be 'good Czechoslovaks' and patriots and the clubs were flourishing all over the new country. Although officially non-political, they were vehemently anti-Catholic in their ethos, seeing the Church as the instrument through which their country's subjugation and domination had been achieved over many years. In his final year of high school, young Jaroslav had come to think so strongly about the injustice of this history that he decided to make a public speech in Banov town square. Standing on a box, he expressed forthright views about the corruption of the Catholic Church, and spoke of his support for Jan Hus, the Bohemian protestant martyr who was burned at the stake in the fifteenth century for expressing similar views. This earned him an immediate expulsion from his Catholic school but also made young Jaroslav something of a local hero – my Czech cousin told me that the incident was still talked about some seventy years later. I suspect Martin Bublík was torn between feelings of anger and admiration for his son at this turn of events.

I flicked through the photo album gently and respectfully. Photos were assembled and affixed carefully, broadly in chronological order. Skimming through the familiar pictures of my grandfather as a youth, I traced my finger across each photo, looking for his face in the shot. I stopped on one of him at junior school: looking uncomfortable, with a tie tightly wound round his neck. Then across the page I fixed on one of my favourites. It shows him lined up in a field with a handful of his fellow Sokol members. The boys look to be about thirteen or fourteen and are bare-chested, wearing knee length white shorts which are frayed at the bottom. My grandfather is fourth from the left, staring back at me defiantly with his hair shorn much closer than the others. He is not tall but stands upright, showing a certain cockiness. Like the others, he doesn't look particularly well-fed but he is more muscled and naturally thicker in the leg. Even at this young age, he clearly had a steeliness to him.

I remembered his stories of the difficulties they had at this time. How he would take carrots straight out of the ground and eat them, dirt and all. His taste for what he called 'Kiska' - the sour milk which was all that was practically available - and how there was usually only bread to eat, not meat. These challenges and the effort needed to meet them, are burnt into his eyes.

I looked up at my grandfather and opened my mouth to quiz him about his early life. But I quickly shut it again as I remembered that he was a little like a jukebox when it came to his favourite old stories and I had heard them all before. They would only take time away from the other questions I needed to ask. So I decided not to put my dime in the slot just yet.

"When I was your age," he often used to say to me in my school days, "I would be up that tree, like a monkey, before you could say 'Jack Robinson.'" He had tried in vain to teach me to walk on my hands and managed a pretty good demonstration for a man of his advancing years. My siblings and I had coped better with the low stilts he had made for us from scrap wood, counting almost to a hundred on some occasions before eventually stumbling to the floor. I was aware that the parallel bars had been his forte and this had led to a demonstration, when he was in his mid-seventies, involving him gripping the arms of adjacent sofa chairs with his legs extended out in front of him as his face flushed a deep red. Fortunately, I think even he now recognised that his gymnastic days were over.

#

Masaryk and Beneš knew that Czechoslovakia's precarious geographical position - sandwiched between major world powers and jutting into the side of Germany - meant that guile and cunning would be needed if the country was to mature through adolescence into adulthood. The period after the First World War was therefore one of strategic consolidation. Tomáš Masaryk had ensured the independence of his country by agreeing borders for it which provided the most militarily defensible position. However, the border lands of this new state (in the Czech regions of Bohemia, Moravia and Silesia) contained significant ethnic German populations. The Czech and German populations had always co-existed, but the ethnic Germans would have to adjust to German disempowerment; their status in the new country would not be the same. Tomáš Masaryk established a modern, social democratic constitution which protected the rights of all ethnic minority populations, however as the majority the Czechs, and to a lesser extent the Slovaks, were now ultimately in power. Initially, many of the German speaking population were comfortable with the arrangements, particularly those who were in business; there were advantages of not being in competition with their more advanced neighbours in Germany. However, from the outset Masaryk and Beneš were very alert to the dangers that a resurgent Germany could present, and the impact of this on their ethnic German population.

Czechoslovakia's proximity to other major countries made it an excellent place to gather intelligence on the key movements within Europe and in particular of its German neighbour. Masaryk and Beneš therefore sought to maximise this advantage by enhancing the county's intelligence capability. The task was given to a man called František Moravec. Moravec had been a philosophy student of Tomáš Masaryk's before the First World War, with aspirations to follow his teacher into a career in academia. However, when the First World War broke out, he was somewhat unwillingly drafted into the army to fight for Austro-Hungary against the Allies: France, Great Britain and Russia.

Like Masaryk and Beneš, Moravec saw the collapse of the Habsburg empire of Austro-Hungary as an unmissable opportunity to finally deliver the self-rule over their homeland that the Czechs and Slovaks had been struggling for, for centuries. So as a young cadet officer in 1916, Moravec – like my great grandfather Martin Bublík - made the decision to desert from the Austro-Hungarian army. He crossed enemy lines with his platoon to surrender and offer his services to fight with Russia. This led to service in the Russian 'Czech legion,' fighting his former rulers on the Western Front and in Greece. Moravec distinguished himself as a soldier and eventually found himself part of the presidential guard for Tomáš Masaryk as he entered Prague in 1918. His old Professor was now the leader of the newly liberated Czechoslovakia and the whole country was giddy with excitement at what had been achieved.

After the First World War, Moravec settled into a successful military career, working to help secure the new country. Although this meant an end to his academic aspirations, it was a role with purpose which he enjoyed for many years. It was in 1929 that he was called upon to revamp the county's dormant and outdated intelligence service. Moravec was not initially enamoured with this opportunity; an intelligence posting was not seen as an honourable one to many military men. But he turned to the task with resolve and steadily professionalised the intelligence bureau. As his early years in post progressed he brought in increasing numbers of high value agents from across the border in Germany and completely modernised working practices. Beneš and Masaryk had chosen well.

\#

I picked up my teacup and noticed that the book below was in a foreign language – Serbo-Croat based on a glance at the dictionary lying adjacent to it on the coffee table. This was quite typical. Even at his advanced age, my grandfather was still seeking to deepen his knowledge of languages. He spoke six fluently and had a working knowledge of several more. I glanced up at the painting which always held pride of place on his sitting room wall: an oil painting of his school in Banov, with all of the children filing out in an orderly fashion in traditional Moravian attire, a serene duckpond in the foreground. He had been a good student from a very respectable family. On his mother's side they were Baráneks, and his maternal grandfather had been the Mayor of Banov. That was one of the reasons why his soapbox oratory in the town square (and subsequent expulsion) had been so controversial: it was scandal and heresy combined.

Despite his good education and linguistic skills, his relationship with English could best be described as functional. The languages he was most comfortable with were those it had been essential for him to know - Czech, German and Russian. He was a relative latecomer to English and the tongue of his adoptive home never sat entirely comfortably with him. Like many of his Slavic kin, he rarely used the definite article in his conversation and his W's were always pronounced as hard V's. All these years after his arrival his accent was still as thick as a Czech dumpling.

#

Over time, developments across the new border in Germany began to alter the dynamics of the uneasy truce between Czechoslovakia and its German speaking populace. The Treaty of Versailles, signed at the end of the First World War, had required Germany to fully disarm, give up significant territorial claims (including those within the new Czechoslovakia) and to pay reparations to the victors. The terms were certainly demanding and in the 1930s, as the Great Depression hit Germany hard, the population became frustrated and angry. An extreme right-wing populist and ideologue, Adolf Hitler positioned himself and his nationalist socialist (Nazi) party on the crest of this wave of disaffection.

In 1931, Moravec's team infiltrated the 'Volksport' group in the Sudetenland, on the Czech side of the border with Germany. The 'Volksport' was essentially a homegrown version of the Nazi 'brown shirts,' who were doing Adolf Hitler's dirty work in Germany. Through an informant, Moravec discovered that the group was forming a military plan - in cooperation with the Nazis - to subvert Czech rule in its key defensive border area. Through Moravec's work, the key culprits were arrested and convicted. The resulting court case woke many in Czechoslovakia up to the growing threat of German aggression. As Hitler came to power in 1933, Moravec continued to extend the breadth and quality of his intelligence and of his understanding of the precise nature of German rearmament.

In 1933, parliamentary rule was overthrown in Germany and Hitler was installed as Chancellor and dictator of a one-party state. The country was strongly united behind Hitler's Nazis in its delusion, hatred and xenophobia, and in asserting the superiority of ethnic Germans. The conditions of Versailles were rapidly unpicked, and Germany ceased reparations and began to openly re-arm. As Hitler increased his lobbying and demands to begin redrawing national borders, the German speaking population of Czechoslovakia – by now collectively referred to as the 'Sudeten Germans' – were a prime audience for his messages. Empowered by developments, many became rabid Nazis.

In December 1935, as Beneš and Masaryk became utterly convinced that a second world war was inevitable, an ageing Masaryk stepped down from office and Beneš took his place as the second President of the republic. Political events were moving quickly across continental Europe, with both fascism and communism on the rise and Czechoslovakia becoming increasingly tense for its future.

#

"You know it's very strange you working in Hockliffe," he eventually continued, brightening. "I was based there during the war. Just where you are."

I had a flicker of excitement and a little apprehension as I was reminded of my mission for the day. "Yes…I remember that you said that. What were you doing there again?"

"I worked at the radio station there. We kept in touch with the Czech embassies in Europe and with the underground in Czecho. It was just some huts in a field. My friend Novák still lives near there. In Dunstable."

I prepared myself to pounce on this but as I opened my mouth for the follow up question, the words I heard were my grandmother's, not my own.

"Oliver Twist…"

I turned. My mouth was still open but my brain was now completely disconnected.

"That's where the workhouse was supposed to be in Oliver Twist," she continued "…in Dunstable."

"Have you heard from Novák lately, Jarda?"

I sank back in my seat while they began to speak – the moment now completely lost.

#

In early 1937, with the need for intelligence only increasing, Moravec had a stroke of fortune that was so remarkable, and so far-reaching, as to restore ones faith in the destiny of the world. He received an unsolicited letter in the mail, seemingly from a high-ranking German military officer, offering high grade military intelligence for a not inconsiderable fee. This sort of direct approach was highly suspicious in the intelligence world, indicating a trap of some type. However, the nature of the information promised was of such potential significance to the defence of his country, that Moravec overruled the advice of his senior advisors and despite the risks replied to the letter. After a period of correspondence, Moravec decided to meet the agent himself in the square of Kraslice, a town near the German border. The man, who came to be known to intelligence services by the code name A-54, introduced himself as Karl, and from his bearing and the information he imparted, Moravec very quickly established that he was genuine. A high-ranking member of the Abwehr – the German military intelligence - he was committed to providing high grade intelligence, with the intent to fatally undermine the plans of Adolf Hitler. Moravec had tapped into a seam of intelligence information so rich that he could scarcely believe it. It ranged from information on key military hardware production and troop build-up, to eventually covering detailed invasion plans.

It was through this network that Beneš' suspicions were confirmed and he was made fully aware of Adolf Hitler's private intentions for Czechoslovakia. He immediately began using this intelligence to alert other nations to the growing threat, the need for resolve in meeting their treaty obligations to protect his country from invasion, and to guard against what he saw as the inevitable wider European war that would follow.

EXILE

As my grandmother departed the room again, I felt it was the right time for a concerted push on my questioning. So, cutting a swathe through our family culture, I finally asked that first fateful question.

"How did you come to leave Czechoslovakia at the start of the War?"

A pause, and shallow breath came before any words. He nodded gently, in recognition that he had remembered my phone call.

"When Germans came, I was taken by them and put into labour camp."

"Where was that?"

"…near Kiel."

I searched my brain for some knowledge about Kiel and almost nothing came back.

"Where's Kiel?" I asked immediately, my keenness to understand dwarfing any embarrassment at my ignorance.

"…In northern Germany. Camp was about four kilometres from the Danish border."

A few words only – but they triggered a flurry of thoughts and half-formed questions. In particular, this was a very long way from my grandfather's hometown of Banov. I sensed a significant story here all of its own.

#

As the 1930's progressed, Tomáš Masaryk and Edvard Beneš watched the rise of Hitler from their front row seat in Prague with a mixture of horror and realpolitik planning. They had predicted this situation but to see it unfold was no less chilling for that. The two men led tireless activity to strengthen the resolve of the great powers from the First World War (Great Britain, France, the United States and the Soviet Union) and to keep together the alliance that had defeated Germany twenty short years before. But these countries were weary, depleted and understandably feared another world war more than anything.

If Czechoslovakia was to be saved and another world war averted, the big powers would have to stand up to Hitler. Its security was fundamentally underpinned by a treaty with France requiring each country to come to the defence of the other in the event of an attack from a third party. France had similar treaties with Russia and Great Britain, so its actions would be critical.

Situated on the map as they were, jutting into Germany's side, Czechoslovakia's future would be decided soon. But Beneš and Masaryk were not warmongers. They continued to discuss possible concessions to the Nazis and the Sudeten German population, despite being increasingly sure that war was coming. Spurred on by continuing appeasement and disengagement from their allies, they set about making preparations for their future. By the late 1930s, they had twenty divisions of troops in place, had heavily fortified their defensive borders and making use of their admirable engineering capability, had equipped themselves with the best modern weaponry; the Škoda Works in Pilsen was the largest arms manufacturer in Austria-Hungary and a hugely significant asset. But more than that – much more - they had succeeded in creating a passionate crop of citizens and soldiers who were ready to fight to maintain their freedom and independence. The Czechoslovak army had a profound faith in the integrity of its countries principles and constitution. Many of the soldiers were also armed with the mental and physical discipline that was intrinsic to Sokol membership.

In December 1936, Hitler sent two envoys to Beneš, expecting him to ally Czechoslovakia to Germany by signing a mutual non-aggression pact. The German tactics here were to seek to separate Czechoslovakia from its allies in the East and the West, and then to use its fifth column within the country to subvert it to Nazism over time. Given Hitler's ultimate aim to wipe out democracy and dominate Europe, signing this pact would have meant Beneš betraying not just his allies but also the sacred principles he shared with his mentor Masaryk. Beneš was not physically imposing but when he turned his intellect to the task, and with the force of truth behind him, he could be eye-wateringly frank. In a unique show of defiance against Hitler, he sent the envoys away with a very straight set of answers that were consistent with Czechoslovakia's position as an independent sovereign state. He was keen to reach an agreement but would do nothing that contradicted his existing treaties and alliances; the status of the

Sudeten Germans was an internal matter for Czechoslovakia to resolve which he could discuss but would not negotiate on. As regards any redrawing of the borders between their countries, this would only arise as the result of a war he did not want but was prepared to fight.

Hitler's men left shocked and disgruntled and never returned. From that time, Hitler railed against Beneš as his greatest enemy and publicly expressed a desire to fight him to the death. This stand left Beneš entirely reliant on his allies. As German rearmament gathered pace, Moravec continued to share his high grade intelligence now bolstered by the information from A-54. But the audience was not a receptive one. France in particular wasn't ready for war - psychologically or militarily - after its horrific sacrifices in the First World War.

In March 1938, Austria succumbed to the internal subversion and Nazification of the type that Hitler had planned for Czechoslovakia, and ceded control to Germany in a bloodless takeover. Emboldened by this, the volume of the ongoing threats to Czechoslovakia was increased and Sudeten grievances were elaborated and stressed to breaking point. Plans were made to invade Czechoslovakia.

Beneš readied his forces in May 1938. He then sent envoys to the French Army to discuss coordinating their joint mobilisation. The message came back that this could not be discussed unless the French government ordered it to happen and that no such instructions had been given. With the whole world watching, Hitler continued to rage against Czechoslovakia and amplify the concerns of the Sudeten Germans. Various plans for their autonomy were discussed, but from Hitler's perspective this was all a pretence to disguise the objective of seizing Czechoslovakia. Events reached a final conclusion in late 1938. At the end of September, Hitler demanded that Czechoslovakia cede the Sudetenland to Germany or they would take the lands by force. After some swift diplomacy, Neville Chamberlain, the British Prime Minister, and Édouard Daladier, the French President, flew out to meet with Hitler and the Italian Fascist leader Benito Mussolini, in order to avert Hitler's planned invasion at all costs. Without Beneš or any other Czechoslovak representative present, Chamberlain and Daladier signed the 'Munich Agreement,' agreeing to the ceding of the Sudetenland to Hitler's Germany. They then informed Beneš of the development and urged his quick acceptance.

#

I had thought very little about my grandfather's life in this period. But there were pieces of information and stories that now began to connect. There was one particular story that I could date with confidence. My brother and I both developed an interest in boxing at a young age. My grandfather acknowledged that he himself had boxed in the army, but still gently tried to discourage us from this interest with stories of the slurring pug-nosed ex-pugilists he had encountered pan handling for change on the streets of London. But there was one story that he recounted with real enjoyment. In June 1938, the heavyweight champion of the world, Joe Louis, was defending his title against the German favourite Max Schmeling. Despite the fact that Schmeling was the challenger, the Nazis were confident that he would win the title. They reasoned that not only was he an Aryan, and therefore superior in every way to the African-American champion, but he had previously beaten Louis, handing him his only loss by a twelfth round knockout at the Yankee Stadium in New York, where the return match was also to be held. At the time, the heavyweight championship of the world was the greatest prize in sport, and given the massive political significance of this return clash, the whole world was engaged; Louis had legions of fans rooting for him across the world – not least in central Europe. My grandfather tuned his radio into the German ringside radio broadcast that night and listened with excitement and interest. The fight didn't last long. Louis had prepared meticulously for the bout and was a different fighter this time, taking control in the very first round and knocking the German to the floor repeatedly with fast concussive punches. As Schmeling lay on the canvas staring up at the ring lights, his senses smashed to pieces, the radio commentator with loss of all shame, spoke for his compatriots in Nazi Germany in his confusion and upset as the broadcast was suddenly cut.

"Max, get up….for goodness sake Max get up…"

My grandfather had laughed hard when recounting this story. Unfortunately, it would be a long time after this event, until he felt any more satisfaction at Germany's expense.

#

Accepting the Munich agreement was not a simple decision for the Czechoslovakian army command or for Beneš. Geo-politically, this was the best opportunity to stand up to Nazi aggression and stall German expansionism. The military leaders knew it would not win a war against the might of Germany on its own but it was capable of a stubborn resistance that would degrade German forces seriously and despite the inevitable outcome, many in the army genuinely wanted to fight. Perhaps Czechoslovakia's allies would feel compelled by public opinion to come to their rescue once the battle was underway?

But Beneš knew better than anyone that the western powers had made their position clear and that this was wishful thinking. He had understandably lost faith in his 'allies' and did not want to see his countrymen and women slaughtered in a futile fight. With a heavy heart and the sacrifice of his own reputation and pride, he accepted the agreement and ceded the Sudetenland to Germany. Supported by a German assertion that he must go, Beneš went into exile, determined to bide his time for an opportunity to right this fundamental wrong that had been done.

The Czechoslovaks felt an immense sense of betrayal from both the western powers and from their own leadership. The outcome was a moral challenge that was of itself an existential threat to this young country. The people of Czechoslovakia - both soldiers and civilians - were deprived of what they saw as their right to fight for their country's existence, whatever the final outcome. In giving up the Sudetenland, the country was also elegantly shorn of its natural and manufactured defences, and the rump of Czechoslovakia could be saved by Hitler for a later day.

Russia was tied up in treaty obligations too, and had equally abandoned its ally, and Slavic kin. But, under its leader Joseph Stalin, it kept its distance from the politicking, happy for Munich to be seen as an entirely western betrayal.

Soon afterwards, Emil Hácha, a lawyer whose political career was untouched by Munich, was nominated as the new President of the diminished Czechoslovakia.

From his position in exile, and despite maintaining a public façade that he was no longer involved in politics, Beneš stayed in close contact with key Czech political figures, leaders of underground groups and of course with his erstwhile Head of Intelligence, Moravec. Moravec continued to work for the increasingly ineffectual regime at home and grew more and more frustrated with their inability to heed his warnings of the eventual invasion of the Czech rump state by Germany. But regardless of those developments, the line to A-54 had to stay open. Eventually, his key agent passed on Hitler's plans for four German divisions to occupy Prague at dawn on March 15, 1939. One of their first targets was Moravec's own office; plans were in place for he and his staff to be hunted down and eradicated.

Moravec reported this information to his superiors who downplayed it and chose not to act. He therefore decided, in the interests of his country, that he must act against what he saw as a discredited government. He contacted his counterparts in the British Secret Intelligence Service - SIS - who immediately arranged for a flight to take him into exile. The British offered eleven seats: four for him, his wife and his two daughters, and the rest for his seven best agents. Moravec grappled overnight with what to do in the best interests of all. Each additional member of his team would provide incalculable benefit to their historic cause. Men like his deputy, Emil Stankmuller and his undercover lead, Karel Paleček and their colleagues were simply indispensable. In his own words, "There comes a time in the life of every man when he must stand agonisingly confronted with his conscience."

He carefully ranked them in order of the value that they could provide and, in the most striking example of leadership imaginable, he made the choice to fill all the seats on the plane with his ten best men. He called them in one by one, to inform them that they, like him, must leave alone the next morning, without informing their families. Moravec then went home that night and simply asked his wife to pack him a couple of shirts and a toothbrush for an overnight trip to Moravia, with only a casual instruction that his daughters should stay home from school the following day as he thought there might be some disturbances.

Key files were given to Major Harold Gibson of SIS at the British Embassy for transfer to England and the rest were burnt. Moravec emptied his safe of foreign currency and went to meet his staff. They then boarded the plane that would take them to England in the nick of time, as columns of tanks approached Prague in a heavy winter snowfall. Moravec's own words at this critical juncture paint the picture well:

"I found myself suddenly swept by black thoughts. The bitter struggle of the past years, the blood and sweat of so many, what had it all amounted to? The republic of Masaryk was dead. For the second time in my life I was in exile. My wife and children lost to me, abandoned in the stricken country below, somewhere under the swirling flakes, left to the mercies of the invaders. Bitterness welled within me. As our plane passed over the frontier mountains of Czechoslovakia, I put my head in my hands and cried."

A few short hours later, Admiral Canaris, the chief of German Military intelligence, arrived and ordered everything to be handed over. There was nothing. Just a polite greeting from Moravec's remaining staff and the dance of floating ash mocking him.

Immediately upon occupying Bohemia and Moravia, the Germans began to select young men and women from their new stolen land to deport to different parts of the Reich to undertake manual labour. Over time, the Czechs developed a word for these compulsory appointments: *Totaleinsatz*. It is estimated that up to 450,000 Czechs were used in this way during the Second World War. Jaroslav Bublík was placed in a labour camp run by Hamburg-based construction company, Richard Ditting Rendsburg – a company that is still in business to this day. He was brought there on April 30 1939, just weeks after the occupation.

#

"What did you do in Kiel?" I asked.

A grimace came before the response, "Hard work….I was labourer. I was sent there on forced labour to help build naval barracks for the Germans," he said, his voice hoarse.

"Was Josef there?"

He shook his head slowly but with certainty. "No – he was younger than me. He was still at school then."

"The conditions were appalling. Most of our time was spent on hard manual labour. Breaking roads…loading and unloading trucks."

I reached forward, grabbed my tea and took a sip as he gathered his thoughts, before continuing with his recollections.

"Sometimes they made us run up and down towers with rocks for no reason. It was very tough. There was no real food," - he waved his hand through the air - "…just thin vegetable soup."

I waited for a moment – watching him in silent recollection. These memories were clearly painful and not often turned to voluntarily.

"They terrorised us…on one occasion I was hit in the head with an iron bar." He touched the top of his head gently, feeling an invisible scar, and fixed me with an earnest stare, before addressing me softly but firmly, "I was very unwell because of that."

I was immediately reminded of another story that he had recounted years before. He had told how he had approached a camp guard and pointed at a large picture of Adolf Hitler on the wall of the mess room hall asking, with feigned ignorance, "Who is that man? I keep seeing his picture everywhere." The guard had been utterly flummoxed by this question and launched into an impassioned explanation. "That is Adolf Hitler," he had stammered, barely able to get the words out quickly enough and gesticulating wildly to urgently cover this impossible gap in the collective knowledge of the human race. "He is our Fuhrer...he is the greatest man in history," he had implored. He had called others over too, to share in the impossible mystery of this Czech fool's ignorance: "This man does not know who our Fuhrer is?" My grandfather had continued to appear unmoved, staring blankly at the picture of Hitler and the display of incredulity from the prison guard. He had chuckled heartily as he recollected this story. I have no idea what caused him to be hit in the head with an iron bar but if it wasn't this specific incident, it surely was a similar act of combined stubbornness and self-amusement.

#

Moravec's actions were a minor blip in the Nazis' plans to dominate and control Czechoslovakia. They were otherwise able to move quickly and effectively to grab their spoils. Slovakia became a puppet Nazi state and Bohemia and Moravia a 'Protectorate' under the oversight of the German diplomat, Konstantin Von Neurath and the ruthless Sudeten Nazi chief of police, Karl Hermann

Frank. This gave the German war machine significant prizes, like the Škoda industrial works outside Pilsen. Plans were made to steadily turn the whole country's resources to the support of the war.

At the start of 1939, Beneš took a teaching post at the University of Chicago. This was not a purely academic pursuit. A real attraction of the role was the opportunity it provided for him to influence US policy and engage with the local expat community there. Jan Masaryk, the former Czechoslovak Ambassador to London, was also in America. The son of Czechoslovakia's revered founder, the younger Masaryk held a symbolic power, given the turn of events. Having also resigned after Munich, he and Beneš both gave political lectures, and developed relationships with key figures, including leading Czech and Slovak Americans.

When Czechoslovakia was overrun, Beneš immediately went into action. He reasoned with conviction that the German invasion had rendered the Munich agreement morally and legally void. All actions since Munich had occurred under duress, so Beneš' view was that this left him as the rightful president of the country. He felt clearly that not only did he have the right to act, but that it was his duty to do so. He immediately began implementing his plan to reclaim his authority, sending telegrams to US President Franklin D Roosevelt, Prime Ministers Chamberlain of Britain and Daladier of France, and also to Russia and the League of Nations.

"Last September, the Franco-British proposals and a few days later, the Munich decision, were presented to me. Both of these documents contained the promise of the guarantee of the integrity and security of Czechoslovak territory. Both of these

31

documents asked for unheard of sacrifices by my people in the interest of European peace – these sacrifices were made by the people of Czechoslovakia. Nevertheless, one of the great powers which signed the agreement of Munich is now dividing our territory, is occupying it with its army and is establishing a 'protectorate' under the threat of force and military violence. Before the conscience of the world and before history I am obliged to proclaim that the Czechs and Slovaks will never accept this unbearable imposition of their sacred rights. And they will never cease their struggle until these rights are reinstated for their beloved country. And I entreat your government to refuse to recognise this crime and to assume the consequences which today's tragic situation in Europe and in the world urgently requires."

At exactly this moment, Beneš received a letter from František Moravec, notifying him that he and his men had arrived in England with their valuable cargo, and that Moravec, having come to the same conclusions as Beneš, wished to put himself unconditionally in Beneš' service. Moravec and his men immediately set about establishing their intelligence and communication centre in London. Contacts were quickly reasserted and strengthened with the key intelligence outposts at embassies in Paris, Belgrade and Zurich. Prior to their departure, arrangements with key underground and intelligence contacts in and around Prague had been put in place and desperate work began to connect with them via courier networks. In exchange for a very credible promise of future intelligence, Moravec refreshed his relations with British intelligence, who began providing him with the technical assistance that he would need to set up his operations centre and build a radio communication capability. Beneš positioned key political supporters and advisors around him to form his government in exile: democrats and proven patriotic Czechoslovaks like Jaroslav Stránský, Hubert Ripka and Prokop Drtina, who Beneš had worked with before the war as ministers and members of the Czech National Socialist Party. With military support a critical requirement for any national political leader, the Czech and Slovak army Generals Sergěj Ingr and Rudolf Viest put themselves at Beneš' disposal too - Ingr becoming Beneš' minister of defence.

There were also political developments at home in Bohemia and Moravia following the German Invasion. Emil Hácha lost any remaining powers and was increasingly required to implement the policies of Von Neurath and the Nazis. But General Alois Eliáš, a Czech war hero and general, was appointed as prime minister. The Germans were happy with this appointment because Alois' popularity supported the practical effectiveness of a 'puppet regime' – but Eliáš had other ideas. He took the role because of the opportunities it afforded for supporting the home resistance and began actively maintaining contact with Beneš in secret.

#

"How did you escape?" I asked, dimly aware that in fact he had.

He shrugged. "I just walked out. It was not guarded heavily…there was nowhere to go."

"So what did you do?"

"I left with two Jewish men, Levy and Jostem."

The men left on Christmas Eve 1939, when a few rare hours of rest gave them a moment to regroup and recover their strength of will. As their bosses relaxed their attention for the Christmas celebration, they slipped away unnoticed.

Although considered 'inferior Slavs' in the strict hierarchy of the camps, the Czechs were treated slightly better than the 'Osterbeiter': forced labourers from Poland, Ukraine and Russia. But Jewish labourers were treated the worst of all and were constantly on the brink of starvation. When Jaroslav's food parcels had sporadically found their way to him from Banov, he had been compelled by his conscience to share them with the Jewish workers around him, despite his own extreme hunger. It was no surprise that two of these men would want to leave too when the time came, and also that they would return the favour when circumstances permitted it.

"We had help from other Jews as we travelled," he continued. "They provided us with food and places to stay.

"Eventually, I found my way back to Banov.'

I flagged the need to check later, but my geography was good enough to know that this meant a trip of hundreds of kilometres, right through the heart of Nazi Germany. Wrong footed, my questioning stopped as I struggled to comprehend the challenges he must have faced.

I took a long breath and found myself aligning and pacing myself to the rhythm of the pendulum clock on the wall: consciously curbing my natural impatience. We were in new territory here. I felt like I was tracking a skittish deer.

#

The practical work of the home resistance in Prague was actively overseen by the 'Three Kings': Colonel Josef Balabán, Colonel Josef Mašín and Captain Václav Moravek. These three would become the swashbuckling heroes of the Obrana Národa – 'defence of the nation' - the Czech home resistance organisation formed by members of the disbanded army. Intelligent, experienced, and with a passionate hatred for the Germans, the Three Kings recognised their role to provide visible resistance to inspire the nation and embraced all of the risks that came with their chosen role. Recognising the value of loyal, home grown technical talent to strengthen radio links with Beneš and the exiles in London, Colonel Balabán approached one of the most capable signalling experts in his network. The young man, named Václav Modrák, would in time become one of Jaroslav Bublík's closest friends and colleagues. "There will be a war." Balabán said to Modrák at a hastily arranged meeting in his mother's house in Prague. "We need radio operators to make contact [between] our homeland and those abroad. Do you wish to serve?" Modrák agreed immediately and set off on what would be a gruelling and convoluted journey, via Poland, to reach London.

Beneš requested that Jan Masaryk return to London from his US tour, while he continued to organise Czech and Slovak organisations in the USA. He also continued to lobby the key political figures and the League of Nations, culminating in a personal meeting with US President Franklin D Roosevelt, who received him as the rightful president. In their conversation, Beneš set out his predictions of the future course of events in Europe, leading to a second world war. Beneš' prescience and knowledge left a lasting impression on Roosevelt, who became convinced that Beneš was a man who understood European power politics like no other.

In July 1939, Beneš finally returned to England to form his government in exile. Despite a lukewarm welcome from Neville Chamberlain – the architect of the Munich Agreement - he was received by a low key, but heartfelt and much appreciated political gathering of support, organised by the veteran British Parliamentarian, Winston Churchill. Beneš' situation on arrival in England was complicated. Any peace would leave Czechoslovakia forever a part of Germany. Beneš' great political foresight and optimism made the mission clear to him: to encourage a flow of events that would set the great powers against Nazi Germany and ultimately liberate the country with its pre-Munich borders intact. He was not in a strong position but his strengths lay in his clarity of vision, his political experience and crucially his control of the information from A-54.

Jan Masaryk became Beneš' foreign minister. On arrival in England, he immediately began broadcasting to his homeland on the BBC, along with another of Beneš' key cabinet members, Prokop Drtina. Masaryk was very different to his father. He was a large, humorous man with a gift for music. If his father had been the stern patriarch and Beneš the distant intellectual grandfather, Masaryk was the warm and friendly uncle. He had a common touch and a natural rapport with all people, in particular with the people of his country. The situation was dire and in his very first broadcast he set the tone, whilst also sending encouragement for young men considering exile to take an active part in the war:

"We have declared through the lips of Edvard Beneš that we are in a state of war with Nazi Germany, Hitler and his gang.......in a short time Czechoslovak legions will again stand in the line of battle beside the Allies. The day will come when Nazism and with it your oppressors will disappear from the face of the earth. Already the Czechoslovak nation summons them to the judgement of God. By the name I bear, I declare that we shall win this fight and that truth will prevail'.

Through the words of Jan Masaryk, the Czechoslovak community was once again brought together under a common purpose and was galvanised to regroup.

#

"I spent Christmas there…in Banov," he said, finally.

"But I couldn't stay…I would be found and sent to prison or back to labour camp. I knew what I had to do. I knew that Czech army was being formed somewhere in France. I decided to go there. To fight the Germans. To get our country back."

He edged forward slightly in his seat, a faint tautening of his cheeks betraying his physical discomfort.

#

Following the Nazi takeover, an untenable political stasis had been in place in Czechoslovakia. Formally, the Protectorate of Bohemia and Moravia was under the protection of the Reichsprotector Konstanin Von Neurath, who had a degree of trust in the international community. He was not a natural supporter of Nazi and SS ways of working and had no real interest in the day-to-day goings on in Bohemia and Moravia. Because of this light touch, Beneš was able to exert a degree of control at home. Prime Minister Eliáš and President Hácha recognised his authority and were secretly in contact. With Beneš' support, the home government avoided dramatic acts of resistance. Instead they advocated undetectable sabotage, go-slows in factories, and intelligence gathering: the classic Czech 'passive resistance' of former times. They sought to bide their time until the Reich was at some point in the future on the verge of collapse.

However, this stasis was inherently unstable. In August 1939 - in a move which shocked many - the Molotov-Ribbentrop pact was signed and Germany and Russia were now formally working in concert to share the spoils of a defenceless Eastern Europe. In September 1939, the Germans launched their 'blitzkrieg' on Poland. The Poles fought bravely but were ultimately poorly armed and ill-prepared and no match for the Germans' modern methods of warfare. Great Britain and France, in observance of their treaties with Poland, declared war on Germany and the Second World War had formally begun. On the occasion of Czech Independence Day in 1939, Jan Masaryk made one of his broadcasts on the BBC foreign service:

"Today on the twenty-eighth of October we are meeting once more. Though physically far apart we are close in heart and spirit, and we are bound together by a common love of our country which transcends all distances and obstacles. You in the temporary purgatory of Hitler and Neurath are not allowed to commemorate this solemn day in public, nor celebrate it with Czechoslovak flags. The invader and his blackguard has forbidden it…In France and Great Britain our boys are joining the army, determined to consecrate your struggle with their blood…we stand together on one front, you at home, and we abroad."

He then invoked his father's name, extolling the values that Czechoslovakia shared with the West: social justice and freedom of the individual. But he ended with a note of caution: "Beware of provocations, don't rush into actions which might aggravate your situation and weaken you."

Despite Masaryk's advice, large demonstrations occurred in Prague. There were outbreaks of violence and a medical student, Jan Opletal, died as a result of being shot in the stomach by a German policeman. His funeral a short time later on November 15 became the catalyst for a student demonstration. This was the opportunity that Karl Hermann Frank had been waiting for. He had for some time been intriguing against Von Neurath and disapproved of his laissez faire approach to overseeing Bohemia and Moravia. He also wanted an opportunity to prove himself to his Nazi masters in Germany and climb the ranks of the party. Frank was also keen to take some personal revenge on the Czechs, who disparagingly nicknamed him 'Kah-Hah' and referred to him as the 'one-eyed bookseller', on account of his partial blindness and pre-war occupation. With the support of his SS bosses, he went into overdrive. Two days after the demonstration, nine student leaders were shot, a large number of students were sent to concentration camps and all Czech universities were closed indefinitely.

With his legal studies curtailed, my grandfather's cousin, Josef Bublík, found himself back in his hometown of Banov. There he was reunited with his older cousin.

#

He coughed and cleared his throat before continuing, hoarsely.

"Josef and I - we decided to leave for France. But it wasn't so easy as that...all the borders were heavily guarded."

"What was Josef like?"

He hesitated and thought before he spoke. "He was fine fellow- tall – young – quite naïve...

I nodded as he spoke

"…inexperienced."

"How old were you both?"

"He would have been nineteen. I was twenty-four. Something like that. I was little older. We were both a little…" He grasped for the right word "…foolhardy. We didn't know what we were getting into. But we did it anyway – we did not feel any danger."

I finished the dregs of my tea and fidgeted in my pocket for the small notebook I had brought. Glancing at the empty cup, my grandfather offered me a glass of cider and I quickly fetched it from the cabinet near his front window. When I sat back down he continued.

"So we left - at start of 1940. We had little bit of money and our winter coats. Other than that, just a briefcase with few sandwiches…"

I smiled. Was it naiveite? desperation? or audacity. The confidence of youth.

"…and bottle of Slivovitz."

I smiled, the sizzle from my cider helping me to visualise the story unfolding. I slid a biro from my jacket pocket and pulled the top from it.

#

President Beneš realised that in the longer-term, intelligence would not be enough. To support his claims as the Czechoslovak leader in exile and to allow active participation in the war to liberate Europe, he would need an army to command. Beneš therefore put in place plans to assist as many able young men as possible to leave their country and find their way to the French army. Prior to this point, many men like Václav Modrák, the signals expert who was still making his way to England, had left their country via Poland but the Nazi invasion had removed this option. The only possible alternative was to travel through Slovakia, Hungary and the Balkans to the Middle East, where the French had a military presence. Although this was the best route, it was by no means a simple one. Slovakia had been formed as a German puppet regime and Hungary was rapidly aligning itself with the Nazis. Any men leaving could be sent back, imprisoned, shot, or even handed over to the Gestapo. A key stopping point was the secret Czechoslovak Military Mission in Budapest, which was hidden inside the French Embassy there. Beneš instructed his team in Budapest to vet any refugees, build a secret network of crossings from Hungary into Yugoslavia, and to facilitate the passage of refugees onwards to the middle east, all under the noses of their Hungarian hosts.

#

"It was cold – snow everywhere."

I looked out of the window behind him at the darkening winter sky.

"We made our way on foot, across countryside to avoid police. Then we crossed border to Slovakia at night. There were guides to help us; taking us in groups down to the border into Hungary."

He stopped and caught a shuddering cough in his cupped hand, his face suddenly flushed.

"So, we got there and went across that border too." he said, haltingly. "When we thought we had just made it, we were challenged."

A stern look came across his face as he composed himself before he finally spoke again:

"….STOP!...We did not stop – of course - we ran for our lives as the gunshots came right past us."

With all of the stories of war and murder that I'd heard and read about these times, the idea of a few shots being fired didn't instantly resonate with me. Just a handful of the millions of bullets that would whiz through European air in those insane years. But looking at his weary, pale blue eyes, it became clear to me that of course the first time someone chases you down with a gun with the intent to kill you is a life-changing experience that stays with you forever.

"I have still not forgotten the Hungarian word for 'stop'," he continued, putting an exclamation mark on my thoughts.

A new atmosphere descended in the brief moment before he spoke again.

"When we got to Budapest, we went to embassy and were put in the care of a man called Schonenfeld, who housed us while next step of trip was planned."

These were all new stories to me and it was somewhat of a revelation. I was no longer sticking my dime on the juke box to hear his favourite tales. I had no idea where we were going to go next.

"After a while we went out - to have look around Budapest. We wanted to see some of it."

The attraction would have been obvious. Budapest at the time was a bustling hive of activity, with streetcars, pedestrians and cyclists all jostling for space on its wide, open streets. The two men would have been eager to see some of the most impressive buildings and monuments in Europe, from the neo-classical splendour of St Stephens Basilica to the Hungarian Parliament

Building and the dramatic Széchenyi Chain Bridge that confidently spans the Danube.

"…But this was stupid idea. As we walked about, I saw someone across the road from us. I said to Josef: 'Here…don't look but there is someone following us.'

I marvelled as my grandfather briefly became his younger self again, sensing the camaraderie and closeness between he and Josef at this time and the general paranoia surrounding them. Hungary had in the 1930's been a safe haven for Jewish Refugees and was still recognised as a key transit point in Europe. But Nazi ideology had steadily infected the country and later in 1940 it would formally join the Axis powers in the evolving war. The city was at this time being watched closely by fascist spies.

"We walked on and then I saw he was still there – this man. He began speaking with Hungarian policeman and policeman beckoned towards us." He acted this out as he spoke.

"I turned and ran as fast as I could and got away. When I looked back to see where Josef was, I saw that he had not run but had approached policeman." He shook his head "I thought I wouldn't see him again," he continued. "I was very worried. After a minute he turned and started walking away. 'What did they say?' I asked him. He said that they had asked him where he was from and he'd said, 'I am German.' 'Not with German like that you aren't,' they had replied. I laughed at that – Josef was lawyer - I was the one who knew languages."

His face warmed slightly with this memory.

He made an officious face and raised his finger. "'I know who you two are. You're Jaroslav and Josef Bublík and you're staying with Schonenfeld.' The policeman had let him go but it was

43

clear we had to leave. We went back to embassy and told them what happened. They said that we must travel on immediately with big group of Poles so we went to meet them."

He paused again, lost in recollection, groping for his memories.

"We got lost on the way, but eventually found them at railway station."

Another pause for recollection came. When he finally spoke, it was with a wistful tone. I felt that he had perhaps found a memory that had been undisturbed since it had been formed. It's in those rare times that you can gather a glimpse of the length of a life: the vast tracts of time and events that have steadily passed.

"On the way there we rescued woman. She was attempting to commit suicide on bridge." As I watched my grandfather reliving these memories, I felt a palpable sense of the despair of those times leaking into the room. The reality of that world, bricked away for generations, behind happier memories. I sat ghoulishly in silence for a moment, groping for more of it.

"What were the Poles like?" I asked finally, as the moment ebbed away.

"They were like us… desperate men who hated the Nazis with passion. You would not have wanted to meet them on dark night."

I nodded in affirmation before he continued, haltingly, but clear in his tone. "We had been assigned a guide and got the train to get us close to border with Yugoslavia. The guide took us to border but he was mercenary and as soon as we got near, he abandoned us. Left us high and dry." He shook his head. "Before he left, he told us, 'If Hungarians shout at you it means 'stop, or we will shoot to kill.' I said, 'Yes – we know all about that.' The problem with crossing border across country is you don't know when exactly you have crossed. Somehow, we got lost. After some hours wandering about, we found peasant's shack. We barged in and it was indescribable scene. People living side by side with animals in squalor. We said to them, 'We will not hurt you if you show us nearest way to border.' Well they showed us of course."

I took a shallow breath, as the words sunk in. I understood better now who the young Jaroslav was. He and his fellow refugees were desperate, angry men with a mission. And they had been taught by their experience that violence was a necessary part of their toolkit. The young Jaroslav was a very different proposition to the aged, reflective and mellowed character in front of me.

"So we finally got across…" he continued, unaware of my reflections. "We saw border guard at his post and shouted to him 'Brother…. we are fellow Slavs…Poles and Czechs.'"

His face warmed again. "They brought us in and gave us wine to celebrate. Things went much better after that. We went on to Belgrade and embassy there. There were a lot of Czechs there, some very senior officers. Josef and I each received certificates declaring us to be patriotic Czechs. Then, ambassador approached me and put me in charge of our group to transfer to the Lebanon and French Foreign Legion there. We went on train through Greece and then to Turkey, Syria, and finally to Beirut. French put us temporarily into Foreign Legion until we could be transferred."

Their brief days in and around Beirut were a happy respite. They were initially housed in tents, in the pouring rain, but were soon moved to lodge with the Legionnaires, staying in bunks in long wooden huts, nestled within the exotic flora: prickly cypress trees, scaly junipers and abundant palms. The weather rapidly improved and the assembled Czechs and Slovaks gathered together each night to take advantage of their freedom, touring the bright lights of the city's Place des Martyrs and taking trips to the Cinema. They were each given a little money and ate well, gorging on lamb and local culinary curiosities. When their money ran out, most jostled through the markets and exchanged their caps and greatcoats for bowls full of bananas and oranges – a decision they would later regret when returning to colder climes.

I sat back to reflect on what I'd heard and then instinctively flicked forward in the photo album to another photo: one which I assumed must have been taken at this time. It shows a collection of men gathered around and on top of a large camel. At the front are some Berbers squatting as for a football team photo, crooks in hands, a couple wearing fezes. Mixed in with them are a handful of other men who I assume are all Czechs. A number of them are wearing matching military outfits. One, standing tall next to the camel's large head, is Josef Bublík. He's the focal point of the photo, wearing a huge grin, his eyes smiling in the sunshine. Another is my grandfather, sitting atop the camel. He looks composed but slightly unbalanced and perhaps distracted by the effort to stay upright. Sitting in front of him, holding the reigns, is another man in a shirt and suit jacket.

"Was this taken in the Lebanon?" I asked, pointing at the photo. He glanced quickly, immediately aware of what I was looking at.

"…a little later."

"Who is this on the camel with you?" I asked. I had a vague memory that he had said previously.

"That's Píška. He is from Banov too."

I leant in and squinted, peering more closely. I saw a young man with fair hair perched atop his head, and a stern, impatient gaze that was a little at odds with the other smiles in evidence.

My grandmother had appeared at the door.

"Marge…. you remember Píška?"

"Oh yes…. Where are they now? Are they in…where is it…Parkstone Road?"

"Yes…that's where they moved." He turned back to me, "He could be very mean, Píška."

He smiled as a recollection came to him. "I remember in the war we were given cigarette rations and Píška didn't smoke. But he took up smoking because he didn't want to share his with anyone."

I laughed.

"When did you last hear from him Jarda?"

A familiar back and forth on this topic began and my thoughts drifted. The photo had reminded me of a story my grandfather had recounted to me several times, which must have transpired at some point between their departure from the Lebanon and arrival in the South of France; perhaps somewhere in North Africa. He, Josef, Píška and one or two others had been on shore leave and milling about the markets and entertainments when they had an unusual experience.

A man described by my grandfather as a 'fakir' approached him and offered him his hand, asking if he wanted to see some entertainment. My grandfather grasped his hand back and as he did so, he felt an electric shock go right through his arm and up his elbow. He was dazed by this and went and took a seat with the others who were also greeted in a similar way. As he gathered his senses, the show started. The man who had greeted them began by acting out an animated discussion with a young boy. He then threw a thick rope up high into the air, and rather than falling back down again, it hung there, suspended vertically. Astonished, my grandfather looked up and the rope seemed to keep going, eventually disappearing into the clouds. The magician then pointed at the boy and pointed up to the top of the rope. The boy scuttled up and up – eventually disappearing into the clouds. After a moment, the 'fakir' called for the boy to come back down animatedly a couple of times and then became furious and drew a large sword. He then quickly climbed up the rope. After a while there were screams and a severed arm flew down, then a leg, and so on until finally a head and a torso thudded to the ground. My grandfather was transfixed by this unreal spectacle and as the show came to an end and the crowd dispersed, he spoke with Josef and the others who had all seen exactly the same thing. This remained a topic of conversation until they arrived in France and Josef was able to get a photo he had taken at the climax of the show developed. The photo showed the man and the boy standing together: the boy – perfectly intact - leaning against a wall looking very bored.

#

In February 1940, just one month after Jaroslav and Josef had left Czechoslovakia, Karl Hermann Frank was rampant again. Hundreds of their fellow Sokol were arrested. The Central Committee of the Communists of Czechoslovakia was attacked. Even the boy scouts were dissolved.

At about this time, Václav Modrák finally arrived from his arduous journey across a war-torn Europe. He reported for duty at the Czechoslovak Military Radio Centre, known in Czech as 'Vojenská radiová ústředna – the VRÚ. The centre was based in Rosendale Road, in the south eastern London borough of Dulwich, where Moravec and his ten original intelligence men had been based since their arrival. It was being maintained under the cover of a radio workshop run by a man who was actually an undercover British agent. The location was also close to Beneš, who was headquartered in modest dwellings in nearby Putney.

Technical support from the British had been quickly marshalled to get the communications facility up and running. Desperate for the gold dust of intelligence, SIS had even given Emil Stankmuller and the rest of Moravec's men full autonomy, including the use of their own independent ciphers for coding and decoding messages. A system had been quickly developed by the in-house coding expert Captain Václav Knotek. In return for their support, the British expected the Czechs to start gathering and passing on the intelligence imminently. All had awaited Modrák's arrival impatiently. His skills and knowledge were essential to the success of their operation. Moravec was immensely relieved as he met the young man in the back of the radio workshop and set him the task of reactivating contact with the homeland.

FRANCE

Czech and Slovak men had by this time been arriving from all directions into France. The events of Munich had been a national humiliation and a tragedy that struck at their every sense and instinct. For this significant core of patriots, there was no question that Czechoslovakia was simply lost; they nurtured a deep and passionate desire to take back their homeland. Soon after the Nazis' invaded Poland, Czechoslovak troops who had signed up at Foreign Legion camps all over France, North Africa and the Middle East, were allowed to form their own army on French soil. They were initially housed with the Foreign Legion in Marseille. Jaroslav Bublík and his young cousin eventually arrived at the Marseille camp, after landing on French soil on a liner named 'Le Champollion.'

"What was it like in the Foreign Legion?"

"We weren't there long. Was very tough place. There was lot of fighting there," he said with faint headshake, '…and lot of homosexuality."

I raised my eyebrows with an inward chuckle. We really were breaking new ground in our topics of conversation.

"Lot of the officers were Germans. As you can imagine, they were very unpopular with us."

I could imagine.

"I had hatred of them from my time in barracks at Kiel." He clenched and unclenched his fists lightly. "My hands did lot of hard work there - they had brutalised me," he said, pronouncing every syllable of 'brutalised' in a jagged flow.

"One day we went on run. Several rows in line: one sergeant or corporal followed by three men and so on. The lead man, a German sergeant, started shouting 'Schnell, Schnell…'. Well he was being followed by three big Czechs: they looked like gorillas." He sniggered a little and shuffled in his chair.

"One of them - these big Czechs said: 'I'll 'schnell' you' and picked him up with one hand…" He pawed forward with his own chunky hand to demonstrate.

"…and threw him to the ground. We threw all of them down and we trampled them with our big hobnailed boots."

I felt a mixture of emotions. I couldn't tell whether this tale was being told with pride or shame or a mix of the two. I prepared myself to ask a question about the fate of these men but was too frightened of the answer I might get. So, I asked a different one instead.

"Did you all get into trouble?"

"No," he said with a shrug. "There was Czech major in charge of the legion at the time: Captain Hájek. He got involved."

My mind drifted, as I thought again about the growing evidence of his comfort with physical confrontation. On my tenth birthday, my grandparents had bought me a portable radio cassette player, which with hindsight was one of my favourite ever gifts. Watching me playing music on it, my grandmother had recounted a story of how, at some point in the early 1970's, my grandfather had been on a train on which two young men were playing music at full volume to the annoyance of all of the other passengers, who were being very 'British' about it and suffering in silence. My grandfather had apparently walked over to them, grabbed their cassette player and turned it off before defiantly handing it back to them: almost daring them to switch it back on. Apparently, all of the other passengers in the carriage had burst into spontaneous applause at this act, but the young men were less pleased. "One of them was giving you a really bad look I remember, Jarda," my grandmother had commented.

"What would you have done if they had fought you Granddad?" I had asked, genuinely concerned about the thought of him picking a fight with these two young men. He had looked at me as if I were insane. "I would have made mincemeat of them," he had then said, in such a tone that I was convinced he was speaking literally.

I realised that I had paused a little too long and I suddenly felt very self-conscious scribbling my crude notes. He glanced down, noticing my writing for the first time but with no notable interest.

#

The Czechs and Slovaks who had flooded into France, were soon moved wholesale to a former internment camp at Agde – an ancient port town on the Mediterranean. It wasn't just soldiers who were arriving; men of all ages and of all backgrounds were now converging to form this exile force that would be the seed of all that was to come.

The morale of their French hosts contrasted sharply with that of the Czech arrivals. The French were not prepared practically or psychologically for war and had sought appeasement over all things. Neville Chamberlain's Britain had orchestrated Munich but unlike the French, Britain had no direct treaty obligations with the Czechoslovaks, so the principal betrayal was not theirs. Perhaps to assuage feelings of guilt and responsibility, there was a strong thread of thinking amongst the French that the Czechs were to blame for the situation. These contrasting positions impacted on the relationships between the Czechoslovak exiles and their French hosts from day one. When they arrived in France, ready to give their lives for the defence of this foreign country, they were given the dregs of French equipment. Many were made to wear First World War uniforms and, in some cases, given rifles from the Napoleonic wars. Rather than shoes they were provided with wooden clogs to wear.

#

Until Václav Modrák's arrival, the men at the VRÚ were transmitting blindly – hoping that the home resistance was picking up their messages and vice versa. However in April 1940, just a month after his arrival, Modrák managed to receive three direct responses from the wireless station in Prague. He went immediately to inform Moravec. Modrák thought he sensed a tiny flash of satisfaction in the colonel's usually inscrutable face as he relayed the news. So began the direct link between the men on the ground in the Protectorate and the small collection of technical experts in London that would remain of critical importance to world events for the next five years. In the Protectorate, there were two transmitters: Sparta 1 and Sparta 2, which passed information from the home resistance through to Modrák, Emil Stankmuller and the others at the VRÚ in Dulwich. All intelligence was reviewed by Beneš and Moravec before being sent to SIS and used to maximum political effect. As Beneš had control of his own codes, he could filter what he did and did not show to the British and the other allies. At this time, the Poles were the only other government in exile that had this privilege. Given his still diminished status, Beneš desperately valued this arrangement for both practical and political purposes.

Modrák and his workmates well understood the criticality of their role and its intensely human dimension. Those transmitting intelligence to them were in great danger. The problem was that the Gestapo was able to track the use of transmitters when they were switched on. Any underground agent had a limited window of time to pass communications and if they were caught, they faced torture and death. The VRÚ was constantly alive to these dangers and the speed of the beeps and buzzes coming through their headphones were pregnant with huge significance. The most alarming indication to them was sudden silence: the urgent aborting of a transmission.

The men had quickly settled into a pattern of working. They would wait for reception on certain frequencies at specifically agreed times, usually at night. Sparta 1b was the main transmitter. It was listened to from the VRÚ and also from stations in Paris and Belgrade. This meant that the information received could be cross checked and corrections made, if necessary. Transmissions to

Sparta were at random during the day and anywhere else where there was no two-way communication.

Information from A-54 was at this time being obtained by courier through Captain Moravek of the 'Three Kings,' who oversaw its communication back to London. Moravek was the only man in continental Europe entrusted by František Moravec, with the identity of A-54. A task this dangerous required someone with a very high-risk appetite, and Moravek certainly fitted this description. This also meant that he would take risks that were excessive given the potential consequences for the war effort of blowing the network.

The 'Three Kings' have passed into Czech folklore. There are many stories of the daring of their actions at this time and they certainly understood their role in setting an example of defiance to their countrymen. Moravek, a wiry war veteran and devout Christian, even had his own motto: "I believe in God and my pistols." He had been conducting a long running and very personal battle with Oskar Fleischer, the deputy chief of the Prague Gestapo, as part of the broader sabotage role that he, Mašín and Balabán were playing. In one instance, as Fleischer arrived at the location of a transmission just too late, he was greeted with a steaming pile of excrement, topped with a handwritten note explaining that it was all Fleischer would get of him that night. On another occasion Moravek sent a postcard to Fleischer thanking him for lighting his cigar in a Prague street, "without recognition, only with courtesy." These tactics enraged the police, and Fleischer in particular, who was a laughing stock amongst his colleagues and the Prague populace. The risk was that these actions were strengthening their determination to hunt the local network down.

Meanwhile, as the VRÚ was seeking to secure its communications with Prague, Jaroslav Bublík was someway away in the South of France beginning the development of the telecommunications skills which would eventually lead him to their door.

#

"Initially, I trained in the signalling school."

"What about Josef?"

"He was gunner."

He cleared his throat and took a sip of water.

"In one of first classes at school, we were making disparaging remarks about French officers in Czech, as one came into the room. He looked around at us with smile and said, in perfect Czech, 'How do you like it here?' We felt very small. He turned out to be very capable man – a colonel meritorious."

I scribbled this down with a knowing nod, although unclear exactly what this rank meant.

"I did very well at signals school – I knew languages and had logical mind, so this was natural." I smiled, in no doubt that he had excelled but also being reminded that he was not traditionally one to play down his capabilities. He looked up briefly, as his thoughts fell into focus.

"One day on parade ground the 'news of the day' came through the loudspeaker."

He sat to attention ever so slightly and looked into the middle-distance, ready to ape a stilted, authoritative voice. "'Jaroslav Bublík has passed out top of class. He is promoted to sergeant.' There were sixty in class," he said, looking back at me as he reverted to himself again.

Even after all these years I could see a glimmer of pride in his eyes and his tautened cheeks. I reflected on what I already knew about the criticality of these skills to his country, and where they would lead him. Was it fate or coincidence? It depends on where you're looking from I suppose.

#

Jan Masaryk spoke on the BBC foreign service again at the start of May. Norway had been occupied by the Germans and the 'phoney war' was coming to an end. He spoke with resolve and empathy to the Czechs and Slovaks, huddled in their homes secretly listening to their radios. In his address he invoked the name of a Slovakian folk hero and the Czech gymnastics movement in his call to arms.

"Soon our lads too will fight for the sacred cause of world freedom – the Czechs and the Slovaks! Thanks be to you mothers of Slovak Jánošíks and Czech Sokols. Our cause could not indeed be in better hands."

Just over a week later, the Germans came through the Netherlands and Belgium towards France at rapid pace, employing their "Blitzkrieg" tactics. Their observation aircraft surveyed the Allied formations which were then followed by Stuka dive-bombers, to sow fear at the point of attack. Columns of tanks then came flooding in, penetrating deep behind the French lines. This was the cutting edge of modern warfare, recently honed in Poland, and equally effective against the French first army and the British Expeditionary Force, who were still not sufficiently bedded into their defensive positions. The Allied troops also had to cope with mass civilian evacuation from northern France filtering through their lines.

It was at this point, with French morale and commitment already broken, that the Czechoslovaks were called into the fray. The influx of exiles had continued right through the first half of 1940 and they were able to form two regiments, each of about two and a half thousand officers and men. The Czech forces, under the command of General Ingr, were loaded onto boxcars, trucks and buses and clumsily brought to the front line. Crushed into any available space, few were able to grab any sleep on their trip to the battle. As they progressed on their journey north, their path was increasingly hindered by crowds of despairing French families heading south, with their possessions piled high on carts or trucks behind them. As the civilians disappeared, they were replaced by abandoned cars and wreckage, urgently swept to the side of the road. The soldiers know they were near their final destination when they heard the din of the cannonade swelling in their ears; huge guns on the horizon exploding fluidly and violently, belching smoke and tearing scars into the landscape.

The German advance had continued and at the end of May, as the Czechoslovak forces engaged, the British launched Operation Dynamo to rescue trapped British, French and Belgian soldiers from Dunkirk. Italy had also now entered the war on the side of Germany.

#

"Josef and I were in separate regiments. I was in the 2nd infantry, in the 2nd company as a signaller. My unit was placed in the north of France near Gien. Josef was gunner in the first infantry, and he was sent up to the river Marne to defend Paris. We knew things were not going well, as on our way there we could see many French and Moroccan soldiers. They were heading the blinking other way already." He shook his head, reliving the frustration. "We managed to get some of their weapons though. We were desperate to fight. We defended our positions well, but we had to keep retreating as the French forces collapsed, or we risked being encircled by the German motor units. The French kept retreating at night without telling us, which was not helpful. We were forced back further to south."

"At one point, Italians blew up a bridge just as we had gotten across. Our unit set up a machine gun post and fired back over at German troops across the river. We got a few of them." I observed some grim satisfaction in this statement, "…but they waved a flag back across to us. To indicate 'no hits'…as on a shooting range exercise." He framed his mouth into a bitter smile. "Our morale was low and got worse as time went on and we retreated further and further south. It became forced march to stay ahead of Germans. We were so tired. For long periods, I slept while I marched."

"What do you mean?"

"I mean I was dead asleep – unconscious - but my body continued to march forward."

As they had nowhere to retreat to, they headed like stray dogs back to the only place they knew: Agde, their former base, which was some seven hundred and fifty kilometres from their northern battle posting. The country around them was in chaos and even their brisk treks through the rolling green fields and woodlands were filled with tension, as confusion and drama threatened to erupt at any moment.

"One officer was very concerned that if we were caught, we would not be treated as soldiers but as deserters." I nodded, recognising the logic of this.

He gazed sideways for a few moments, his eyes gently darting up and down. There was an unusual calmness to him as he finally spoke – a sense of melancholy, wistfulness even.

"He stopped under a tree…and shot himself in the head."

I swallowed.

"We had to just leave him there… we didn't have any time to bury him."

#

Political developments in Great Britain moved in Beneš' favour as the war in France raged. Neville Chamberlain resigned as British prime minister and the man who had welcomed Beneš solemnly to Britain, Winston Churchill, was now leader of a British government of all parties. Appeasement and peace without victory were anathema to Churchill and therefore the immediate possibility that Czechoslovakia might be permanently incorporated into the Third Reich as part of a peace agreement with Hitler, receded significantly.

At this time, Beneš learned that A-54 had been posted to Prague by his bosses in the Abwehr. This and the recently re-established communications with the Protectorate created the opportunity for Moravec and Beneš to run their network (and the line to A-54) directly through the VRÚ and the Prague underground. This was risky, in particular given the febrile environment in Prague caused by the ongoing battle between the 'Three Kings' and the Gestapo, but Beneš considered it worth the risk. It would allow Beneš immediate and direct contact, helping to maintain the close control of intelligence that he desired. With the resistance of France crumbling, Britain was increasingly isolated and desperate for intelligence. However, putting the new arrangements in place would be complicated. A-54 was temporarily out of contact and re-configuring liaison might expose him or other Czech agents. Beneš was very concerned that they might lose contact altogether. In June 1940, František Moravec assigned the task of establishing radio contact with A-54 to Captain Moravek. At the same time, a rapid development of the VRÚ occurred, with it being moved from Dulwich to a base just outside London at Woldingham in Surrey. This move was accelerated by a bomb landing on the Dulwich address, which obliterated much of the exiles' equipment and almost wiped out the precious intelligence files they had smuggled out of Prague.

#

Josef Bublík and the 1st regiment had a very similar ordeal to the 2nd. They went to defend Paris on the Marne but upon arrival the French had not thought to tell them that they had decided to desert Paris to save it from destruction. So once again, the Czechoslovaks found themselves fighting a violent rear-guard action. One soldier who distinguished himself in particular in these battles - overseeing the positioning of gun posts - was a professional soldier from Slovakia named Sergeant Jozef Gabčík. Gabčík had been demobilised after Munich but fled to Poland when the Germans took his country; from there he had made his way to the Foreign Legion camp in Marseille. Unknown to the two Josefs, they would fight side by side again, two years later, in another pivotal battle.

So, the two Czech regiments found themselves retreating across the entire length of France. All the way, they were followed by heavy bombing from the German and Italian troops. They were more likely to find abandoned bottles of wine than food. There was nowhere to stop and rest as local families would not help them: they were outcasts. One soldier said that only prostitutes showed them any kindness - letting them come in to wash. The Czechs were in a foreign land, militarily beaten, abandoned by their allies, and with no idea of what the immediate future held or where they could go. The men were mentally and physically exhausted to their very limits.

Eventually, the two infantry units got as far as Nontron, where they were forced to give up their heavy equipment. It was here that the Bublíks were reunited and they continued their retreat together, eventually reaching the Mediterranean, their former depot at Agde, and the neighbouring fishing village of Sète.

When news of the armistice came those Czech and Slovak soldiers who had resided in France before the conflict were demobilised. For the other men, things weren't so simple. They became aware that General Charles De Gaulle had escaped to Britain to lead a French exile movement and the French government were already seeking an armistice with Germany. On June 17, the French surrendered and a condition of the Armistice was that they must hand over all German subjects to their fate; that included citizens of the Protectorate of Bohemia and Moravia. Struggles with French Garde Mobile ensued, as attempts were made to disarm them completely.

On the night of June 24, the troops spent the night on the beach, while Jaroslav Bublík and the other signalmen tried to contact any ships passing by that they could disembark on.

One of the boats they contacted was an Egyptian boat travelling under a British flag – the 'Rod el Farooq'. This boat picked up several hundred of the men, including Jaroslav and his cousin Josef. Others boarded another large ship, the 'Mohammed Ali et Kebir' and both boats sailed out into the Mediterranean.

France had collapsed in under a month. With their desperation to fight and their fundamental need for an allied victory, Jaroslav, Josef and their compatriot soldiers had fought hard and well. The Germans never pierced the sectors that they protected and they only retreated from their positions when ordered by the French infantry or when they had been abandoned by their allies. This was a source of both pride and frustration for the Czechoslovaks. Despite their desperate efforts, France was now lost.

ENGLAND

At the very end of June, these Czech and Slovak men from all walks of life were now floating, hungry and abandoned in the Mediterranean, on a heavily overloaded Egyptian passenger ship. The Rod el Farooq sailed away in a south westerly direction, while the men on board scoured it desperately for any remnants of food, clothing or equipment. Unbeknownst to them, they were being trailed by an Italian submarine which, thankfully, was obeying the boat's neutral Egyptian flag by holding back from an attack.

The men lay across the ship, utterly demoralised but craving some desperately needed rest. However, as they cut through clear blue water to the jagged terrain of Gibraltar, they saw a sight which caused them to stagger back on to their blistered feet. The West Mediterranean Fleet under Admiral Sommerville was about to travel to Oran in Algeria, to stop the French fleet there from returning home. With the French surrender, Churchill had decided that he must prevent its navy from falling into German hands and he had sent a formidable task force to see through this task: eleven destroyers, the battleships Valiant and Resolution, the battlecruiser Hood, and the legendary aircraft carrier the Ark Royal. Seeing the sailors standing to attention on the decks of these warships, as the sun lit the giant rock behind them, was something that each of the Czechoslovak soldiers would remember forever. All was not lost. Great Britain, that mighty sea-faring nation, was still their ally.

The Rod el Farooq slipped past the Armada and through the straights of Gibraltar into the Atlantic. It then came up through the Atlantic and eventually into the Irish channel. It was a relatively uneventful journey from a seafaring perspective, but there was very nearly a mutiny on board, as the ship's crew threatened to down tools in protest at the complete disappearance of their rations.

#

"We arrived in Liverpool in a sorry state. We were absolutely covered in lice - it was a dirty boat – so we were taken and all deloused in turn in an oven." He shook his head before continuing. "As I came out, I was inspected by Czech doctor – young fellow he was. I handed him my clothes before I put them back on, and he looked them over, inspecting the collar and cuffs of my shirt."

The inspection was mimed, with a deadpan face.

"…and finally, he handed my shirt back. 'This is fine,' he said 'it is so dirty that nothing could possibly live in it.'"

#

The troops boarded a train to Beeston Castle in nearby Cheshire, greeted enthusiastically with eccentric but much appreciated English fare: jam sandwiches and cups of tea. As they sank into the comfortable upholstery of the train carriages, they took some much needed rest. The men were utterly dejected but as the songs of support drifted in through the train windows, their spirits were gently rekindled by the certainty that there was no defeatism here. On arrival in Cholmondeley Park, they settled to a sound sleep in the open summer breeze as they awaited the tents which were to arrive the next day.

Beneš was, like his men, at his lowest ebb. But Great Britain was now also in a desperate state. France had fallen and Russia had formed a cynical truce with the Nazis. Britain stood alone in Europe against the might of Germany and its allies. At this exact moment, Captain Moravek finally made contact with A-54 in Prague. Information on the planning of the operation to invade Britain by sea – codenamed Operation Sealion - collected during the time he had been out of contact, came flooding in, pulse by pulse, through the receivers of the VRÚ. This was vital nourishment to the Czechoslovak cause. The Battle of Britain was underway, with a sustained aerial bombardment being repulsed by the Royal Air Force; the threat of England being invaded was a real and present danger. Beneš sent a personal note to Stankmuller and the men of the VRÚ, stressing the value of their work to the good name of the whole nation and how they were providing something that neither the Poles, Dutch nor the French could match.

Picking their moment, Beneš and Jan Masaryk reasserted their push for Munich to be repudiated by the British and for Beneš to be fully recognised as the leader of Czechoslovakia. However, the British only agreed to recognition of Beneš as the leader of the 'provisional' government. The 'provisional' epithet humiliated Beneš and his countrymen and was hurting his practical ability to get things done. Jan Masaryk made pointed comments asking British officials if the Czechoslovak pilots who were dying courageously flying in the Battle of Britain were 'provisionally' dead. These appeals, and the intelligence push didn't have the desired effect but they at least bought some of the time that would be needed to consolidate the exile position.

Beneš now had the men he needed to form the kernel of a Czechoslovak army on British soil. He would also have to demonstrate his ability to direct action within the home country for an eventual uprising there. Both things were essential to give him the authority to act as a statesman and to demonstrate that Czechoslovakia was still a viable country.

#

"It became village of tents." My grandfather continued, recalling his time in Cholmondeley Park.

"We made our beds from saplings…. We had a large tent for ten."

"Who was in your tent?"

"One of the men we shared with was Vlado Clementis. He was made foreign minister for the Czechoslovak government after the war."

He glanced up, drifting into his memories once again:

"He was executed with Slánský in 1952," he said sombrely, holding my gaze as he spoke. "He was a good friend of mine – I worked with him later on in post-war government in Czecho."

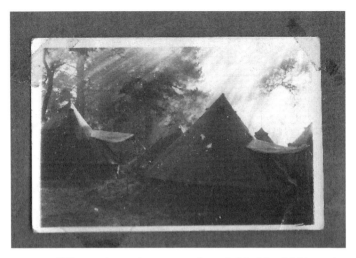

"Clementis was in my tent through his friend Majer, who was Minister of Food after the war." He threw me another look. "Majer was not executed."

I nodded, feigning understanding of the significance of all of this. This was something to research later.

"Who else was in your tent?"

"There were few of us..." he thought again.

"Novák was there..... Karel Svoboba...'

I knew that name from some of the books I had read. Svoboda had been involved with taking down Heydrich, I was sure of it. He had been selected for the mission before anyone else.

"It was a good place and many senior officers were buried there after the war."

He sat back.

"They were good times. We played cards a lot."

A faint smile came as some thoughts flooded back.

"They would bet on anything you know. I remember soldiers betting on which dewdrop would start to run down a windowpane first."

#

Although the Czechoslovaks would in time come to remember Cholmondeley Park fondly for the essential sanctuary and recuperation it provided, their morale initially remained low. As well as having suffered a crushing defeat in France - losing many of their comrades - the mood in the camp was affected by other circumstances. There were too many officers as a proportion of the three and a half thousand men who had made it to England. General Ingr therefore made a pragmatic and necessary decision that most officers should renounce their rank. This hit the men hard as it impacted their pay and rations, as well as their status. It also led to questions about Ingr's authority to make such a decision, and by implication undermined Beneš' authority at the worst possible time. The communists in the army were also a disruptive influence. Unofficially led by Second Lieutenants Schwarz and Vroc, they were close to Russia and sought to turn the embers of any discontent into a raging fire to damage Beneš irreparably.

News that Churchill had recognised Beneš as the leader of the provisional government in exile of Czechoslovakia had been greeted rapturously by the bulk of the exile army. However, the communist element – nicknamed the 'Spaniards' as many of them were veterans of the Spanish Civil War - were under instruction to foment rebellion, so that Russia would have no rivals for the political leadership of Czechoslovakia. This represented in many ways the first real post-Munich skirmish between the democratic founders of the state of Czechoslovakia and communist Russia for the soul of the country. It needed a strong response.

#

His face turned a little darker as he continued to reflect.

"One night, not long after we arrived, it was very windy and a tree fell on the tent next to us. There were four young officers in the tent who were crushed. We knew them well – we had played cards with them. We got very angry and chopped down another of the farmer's trees in case that fell down too."

"There were some members of our army who were communist and at that time Hitler was in a pact with Stalin. These men exploited the situation and the low morale. They started to say that we were being used in a capitalist war. They refused to carry out legitimate orders and tried to introduce a state of anarchy among us."

"That was something to do with Robert Maxwell wasn't it?" I said in reference to the infamous newspaper boss. I had remembered a previous discussion about this. My grandfather had seen Maxwell, who was one of the 'Spaniards' in Cholmondeley park, interviewed on television by the journalist Brian Walden in the late 1980's. He had been apoplectic with rage at Maxwell's description of events – in particular his description of Czech officers as cowards – and had written to several newspapers to voice his disapproval.

"Oh yes he was there. He was called Hoch then. He was a young soldier, not remarkable, but a cheeky swine. I remember, at that time, I saw an officer walk past him and the officer turned to him and shouted: 'Why didn't you salute?' He replied back 'I only salute from lieutenant colonel up.' The cheeky so and so.

Eventually Beneš came. We all marched out onto the parade ground and the five ringleaders were brought out."

"Was Hoch one of them?"

"I don't remember…he might have been. Beneš saluted them and then spoke. 'I understand you have some concerns,' he said, 'What exactly is the problem?' The ringleader brought out a piece of paper to read his grievances." He turned the corners of his mouth down in disgust, as he acted out the scene. "Beneš became very angry and pushed the paper away, 'Tell me - don't read it out.' He wanted to know genuinely what their concerns were, not what they had been told to say. The man was so nervous that he couldn't speak and started stuttering."

He shook his head.

#

Four hundred and eighty of the legionnaires who took part in the rebellion – mainly those veterans of the Spanish Civil War - were temporarily interned at York and then drafted into the pioneer corps, where they could support the war effort put to work in safe activities. With the core of disaffection gone, morale soon returned to the now legitimately recognised Czech army.

COUNTER OFFENSIVE

As the summer of 1940 subsided, the waters surrounding Britain became choppier and colder and the trees in Cholmondeley park wrinkled and wilted. The Battle of Britain had steadily, painstakingly, been won, and as the threat of immediate invasion from the continent subsided, Germany secretly began to turn its thoughts instead to the invasion of Russia. Jaroslav Bublík, his cousin Josef and the rest of the free Czechoslovak army were moved from the tents of Cholmondeley Park to a more permanent base near Leamington Spa in the midlands of England. The forces were spread throughout a number of properties including Harrington House a grand Victorian villa in the town, and Walton Hall nestled in the nearby countryside. Many of the men were billeted with local families and hutted accommodation was built for them ten miles away near Moreton Paddox. Beneš had by this time moved to a large house in Aston Abbots in Buckinghamshire, to the north west of London, which was just fifty miles from his troops' new base.

The scale and activity of the war was growing exponentially in the autumn of 1940 and Beneš needed to respond to the new challenges and opportunities this created. The relationship with SIS remained strong. Intelligence had continued to flow to England through from Prague via the VRÚ. Moravec had consolidated this operation, fully equipping the new centre at Woldingham – known as Funny Neuk - with SIS support, whilst ruthlessly maintaining independent control of his codes, contacts and intelligence to a system devised by Václav Knotek. This intelligence continued to be cherry-picked to support Czechoslovakia's strategic objectives.

Meanwhile, a new organisation had sprung up that offered Moravec and Beneš more immediate opportunities to take the battle back onto Czechoslovak soil. At Churchill's instruction, a new secret organisation - the Special Operations Executive or SOE - had been set up with the mission to 'set Europe ablaze.' The British had learned much from operations in Ireland at the start of the century and understood - from the occupier's position - the great value that could be achieved by irregular forces operating on their own turf to disrupt an occupying army. The SOE started to work with all of the exiled armies in Britain to develop and encourage partisan activity inside the occupied countries. The priority was to damage war production and tie the Nazis resources down in their occupied countries. Longer term, the objective was to build the conditions for uprisings that could be synchronised with the Allies efforts to retake the continent. The SOE saw real opportunities in Czechoslovakia for both of these strategies, particularly given Beneš' continued talking up of the underground capability at his command. Moravec's right hand men, Emil

Stankmuller and Karel Paleček, therefore began to engage heavily with the SOE.

I heard the doorbell ring and a kerfuffle of noise and movement as my grandmother answered it. I wasn't sure who it was – someone selling something or the post maybe. My grandfather looked up – jolted out of our conversation. I picked up the album from the coffee table again and leafed through it, trying to use this break to make sense of all of the information I had taken in. Although some of the pictures were now loose from their mountings and other photos had been inserted over time, it had originally been meticulously arranged to tell the story of my grandfather's war. Little was annotated but with the knowledge I'd gained, I was increasingly able to piece things together. There were photos from all points on his journey of exile and his days at both Cholmondeley Park and the bases near Leamington Spa - Moreton Paddox and Walton Hall.

As I flicked forward, I saw stock photos of Edvard Beneš were placed in chronological order, along with various photos of my grandfather and his colleagues on military manoeuvres. There were other senior officers dotted amongst the photos; one face I recognised immediately from the tattered book cover of his memoir was that of František Moravec. I examined a photo of him smiling next to Major Gibson of SIS, President Beneš and a few others at Woldingham.

#

The political situation in the Protectorate continued to be delicately balanced and very complex. Hitler had continued to turn a blind eye to Hácha and Eliáš' complicity with Beneš on the basis that in reality the Czech population were indeed providing very significant input and material for the Nazi war effort. Hitler didn't want any disruption to that, or to create martyrs to the Czechoslovak cause. Beneš was continually seeking to downplay any intelligence that indicated compliance with the Nazis. There was one character in particular who made this a difficult task: the minister of 'propaganda and education' in the Protectorate, Emanuel Moravec, yet another character within the troop of Moravecs and Moraveks that people this story. This Moravec was a veteran of the First World War and a career military man, much like his namesake František. He had been a fierce critic of Munich and a strong nationalist prior to the German invasion, who had robustly advocated fighting to defend the country. However, in the time since then he had turned his allegiances fully and become the strongest Czech advocate for active cooperation with the Nazis. He had taken on his ministerial role with relish and his key objective was to deliver the submission of the Czech population to the Nazi machine. Every utterance by him was in fierce opposition to Beneš' entire strategy and caused huge embarrassment for the exile government, forcing Beneš' activity into the searchlight of allied and Nazi consideration, when he would much prefer to work quietly in the shadows with his contacts at home.

The fragile balance in the Protectorate threatened to tip over into more overt oppression at any time. The SS were continuing to intrigue against Von Neurath through their instrument Karl Hermann Frank. From his observation point in Prague, Frank continued to gather evidence of the failings of Von Neurath and what he viewed as the clearly traitorous behaviour of Hácha and Eliáš. Frank took any opportunity had to strike fear into the populace.

The home network that was allied to Beneš was known as the Central Leadership of Home Resistance or in Czech 'ústřední vedení odboje domácího' - UVOD. It comprised of all non-communist resistance groups and had a strong link to the military via the 'Defence of the Nation,' the organisation to which the 'Three Kings' were affiliated. UVOD was far more influential than its rival communist groupings. But Beneš knew that relationships with Russia and its communists were also important and needed nurturing. Despite the Nazi-Soviet pact, the Russians had been secretly working to support home grown Czech communists in their fight against German occupation. Should Czechoslovak independence be won again, a reconciliation between Beneš' factions and the communists would be needed. Unbeknownst to the British, Beneš and his team were therefore also in touch with Russian intelligence. This was a key reason for maintaining their independent communications.

As autumn turned to winter, more and more information was emerging from A-54 and other sources about 'Operation Barbarossa' – Hitler's plan to break the Nazi-Soviet pact by launching a sudden attack on the Russian front. Beneš began to feed this information to Russia aggressively, seeking to warn of the attack, but principally to drive a firm wedge between Hitler and Stalin. Frustratingly little feedback came from Russia on how they were interpreting this information, but it would have certainly been difficult for them to disregard it when, in Feb 1941, the central committee of the Czech Communist Party was arrested by Karl Hermann Frank and their radio links with Moscow were destroyed.

#

Looking down at the photo album again, my eyes were drawn to a very familiar face. I smirked as I remembered an exchange with my grandfather many years before:

"Why have you got pictures of Winston Churchill in your photo album, Granddad?" I had asked, hoping for a fairly detailed and well-rounded explanation.

"Well," he had replied curtly, after a very brief pause, and leaving no room for a follow up question "...he was there."

#

The British were increasingly concerned about Operation Barbarossa. Their fear was that Russia, like France, was completely unprepared for the Nazi onslaught and would collapse in a matter of weeks. If this were to happen, Britain's defeat would only be a matter of time. In April of 1941, Beneš invited Churchill to visit the Czechoslovak troops and discuss developments while he was there. He took the opportunity to invite the American Ambassador to Great Britain and the Commander of the American Airforce too. Making use of his up-to-date intelligence on the matter, Beneš held the men spellbound over a lunchtime discussion, with his erudite and nuanced outlining of the political and military situation. He made a clear prediction that war between the Nazi and Soviet empires was imminent and would be initiated by Hitler. Churchill's separate intelligence corroborated Beneš' account. When questioned by Churchill on the Soviet's strength and ability to hold out against an attack, Beneš' response was firm and unqualified: he had every confidence in the Soviet Union, its officer corps and its soldiers to stand up to a German assault.

Further discussion on the moral and political preparedness of the Red Army, continued in Churchill's car as the men drove out to inspect the troops awaiting in Leamington.

#

I smoothed out the bent edges of the photo to get a clear look at it. Churchill was wearing his traditional overcoat and a spotted tie but not his usual homburg. He's next to Jan Šrámek – Beneš' Prime Minster - and General Ingr, a showery looking British sky overhead.

A couple of pages on, there's another one. This time it shows Churchill – in the same attire - stood next to Beneš with a stern and statesmanlike look on his face, shadowed by a large tree. And finally another of Churchill inspecting rows of well-ordered troops – his overcoat billowing out and his walking cane firmly in hand - as he strides forward.

#

Jan Masaryk had a surprise in store for Churchill as he boarded his car for the journey back to London. Masaryk may not have been an intellectual or a skilled administrator, but he knew 'people' and he'd seen in Churchill a man who like him, had an emotional centre. It was no coincidence that the two of them were the prize attractions on the BBC's Czech broadcast; the illegal device that those in the Protectorate affixed to their radio sets to tune in was even nicknamed the 'Churchillky.' Prior to the Prime Minister's visit, Jan had suggested that the exile army should be taught some English songs and that they should sing them to the visiting Prime Minister. As Churchill made his way to leave, the soldiers broke into an impassioned rendition of "Rule Britannia" in their well-rehearsed English. Although I know that at least one of the men there could not carry a tune, many were fine singers and they all sang with genuine appreciation and rekindled hope to the country that had given them succour. Churchill paused and then clambered back out of his car and made his way amongst them. He joined with them, conducting with his fist as he sang words that surely resonated with all present:

> "The nations, not so blest as thee,
>
> Must, in their turns, to tyrants fall;
>
> While thou shalt flourish great and free,
>
> The dread and envy of them all."

Churchill knew the lyrics well and harmonised with the men, as they began the rousing refrain:

> "Rule, Britannia! Britannia rule the waves,"

As he sang, tears welled in the British leader's melancholy eyes.

> "Britons never, never, never shall be slaves."

The Prime Minister thanked the men heartily and left deeply affected, carrying with him Beneš' latest note requesting full recognition of his government and the repudiation of Munich. He had the drive to London to think and on arrival he handed the note to Anthony Eden, his foreign minister, with a handwritten annotation.

"I do not see why the Czechs should not be placed on the same footing as the other allied governments. They have deserved it."

"I agree," wrote Eden underneath, on receipt of the note. Masaryk's human instincts had proved correct and effective, although the friction of bureaucracy and law would mean that it would still be a matter of months before this was formally enacted.

\#

The VRÚ was now in full operational mode at its new base in Woldingham. Initially, it was under the command of Lieutenant Jaroslav Suchy and in time would come to be led by Lieutenant Zdeněk Gold. Václav Modrák was hard at work on wireless operation with two other colleagues. Equipment maintenance was overseen by Antonín Simandl - an electromechanical expert who worked non-stop evolving and improving the designs for the transmitters and receivers, when not doing more urgent repairs.

The staff were working long hours in this tense and demanding environment and were gaining experience rapidly. The team were highly motivated and felt immense satisfaction when they were able to successfully do their job. As Modrák, wrote in his later memoir:

"Contact is a magic word, expressing satisfaction for all of those who were part of it in World War II, either home or abroad."

The nature of their work ensured that they were intimately connected to the activities in their homeland. Over time, the men became able to interpret the most subtle distinction between different sounds, being able to work out which stations they were in contact with by the tone and rhythm of the signals received. They were able to instinctively discern the degree of risk operators were facing, in making their transmissions. The highs of success were therefore tempered by regular lows when communication broke down. Modrák would later describe these feelings and in particular how they resonated with him, as someone who had, not so long ago, been active on the other side of the radio network in Prague.

"Along with these [received messages] came memories of those back home and of the courageous spokesman of the resistance Lt Col Balabán, that fighter and organiser who gave the call to join, which I answered. As I was working on my receiver I could see him bent over the table, the finger of one hand moving along the text of the message, and the other punching out the symbols of the communications."

Modrák was right to discern danger in the ongoing work of those at home and of Lieutenant Colonel Balabán in particular. In April 1941, he was finally caught and arrested after a gunfight with the Prague Gestapo. The 'Three Kings' were now two. Shortly afterwards in May, Moravek and Mašín were located in an apartment mid transmission by the Gestapo too. In a selfless attempt to buy time for Moravek and the wireless operator Peltan, Mašín shot one of the Gestapo men as they burst through the door and grabbing the others, tumbled down the stairs with them. Mašín was caught but Moravek and Peltan tied a steel cable to the sofa and dangled it from the window, before sliding fifty feet down it to the ground. One of Moravek's fingers was sliced clean through on the descent, but the pair managed to escape in a passing streetcar. The loss of this transmitter came close to cutting off Beneš' contact with A-54 on the very eve of Barbarossa. Moravek was able to find a transmitter from another group but he had the Gestapo very close on his tail. The Gestapo also had Mašín and Balabán, and therefore in theory an opportunity to torture out of them the information they needed to track down the last of the 'Three Kings' and get to A-54. They should have known better: the men betrayed nothing.

News of these developments reached Stankmuller and Moravec almost instantly via the VRÚ. The view was quickly formed that this fragility of communications was unacceptable. More support was needed in the home country to keep it intact – both people and equipment. Stankmuller's work with the SOE would need to be accelerated and men with the right skills would have to be found to go back to the Protectorate. In April 1941, almost as Churchill was departing from his visit, Stankmuller came to Leamington. He was looking for men of special qualities – the qualities they would need for extraordinary tasks in service of their country. Fate would now put Jaroslav Bublík at the very centre of the story.

#

I had made real inroads in my questioning but it was time to get specific.

"Did you know František Moravec?" I said, pronouncing his name with a hard c.

"Mor-a-vetz," he corrected. 'Yes I knew him very well. He was my boss for much of the War."

I nodded, thankful for this validation. He looked at me sternly.

"We Czechs would have done nothing if not for Moravec."

#

Beneš and Moravec needed men who were loyal to them on the ground in the Protectorate. Primarily, and most critically, they needed men to strengthen communication links with the Protectorate. This would allow them to coordinate a range of actions in their home country. Initially they would focus on sabotage of armaments and logistics behind axis lines and link with the home resistance. Ultimately they sought to prepare for the coordination of the eventual uprising against the Nazis. But an uprising was not imminent. They felt a need to make an immediate statement that would strike down any notion amongst the Allies that Czechoslovaks were docile and subservient to the Nazis. They were going to conduct a political assassination. The target? Emanuel Moravec, the dreadful quisling who embarrassed the exiled intelligence bureau constantly by the coincidence of his surname. If not him, then the ruthless chief of security, Karl Hermann Frank. The turncoat or the oppressor must be killed. By mid-May, František Moravec had selected a group of both commissioned and non-commissioned officers for parachute training. In his memoir he explains how they were chosen:

"The selection would not be easy. The requirements were rigorous. Besides all the qualities of a commando, such as physical fitness, mental alertness and various technical aptitudes, one more quality was needed. The nature of the task, I knew, would almost eliminate chances for escape, and apprehension meant certain death. The first question I had to ask a prospective candidate was: "Are you prepared to die for your country?"

"The men most highly recommended were interviewed by my deputy and me. The top candidates, after this scrutiny, were asked if they would volunteer for special training. All agreed. At this stage that was all that they knew…They were an attractive group. Young, fit, well-motivated, they all had good military records. They were all unmarried and none had been a resident of Prague."

#

"When did you first meet him?" I asked, keen to coax out more.

"When they first began to recruit for parachutists. To be dropped behind enemy lines."

I wasn't sure where to go next. There were too many questions to ask. I dug deep into my brain for something, anything I'd read about this time.

"In Moravec's book he says that he didn't select any gamblers or womanisers?

He eyed me curiously, and gave a slight shrug.

"…some were…some weren't…I was selected as one of the very first batch of parachutists, along with Opálka, Gabčík and Novák."

"What about Josef?"

"No - he was not chosen then – he was later."

"What was your mission?"

"I was recruited initially for an assassination mission."

"With Karel Svoboda?"

"No – before him. Right at the start."

"Did you know who you were going to assassinate?"

"No. Everyone knew who Moravec was though - so we knew it was something big."

My brain started to itch with a thought and I flipped forward to the last page of the photo album on my lap. My eyes fixed on the main addition to the very last page. I had seen it dozens of times over the years. Although I'd never paid much attention to it, it was as familiar to me as the perfumed smell that infused the whole album, but I now looked at it afresh. It was a rectangular card, aged from an original white to a grainy beige, affixed at the corners with squares of thick, yellowed sticky tape. Although I didn't speak Czech, the translation was easy. It was a personal invite from Dr Edvard Beneš, President of the Republic of Czechoslovakia to "Bublíka Jaroslava"- to attend a dinner at Walton Hall, in Warwickshire, where Churchill and Beneš had just dined. The date? May 26, 1941: just a month after Stankmuller's visit.

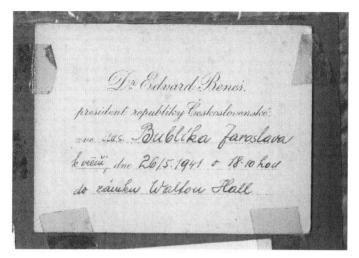

I remembered him mentioning this appointment with pride, if not with much detail, on a couple of occasions. The farmer's son from rural Moravia had surfaced literally at the top table, with the intellectual and political elite of his beloved country. And the reason why? They needed men like him.

#

The Czechs were very impressed with the professionalism and quality of the SOE training and sought to make the best use of it. Plans rapidly began to take shape to drop these Czechoslovak soldiers behind enemy lines. But at the same time, as with their communications, the exiles needed to maintain the right degree of independence from their hosts. The various SOE schools were used to build a training programme, but this was under the ultimate oversight of Emil Stankmuller and Karel Paleček, starting from this small core of soldiers.

At the start of June, as this frantic activity was underway, Hitler finally invaded Russia, just as A-54 had predicted. This development led to a complete pivot from the Soviets and their communist diaspora. Of particular note, the Czechoslovak 'Spaniards' who had sought to undermine Beneš just a short while earlier, no longer saw an objection to being part of the 'capitalist' army and were gradually released to front line roles, many distinguishing themselves in the fight against the Nazis. Soon afterwards, on July 18, the Russians granted the Beneš' government in exile full recognition. Britain's recognition, despite the successful manoeuvring of Jan Masaryk some months before, came three hours later. This was significant; the Russians had acted first, outflanking the West in the field of Czechoslovak opinion once again.

Beneš was now the recognised leader of Czechoslovakia, and he would need the actions of his country to reflect that. Given that many Russian soldiers were now being slaughtered by armaments produced by Czechs at the Škoda works, this was no small matter. Paying lip service would no longer do; parachute missions had to be progressed, but for them to be possible, the communication network first had to be strengthened. It was 'contact' that was the most important as always - without that there was nothing.

#

"Were you dropped?"

"No. Not then – I was dropped later. As things developed, it became clear I was too much use as a radio operator to go. Novák and I were kept to train the radio operators and build our capability."

I felt some satisfaction at this clarity. I now knew for sure, from his own mouth, that he had been parachuted into his homeland. But it wasn't at this time. I ultimately needed to understand the details of his later mission: the culmination of his story. But there was more to know first about the roles he and Josef played in those first missions.

#

In terms of the public record, there is very little documenting the activity of Beneš, Moravec and the exiles at this time. Events that were about to unfold were to be hugely emotive. Even František Moravec's memoirs, written many years later, are selective and in some cases give incorrect dates and information. For many years there were good reasons why some figures remained silent about their part in preparations for what - regardless of the moral or strategic arguments - was to be a political assassination. Jaroslav Bublík and his good friend Miroslav Novák took up roles as instructors helping agents to perfect their telecommunications skills, Morse code and equipment maintenance. Trainees undertook instruction under their close oversight, making use of SOE facilities in Thame Park in Oxfordshire, Chicheley Hall near Newport Pagnell, and at 'Funny Neuk,' the VRÚ centre in Woldingham, where some of the budding radio operators were sent on brief secondments to hone their skills at the front line. Jaroslav Bublík and Miroslav Novák began to train a steady stream of the radio operators who would be dropped into the Protectorate over the following years.

Once their functional training was complete, the candidates were sent to the Czech's own 'holding centre' at a country house called Bellasis in Surrey, outside London. Agents there were commanded by Staff Captain Jaroslav Šustr, who prepared them for their specific operational tasks. This was done entirely independently of SOE control and was the weakest part of training, as the Czechs had no prior experience of running agents into occupied Europe. It's likely that the radio operators were instructed here in the final aspects of their training: coding and decoding messages to the system derived by Václav Knotek and known only to a very select few.

#

"Did you know Captain Gold?" I asked, referring to the head of the communication function I had read about in my research. My grandfather looked quite surprised and confused at this name coming forth from me.

"Yes – very well – I worked for him when I joined the signalling headquarters, until I took over his job. But he was not really a big fish. The big men were Moravec, Stankmuller and Paleček."

I nodded. I remembered from my research that Stankmuller and Paleček were two of the team Moravec brought over on his desperate flight from Prague.

"They were all intelligent men. I liked them all a great deal."

"Marge!" my grandfather shouted, summoning my grandmother clattering down the corridor from the kitchen.

"Marge, you remember Paleček?'

"Oh yes Jarda. Of course I remember him."

"He ended up as machine operator after the war…Paleček."

"Oh yes…I know. Fancy that."

"Did you know Captain Šustr?" I asked.

He nodded curtly, his face still showing confusion at my depth of knowledge. "Yes…him, I did not like so much…He was not big fish either. Marge, you remember Šustr?"

"Oh yes…Šustr…he looked like Nigel Patrick."

"I don't know who he looked like – he was arrogant swine."

I stifled a laugh, and before I could stop myself asked: "Who's Nigel Patrick?"

"He was an actor," my grandmother replied.

"What was he in?"

"Oh…he was in lots of things,' she replied, before abruptly departing the room again.

#

The remaining men from the first cadre of recruits were put through their paces in a commando course at Arisaig in the Western Highlands of Scotland from July 1941. The scenic views out to the islands of Rum and Eigg would have been a wondrous, alien sight to the men from landlocked Czechoslovakia. But the deep blue seas and white sands were deceptive, as a stiff Scottish wind could whip up in a moment and suddenly remind the men of their lofty latitude. A short trek into this rocky coast led straight into a rising terrain of peaks that had broken the spirit of many a prospective paratrooper. The men were taught survival skills, weapons handling, basic sabotage and unarmed combat. After Scotland came a trip to Manchester for parachute training at Ringway airport. Saboteurs were sent on to Brickendonbury Manor, a grand estate in Hertfordshire, to learn more advanced industrial sabotage.

One notable member of that first group was Sergeant Jozef Gabčík, the Slovak artillery sergeant who had distinguished himself in the Battle of France. A professional soldier with a fiery temper, he brought a professionalism to the handling of small arms and stood out from the start. There were various others too, who I would come to learn much more about. There was Lieutenant Adolf Opálka, a career officer who had left Czechoslovakia via Poland and was serving in a machine gun company; Josef Valčík, an affable and gregarious young man who had been a worker in a shoe factory before the war; Jan Kubiš, a quiet and reserved young Moravian and Jiří Potůček, a signals expert who had trained and honed his skills at the signals unit in Agde.

A second course followed in August. This included many of the members of the impending communications operation SILVER A, including its leader, Alfréd Bartoš, who like Opálka was a graduate of the Hranice military academy. The group also included Jaroslav Bublík's erstwhile tent companion Karel Svoboda, a teenage radio operator called Oldřich Dvořák, and the second of the Bublíks, Josef, who had by now followed his older cousin into this secretive domain.

#

"So you and Josef were very close?'

"Yes…but not just Josef. I was close to all of them"

"Gabčík…Opálka?

"Yes….I knew them all…I knew them…'

He paused, seeking the right word to properly convey his relationship

"…I knew them intimately."

"Did you know Valčík?"

A smile came to his face, full of respect, "He was a good friend of mine. We all came over on the boat together. He was fine fellow."

I had read about these men in books and magazines - to me they were semi-fictional characters; archetypal war heroes. I was finding it difficult to think of them as real flesh and blood people; my grandfather's closest cohort of companions and comrades.

I gazed down at his photo album, looking once again at the pictures of the men in their early days in England, seeking a sense of the mood and relationships at this time. There are several of exercise drills. A forest of bare-chested men lifting rifles above their heads.

Another shows a cast of sokols, pristine in their white shirts and trousers, standing on their hands with their legs spinning in the air in unison.

One photo shows a small group of them collapsed on the grass after a workout: A young version of my grandfather staring out at me.

In another one a soldier plays the accordion: a bottle of beer sitting beside him. Then they're sitting in a large group on the grass - in uniform - taking an informal briefing from one of their officers. Most look calm, some look bored, others look downwards, lost in their thoughts: A group of young men thrown together in extreme circumstances.

As time moves on, the photos evolve. Several show the act of radio instruction: soldiers hunched on parkland, fiddling with portable radio sets as notes are scribbled.

In another my grandfather sits in some sort of military briefing in a darkened room. Next to him is a young soldier: wide eyed and earnest with an open notebook.

#

The invasion of Russia emboldened resistance in the Protectorate. A shared purpose now brought closer coordination of the communist and democratic groups with visible results. In a game of tit for tat, the Nazis responded to this increased threat with more crackdowns, including more Sokol arrests. Unperturbed, the populace instigated slowdowns in factories, which reduced productivity in the Protectorate by ten to twenty percent. Finally, in the middle of September, Beneš orchestrated a boycott of the local pro-Nazi press. Its purpose was to demonstrate the influence of the home resistance and Beneš' control of it. The sale of newspapers reduced by seventy percent, indicating widespread resistance to the occupation. From the German perspective, this development was also instructive. In particular, it was noted that the state President of the government, Emil Hácha, and the Prime Minister, General Eliáš appeared to be complicit in the boycott.

The Nazis therefore decided that it was time for a change and a series of long planned intrigues and counter intrigues matured.

In response to this flexing of Beneš' muscles, Karl Hermann Frank confronted Von Neurath with his final demands for the imposition of extreme measures and martial law. When he was rebuffed, Frank managed to negotiate a face-to-face meeting with Hitler himself. He flew into Berlin with his dossiers of information, determined to leave as the new 'Protector' of Bohemia and Moravia. But when he arrived, there was another man present too: his SS boss, Reinhard Heydrich. Heydrich had been the puppet master all along. He had encouraged Frank's plotting against Von Neurath whilst separately collecting additional information from his own sources. Heydrich effortlessly brushed Frank aside, whilst demonstrating to Hitler his knowledge of the situation and his plan for Bohemia and Moravia. These Slavs would be made to know who their masters were. They would be terrorised and offered respite only through compliance. Rewards for those knuckling down and supporting the Nazis would be generous. But for anyone else, punishment would be immediate and severe. Secretly, a longer-term plan would also be implemented: Bohemia and Moravia would be 'Germanised.' Secret racial profiling would begin immediately and all Slav blood removed by execution or deportation to the East. This would set the approach that would also be applied to the vast tracts of land that would open up as Soviet Russia fell. Hitler, still furious at the news presented to him, found the plan very much to his liking and knew that Heydrich was the man to implement it - an inhuman sociopath, cunning, hard-working, pitiless and without any constraints of morality.

A stunned Von Neurath was given a severe dressing down and retired through 'illness'. Just days later, Heydrich arrived in Prague to take up his role as the new de-facto 'protector' of Bohemia and Moravia. A still dazed Frank was in tow; kept on by Heydrich to be the hand that would continue to do the dirty work he needed.

Heydrich was immensely satisfied with the outcome of his plotting, as the black flag of the SS was raised over the Hradčany Castle in Prague. Not only would this posting give him a chance to show how merciless he could be and to position himself to rise above his boss Heinrich Himmler in the Nazi hierarchy, it also represented his complete victory over the German military establishment. Heydrich's SS career had begun when, as a young lieutenant, he had been ejected from the German navy on the grounds of ungentlemanly conduct with a young lady. He had sought revenge since that day and now, as the German military saluted and genuflected, he had it.

His first actions were directed toward the local leaders, who were hopelessly compromised by the information in the avalanche of files he had in his possession. Eliáš was arrested and sentenced to death. Sick and weary, Hácha was confronted on the verge of making a formal resignation and forced to collaborate with this change in leadership, with the inducement that the suffering the Czechs deserved could be mitigated a little by his involvement. A civil state of emergency was declared and martial law was imposed. Five thousand people were arrested - any potential leaders, those suspected of involvement in resistance and black marketeers. Of these, four hundred were immediately and very publicly sentenced to death. The members of Obrana Národa suffered the worst. One of the first to be taken from his cell for execution, at the start of October, was its leader Josef Bílý. His execution was intended to be a demonstration of the futility of opposition and resistance but he had other ideas. Refusing his blindfold, he was marched out in front of the firing squad and sneeringly asked if he had any final words. He had a few.

"Long live Czechoslovakia," he spat.

"Now shoot you German dogs!"

In a cynical attempt to create the impression that the situation was being brought under control and to maintain the illusion to Hácha that his complicity had value, public executions were ramped down over a number of weeks. However, the remainder of the prisoners were sent to concentration camps and murdered gradually in secret, while Hácha was induced to berate Beneš over the Czech airwaves. In combination with increased rations and benefits for armaments workers and others, these measures instantly began to have a noticeable effect on war production and behaviour. Extremely satisfied with his initial work and how power had been realigned, Heydrich sought to ensure he also retained his influence inside Germany, making arrangements to chair the Wannssee conference in Berlin, where an agreement of the 'final solution' to the 'Jewish problem' was soon to be discussed and agreed.

#

At the start of October, Jan Masaryk came onto the airwaves for his latest broadcast. Always genuine in his emotions, he spoke with uncharacteristic fury.

"The blood of the students of Prague has dried on the fat hands of Neurath, but it has not disappeared....Heydrich has come to Prague to break your spirit, and intimidate you all. In that, of course he will not succeed. I am a little ashamed to speak to you today from here, where I am in safety. But you know how fervently I am with you and how I swear to God Almighty, and so with me do all of us in London, that we shall avenge [those murdered by Heydrich] – a hundred Germans for one - and that will be little."

This was tempered with realism and a note of caution for the people his father had united. Almost as if his words would do the fighting for them, for the time being.

"Please do not let yourselves be provoked into the actions for which Heydrich's bloody hands are waiting and go about your business calmly…you have shown the world how flexible you are, for the present that is enough. It is neither your nor our fault that murder is being committed in Prague. Orgies of the Gestapo murderers are at their climax throughout Europe, and it was impossible for you to be left out…it is difficult for me today to wish you a good night."

As the days passed, Beneš' regular meetings with Moravec became increasingly tense. The British were regularly reviewing the resistance activities of the underground movements in each occupied country and Heydrich's approach had rapidly moved Czechoslovakia to the bottom of the list. No amount of cherry-picking their intelligence could now hide the truth. Pressure from both the British and the Russians for action was intense but Beneš' appeals to the home resistance were falling on deaf ears. Beneš and his Chief of Intelligence therefore decided it was time for them to take direct action. Beneš inquired about the parachutists in training. Stankmuller and Paleček surveyed the crop of trainees and deliberated hard, finally settling on two men. The first was obvious. Jozef Gabčík would deliver any mission given to him and his proven ability to handle automatic weapons would serve him well in formulating an effective assassination plan. The second person had to be a more sober, even-tempered character, to provide balance to the team. They settled on Karel Svoboda, a proven patriot and an excellent soldier who had volunteered readily, even supplying the details of his family at home as patriots who would support any parachutists dropped. It was decided: a Slovak and a Czech would together conduct the mission. In early October, Moravec addressed the two young men:

"The radio and newspapers have told you about the insane murderous slaughter that is going on at home, in our own houses…At home our people have fought – now they are in a difficult position…it is our turn to help them…In Prague there are two persons who are representative of the killing. They are Karl Hermann Frank and the newcomer Heydrich. In our opinion, and in the opinion of our leaders, we must try to make one of them pay for all the rest, so as to prove that we return blow for blow…I don't have to tell you that your mission is of the utmost historical importance and the danger is great. Its success depends on the conditions that your own shrewdness and ability to bring it into being…. If you still have any doubts about what I have set out, you must say so."

The two men had no such doubts and left immediately for their final parachute course at Ringway airport in Manchester.

#

I found myself looking at my grandfather afresh. Still a little in shock that he was finally opening up, I was now getting to know a different side of him at this very late hour in his life. As he spoke, I found myself absent-mindedly staring at the deep ridged scar on the bridge of his nose. It was very familiar to me but I'd never really thought much about it. It really was a nasty one; a long purple welt still clearly evident, although the original injury must have been getting on for sixty years in the past. My mum had told me that when she was young she had thought the ridge was there to rest his glasses on and assumed that many people had them. At some point he had briefly mentioned to me what actually caused it. While making a parachute jump, he had apparently fallen awkwardly into a large tree and his face had been thrown into its sharp branches.

#

Arriving in Manchester, Gabčík and Svoboda were tasked to carry out two final practice jumps from a Whitley aircraft and one night jump from a fixed balloon. The first jump went smoothly and the men repacked their chutes and readied themselves to jump again. However, the second jump did not go to plan. As Svoboda left the plane, he became tangled in his static line. His parachute eventually opened but his descent was jerky and inelegant and his landing heavy. He was sent back to London urgently where a doctor examined him for persistent headaches. Gabčík completed the course alone, while confusion reigned about what to do next on this vital, secret mission. When it became apparent that Svoboda could not complete the course, Gabčík took the lead and proposed to Captain Šustr that his good friend Jan Kubiš should take Svoboda's place. This was a sound switch. Kubiš was a good soldier with an even temper. He and Gabčík were the firmest of friends and had a natural trust in each other. In addition, Kubiš was a Moravian, so the Czecho-Slovak flavour of the team would be maintained. The switch was agreed and Operation

ANTHROPOID - as it was now known - was entrusted to the two men. But a delay was necessary while Kubiš' documentation was produced and his training completed.

Meanwhile, Heydrich's reprisals had made other missions essential too. On the night of October 4, the Gestapo's relentless searches took effect and Captain Moravek's replacement transmitter was detected while in use in Prague. One of the operators killed himself and the other was captured. A-54 continued to provide information to Moravek but the last of the 'Three Kings' could no longer share it with the VRÚ in Woldingham.

With contact lost, there was an urgent need for a parachute mission to send in agents to restore Beneš' essential link with the home resistance and A-54. Jaroslav Bublík and his fellow radio trainer Miroslav Novák were urgently engaged with training the team for this mission. It was to be codenamed 'SILVER A'.

PROPHECIES

SILVER A's mission was multi-faceted: re-establish radio contact between the VRÚ and the home resistance, contact A-54 and establish a base to co-ordinate arrival of subsequent groups. This mission was a key enabler to everything else, including Kubiš and Gabčík's secretive and more dramatic mission. It was to be led by Lieutenant Alfréd Bartoš, who although still only twenty-five, had experience that made him a sound choice. In France he had worked as an Intelligence Officer. Eager to see action, he had been one of the first to volunteer for special missions when Stankmuller had come calling. His team would also comprise of two others. Second in command was Josef Valčík – a gregarious, fair-haired sergeant major from Moravia, just twenty miles from the Bublíks' hometown of Banov. He and the Bublíks had in fact taken the same route to exile and their paths had crossed many times in the weeks and months since. The final member was the group's signaller, Jiří Potůček. The oldest of the three (at the grand old age of twenty-nine) Potůček was a gifted linguist and had been working in business in Yugoslavia when his country had been overrun. He had made his way to Agde, where like Jaroslav Bublík he had been placed in the communication unit.

Potůček's transmitter, on which so much rested, was given the name Libuše. This was an appropriate moniker, which clearly underlined the significance and hope that it contained. Libuše was the name of a fabled Czech princess, the wisest daughter of a mythical king named Krok, with a gift of seeing into the future. As the mission was quickly planned, Potůček was put through his paces, coached by Jaroslav Bublík and Miroslav Novák on the practical use and operation of the equipment. Potůček was made to think of how to diagnose and fix any and all faults that Libuše, his temperamental princess, might have. His role was simple: get her somewhere safe, get her working, and keep her working.

After a number of false starts and aborted attempts, seven men – comprising three separate missions – were eventually dispatched together on December 28, 1941 from Tangmere Airfield, close to England's southern coast. In addition to the ANTHROPOID and SILVER A teams, two other men were sent on a separate mission to deliver another transmitter to a separate part of the local underground resistance in the eastern region of Bohemia. This mission was codenamed SILVER B.

The teams knew that they would parachute together at the last moment and were instructed not to talk to each other on the flight. In addition to their equipment, they were given basic clothing and provisions which had been carefully prepared so as not to give away their origin from England. They were also given fake identify papers that had been meticulously prepared by the SOE. Unfortuantely Šustr had clumsily applied the wrong sort of ink to the stamp he used to validate SILVER B's papers, in effect ruining them. For Vladimír Škacha, one of the two members of that group, the result was a 'disaster' which not surprisingly left him feeling even more apprehensive about his return to the Protectorate. Škacha's summary of his feelings about the mission and his part in it were probably very representative of how many of the men most likely felt about their various missions:

"I had joined the resistance when I was nineteen. I was one of a family that was pleased if we could get enough to eat. That means I owned nothing. I volunteered for parachute training out of pure patriotic feeling; I had ideals that seem exaggerated to me now – the sort you only find in novels…nobody offered us the least reward for what we were going to do. And on our side we never asked for any. I looked upon myself as a soldier who had been given an order and who could only expect a word of praise at most, if he carried out what he had been ordered to do properly. So I left the trifles I owned to my parents in a will I wrote on rather humorous lines."

The humour was seemingly lost on Šustr, who concluded in his despatch report that Škacha was unacceptably curt and inattentive in their final discussion. In reality, Šustr was barely a concern for the young parachutist who understandably had other things on his mind. The men all boarded silently with winks, smiles and supportive pats on each other's backs but retreated into themselves for the difficult flight that followed. Crammed together in the hold of the plane, they encountered enemy fighters and anti-aircraft gunfire, before eventually passing the Škoda works and reached their dropping points sometime after two am. Gabčík and Kubiš of ANTHROPOID dropped first and disappeared into the dark. Then the three members of SILVER A waved goodbye to the men of SILVER B and in quick succession leapt from the plane, and plummeted through the open sky above Bohemia.

Potůček descended to the ground in the rolling lowlands near the small town of Poděbrady, about thirty miles east of Prague. He freed himself from his parachute, which he then buried. Despite a search, he was initially unable to find either his precious Libuše or the other two members of his group. After some time, he stumbled across Bartoš in the wilderness. Although the pair were aware that they would have to start moving soon to avoid detection, they waited still longer to search for Valčík and their equipment. With their efforts in vain and dawn fast approaching, the two men set out along a nearby road which led to a crossroads with signs that indicated that they were close to the village of Senice. This was a very helpful steer for Bartoš, who had grown up in the area. They approached the local schoolhouse and tapped on the window, finding the schoolmaster who gave them food and let them sleep. This was their first lucky encounter and with a level of providence they could not have hoped for, many more chance encounters eased their way to success. They continued on the next day to a nearby village and - with the help of contacts they found there - eventually reached Pardubice, a city sixty miles east of Prague. There they managed to find Valčík, who had initially buried Libuše on landing, and had used his contacts to find local support. A patriot schoolmaster in Pardubice had helped him recover the transmitter and retrieve it in a taxi - the taxi driver completely unaware of the critical nature of his cargo.

All three men were now together with their equipment and immediately set out to complete the first step of their mission.

Bartoš set up his command post in a village called Dašice, just west of Pardubice and instructed his local contacts to gather intelligence. With the help of a local policeman who worked for the underground resistance, Potůček set up the transmitter in a quarry at a local mountain range. This vast warren of pitted land provided the perfect place to hide away. Meanwhile, Valčík managed to secure a job as a waiter at the 'Veselka' restaurant in Pardubice. The tactic of hiding in plain sight was in some ways less risky than the alternative and the post allowed Valčík to engage with the community in the area and pick up useful information.

Initially, there was no response to the messages sent via the transmitter. After a number of days of silence, Potůček undertook detailed fault finding on his equipment. He realised that the problem was not with Libuše's transmitter but with her receiver. He was able to use a spare part that had been sent to fix the set and SILVER A finally made contact with the VRÚ on January 15. A key part of their mission had been successfully completed.

Over the coming weeks SILVER A and the local team around it quickly settled into its work to establish a steady stream of information to Woldingham. Potůček would send and receive messages at night and then cycle to Bartoš in Dašice each morning, bringing an envelope with coded messages. He would note his arrival with three short rings and one long one on the door bell. Potůček would then return to the quarry where he would rest through the day while Bartoš decoded the messages. Valčík wore his responsibilities lightly and he cheered them all up with tales from his work in the café. He talked of how he would offer Gestapo officers a light, listening to everything they said as he did so. But the tension was palpable and the environment unforgiving. Heydrich's regime of psychological terror had induced fear and paranoia in everyone.

Two parts of their mission had been achieved: linking with local resistance and the setting up of Libuše. The third goal still remained: they needed to form a link with A-54. The way to do this was through contacting the last of the 'Three Kings,' Captain Moravek. Valčík was entrusted with this task. Unsurprisingly, Moravek was not an easy man to find. He had been on the run since the loss of his last transmitter and the Gestapo were doggedly on his tail. He had nearly been caught in December, when a raid on a safe house had required him to shoot his way free, injuring three security policeman.

Valčík headed to Prague and contacted the underground there. However, he was not immediately trusted. Heydrich's reign of terror had understandably made everyone extremely guarded. Eventually, a message was sent via Libuše to the exiles for their help. A coded message validating Valčík's credentials was broadcast by the BBC. Accepted into the fold, he was reacquainted with Kubiš and Gabčík, who upon landing had gone immediately to Prague and were now being sheltered by the same resistance network. Finally, on March 14, Valčík was put in direct contact with Moravek. A backlog of fresh intelligence came flooding into the VRÚ through Libuše.

Beneš was extremely pleased. This was a major success at a critical time, and all members of the group were promoted in the field. But as the commanding officer, Bartoš was critically aware of the difficulties they had faced and how their success had involved more than a degree of good fortune. He was concerned that

Moravec and the government in exile were not fully aware of the extreme difficulty of the environment they were working in. The network he had pulled together was fragile and the whole of the Nazi machine was ruthlessly seeking to destroy it.

After the briefest moment of celebration, Bartoš sent a very considered note to Moravec. It was nominally a request for improved equipment: he asked for smaller pistols, more concealable suicide tablets and also cases that it was impossible for him to get hold of. But it also spelt out the harsh realities of life in the Protectorate, stressing that Moravec should factor this into future operational planning. Meals and provisions could not be obtained without coupons, bicycles could not be purchased, transport by train was difficult and anti-sabotage patrols roamed nightly. He stressed that no agents were able to work without being at risk of discovery or being taken for use as forced labour, which was a particular concern as spring approached. He finished his note with a very pointed and honest piece of advice for his handlers.

"It is therefore impossible to commit a greater number of secret agents without increasing the risk of the whole system being discovered. That is why I think it more profitable to make the utmost use of those who are here and to limit the number of fresh arrivals to the lowest possible figure."

Beneš and Moravec provided no response to the letter. Meanwhile, in the rapidly shrinking operational space of the Protectorate, time had inevitably run out for A-54.

#

Unbeknownst to Captain Moravek, the Gestapo had discovered the identity of A-54 by the end of February. He had been unmasked as Paul Thümmel, a man of impeccable Nazi and

Intelligence credentials and a very senior member of the Abwehr, based in Prague. He was even a long-term friend and confidante of SS boss Henrich Himmler.

Oskar Fleischer discovered that Thümmel was in contact with Moravek, but the experienced Abwehr man was able to delay the investigation by claiming he himself was seeking to entrap the Czech resistance leader. After a series of interrogations, Thümmel was sent, under surveillance, to set up a rendezvous with Captain Moravek. When Moravek failed to arrive at the designated time Thümmel was imprisoned.

Through the interrogation of a local liaison agent, the Gestapo had coincidentally discovered that Captain Moravek was due to be in a park in Prague at 7pm the very next day. At the appointed time, Moravek sent his liaison ahead of him and the man was captured by the Gestapo agents guarding the park. Moravek set out to rescue him and, in what would be his final firefight, discharged fifty rounds before eventually being hit in both legs. Surrounded and about to be captured, he killed himself with a shot to the head. The 'Three Kings' were no more.

Moravek's death did not stop key intelligence from falling into the hands of the Gestapo. In his discarded possessions were photos of the members of SILVER A – Potůček, Bartoš and Valčík - for making new identity papers. The Gestapo immediately saw that the photos had a Pardubice studio address and swarmed into the region hunting for the men. Valčík's photograph was recognised as that of the waiter from the Veslka restaurant and his employer was interrogated. Valčík managed to escape to his parents in Moravia. Bartoš and Potůček remained in Pardubice with Libuše.

With the situation becoming ever more precarious, and despite Bartoš' very clearly expressed concerns, Moravec, Stankmuller and Paleček continued with the dispatch of still more agents into the Protectorate.

#

"I trained all of the radio operators that were dropped in that period: Potůček, Dvořák…. Gerik."

My eyes darted up at the mention of the final name. It was very familiar to me from the reading I had done.

'You trained Gerik?'

"Yes"

"Was he capable in training?"

"No, no– he was completely unsuitable," he said, shuffling in his seat. "He should never have been sent. I said so in my report and I argued strongly against it. But I was overruled."

I paused to take this point in. Through my research I knew what Gerik had done, and how he had committed the worst crime any agent could. But I hadn't been aware that there were any doubts about his suitability for his mission.

#

At the end of 1941, the Japanese had made a surprise attack on US naval base at Pearl Harbour in Hawaii. This had brought the might of America fully into the war. With America as an ally and with Russia's continued stubborn resistance on the battlefield, Beneš was now more confident than ever that the Nazis would ultimately lose the war. He also felt sure that the careful lobbying of the Czechoslovak-American community and his relationship-building with Roosevelt would now bear fruit. Beneš began to plan earnestly for the end game. In particular, he started to lobby hard for the eventual expulsion of the entire Sudeten German population from Czechoslovakia. In his mind, it had been clearly proven that his country would have no security and no future with this fifth column in its borders. With an eye on this objective, under pressure to demonstrate more immediate tangible success for the war effort and emboldened by the success of SILVER A, Beneš demanded more action. But this was risky. In March 1942 the Germans were at the height of their powers and Bartoš' warnings of the dangers of further missions were on point.

Operation OUTDISTANCE was fast-tracked. This was an ambitious plan to help the Royal Air Force bomb the Škoda works and critically damage Nazi heavy armament production in the area. Like SILVER A, it was staffed with the very best men that could be found. The group leader, Captain Adolf Opálka, was an officer of the very highest calibre and well respected by his men. His number two for the mission was one of the more experienced soldiers in this young crop of men. A grizzled professional soldier, thirty-year-old Sergeant Karel Čurda had stayed in the force for a decade following his military service. The final member was Corporal Ivan Kolařík, a medical student who had fled his home country when the universities were forcibly closed and had then fought his way to and from France with his fellow exiles.

A further mission was to be executed at the same time. With an eye to an eventual Nazi collapse, Operation ZINC was planned to establish a new communication network in Moravia; creating an area of operation closer to the Slovak border. As with SILVER A and OUTDISTANCE, it was headed up by a graduate of the Hranice Military Academy in Moravia, Lieutenant Oldřich Pechal. His deputy was another capable soldier. The lantern-jawed sergeant, Arnošt Mikš, had been a stonemason in central Bohemia before exile took him to France and England. ZINC was fundamentally a communications mission. Radio operators were a critical and scarce resource and anyone with skills in this area was fast-tracked for missions. So it was, that twenty-one-year-old Viliam Gerik came to be the third member of the group. Gerik had been apprenticed as a radio mechanic in his native Slovakia before the war. He was nimble, athletic and physically strong. Small in stature, he was reputed to be somewhat insecure and had developed a reputation as a practical joker. As well as his radio training at the SOE school in Oxfordshire, he was sent on a secondment to the VRÚ in Woldingham, all under the sceptical eye of Jaroslav Bublík.

ZINC and OUTDISTANCE were flown out together on the night of March 27, 1942. Opálka and the members of OUTDISTANCE landed in the planned location near Telč in Moravia. ZINC's mission started to go wrong from the very outset, when they were wrongly dropped in Slovakia. As well as rendering their contact lists useless, this meant that they now had to make a crossing of the heavily guarded border into Moravia. They buried their parachutes and overalls near their landing spot, hid one wireless set in a nearby barn and took their other radio set with them. Gerik's search for a relative who he thought still lived nearby proved fruitless. Pechal decided that their best bet would be to cross the border separately and set off on his own. Mikš and Gerik managed to catch a train into Moravia and found temporary shelter with local patriots. On setting up their radio to inform London of their dire situation, Gerik discovered that it had been broken in the fall and was useless.

In his attempt to cross the border, Pechal sprang from dense tree cover and was surprised by a two-man border patrol. He reacted quickly, freeing his gun from his pocket and shooting both officers dead with clinical efficiency. Appraising his brutal handiwork, he decided that he should quickly flee the scene. However, when his composure returned, he realised that in the melee he had dropped his briefcase which included his false papers. It was too late to return and in panic, Pechal ended up at his parents' nearby house. Their happy surprise at seeing him would have quickly soured. Shortly after his arrival, they received a visit from a Gestapo informer looking for him. Pechal kept hidden in the undergrowth outside the house but the visit made it clear that he had been identified and his parents were in imminent danger.

Pechal, Gerik and Mikš met at a planned rendezvous in the woods near Pechal's parents' house. Cautiously pacing the crunchy forest floor in the cover of tall, ancient trees, they planned their next steps with rising anxiety. Without their contacts to rely on, they had found a local population that was terrified and frightened of contact with them. They decided that travelling together was too risky and that they should seek out their contacts separately. Pechal remained where he was, watching over his parents. Mikš and Gerik travelled to Brno (the Moravian capital) in a sombre mood and then parted company without any fanfare. Mikš went to his fiancé in Bohemia and through her he managed to make contact with local resistance organisations.

Gerik dutifully went to his contact addresses in Prague. The first was for a local midwife, whose son was a Czechoslovak soldier abroad. On enquiry, her fidgety neighbours informed him that she was in prison. An approach to the address of a local tradesman also proved fruitless, his terrified family shooing their naïve young visitor away from their doorstep, whilst quickly explaining that the tradesman was now in a concentration camp.

In a daze, Gerik drifted into the cautious bustle of central Prague and checked in at the Hotel Julia, where he retreated to his room alone with his thoughts. He was isolated, hungry and completely devoid of any idea what to do next. In this pit of fear and despair, he convinced himself that - as a Slovak - if he handed himself into the police and told them everything he knew, he might simply be sent home with a reprimand. So, on 4th April, he walked into the police station in Prague with his equipment and a huge amount of cash, handing himself in to a shocked and disbelieving officer. He was immediately passed to the Gestapo and personally interrogated by Oskar Fleischer. He rapidly disclosed not only important details about his mission but also about the parachute training system in Great Britain, the training centres and the names and details of all the other parachutists he could remember. Gerik stated that as a Slovak he felt no loyalty to the exile movement and had volunteered for special duties only to return home. The Gestapo took him to Zinc's drop site in Slovakia, where he showed them his hidden equipment. Moravec and his teams' entire plans - with all their political significance and gravity – were now fatally compromised.

#

I flicked back to the pictures in the album of my grandfather engaged in radio training and returned to the one of him sitting in a military briefing. I looked again at the young man sat just in front of him with a book in his lap.

His face is upturned, open and earnest topped with thick curly black hair that is swept backwards. I turned the album towards my grandfather, touching the picture.

"Is that Gerik?"

He glanced across the table, calmly.

"No…" he said with a faint headshake.

"That's Dvořák…Oldřich Dvořák. I trained him as radio operator just after I trained Gerik."

He got up shakily.

"He was fine fellow," he added as he ambled out of the room.

\#

OUTDISTANCE suffered misfortune from its outset too. On jumping, Opálka plummeted to the ground awkwardly, his leg jarring on impact. The men buried the homing beacon for the Škoda raid and aiding their injured captain, left the scene as quickly as they could. Unfortunately, the beacon - which was absolutely central to the success of the mission - was soon found by a farmer and handed over to the police. As if that wasn't enough, Kolařík realised that somewhere between the bustle of the jump and the clearing of their drop site, he had managed to lose his false identification papers. This proved a fatal error. Opálka and Čurda had no option but to leave him to fend for himself in no-man's land; the two men headed to Pardubice to rendezvous with Bartoš and SILVER A. Without papers, Kolařík went into hiding in nearby Zlín but was quickly tracked down by the Gestapo. Cornered by them, he knew well what he was supposed to do. The brave young man, who in other circumstances would have channelled his considerable intelligence and resolve into saving the lives of others as a doctor, instead immediately and efficiently took his own.

As their various plans crumbled, the parachutists began to gravitate to the underground resistance in Prague. There were three individuals who were central to the network there. The first was a former chemistry teacher and Sokol official named Ladislav Vaněk, who was himself on the run from the Gestapo. Vaněk's codename was 'Jindra,' and that name was often used as shorthand for the network he ran. When Kubiš and Gabčík arrived in Prague in October, he got wind of their arrival and after a robust cross-examination brought them within the network. The second key individual was another former teacher and Czech intelligence agent called Jan Zelenka, who operated under the cover name 'Hajský.' It was Zelenka's job to provide safe places to stay for people on the run from the Gestapo. Over time, he became affectionately known as 'Uncle' to the people he housed. The third key individual within the network further strengthened this sense of trust and provided the essential matriarchal support for the bewildered young men who were now steadily arriving from England. 'Auntie' Marie

Moravcová was the beating heart of the resistance network. Through her work with the Czech Red Cross, she was well connected amongst patriots and humanitarians across Prague. The historical record does not focus on the commitment and sacrifice of the women of Czechoslovakia in these events, but Marie Moravcová is a figurehead through which one can see and understand their broad and essential contribution. A tireless and dedicated patriot, she continually put her own safety and that of her entire family at risk for the cause of Czechoslovak liberation. In addition to making her own home the transit place for arriving parachutists (until other safe houses in and around Prague could be found), both she and her teenage son, Ata, regularly made trips to and from Pardubice to ensure the free flow of intelligence through Libuše.

Alfréd Bartoš decided to send Opálka and Čurda back to Prague from Pardubice to be hidden by Jindra. There they could make plans for the mission to bomb the Škoda works; instructions had been received that the mission should still go ahead. Beneš and Moravec had made arrangements with the Royal Air Force and there was now a real sense of expectation about the raid and the opportunity it provided to degrade Nazi war production in the Protectorate. But with the loss of equipment and the death of Ivan Kolařík, Opálka and Čurda were now in no position to succeed alone. An operational decision was made – with agreement from London - to draft in the support of ANTHROPOID. While they bided their time waiting for the right opportunity to tackle Heydrich, Gabčík and Kubiš were keen to do something constructive. However, this move broke a key principle of intelligence work. With the men co-located and collaborating, the necessary compartmentalisation of missions began to become blurred. It was from this point inevitable that the other parachutists and the Jindra network would eventually discover the nature of ANTHROPOID's secret mission.

On the night of the raid - at the end of April 1942 - Gabčík, Kubiš, Čurda and Valčík of Silver A all rendezvoused with Opálka in Pilsen, full of anticipation and determined to succeed. Although the works was a vast complex of chimney stacks and brick industrial outbuildings, it was still a very difficult target to pick out from the night time sky. Without their beacon, they had to improvise a way of guiding the British bomber their. They placed large piles of wood at intervals on the plane's guessed approach path. After a tense wait, they heard the growl of engines overhead, as the plane appeared in the distance. The men set the wood ablaze and ran for cover in the undergrowth. But when the sound of the bombs' impact came, it was remote and muffled. They watched the plane – expectant that it would make a second run – but it disappeared as quickly as it had arrived. The next morning they discovered that the munitions had fallen harmlessly on farm ground. With no damage to the works, there was no cover for the ground sabotage that they had arranged either. The workers who had dismantled and wrecked equipment had to return to work the next day to explain what was going on to their irate Nazi bosses. The mission had been a complete failure and the men returned to Prague humiliated and angry. Bartoš felt that support from outside had been half-hearted and was now even more disillusioned with Moravec and the exiles. Under the constant mental stress of worry and responsibility, he began to suffer with flare ups of acute rheumatoid arthritis.

It was in this environment of despair that Arnošt Mikš arrived in Prague. He had been staying nearby with some underground contacts of his fiancé, who had managed to contact Jindra and put him into contact with Opálka. On arrival, he told the story of ZINC's failure and his separation from his leader Pechal and his team mate Gerik. Opálka listened carefully and with his knowledge of the waning resolve of Bartoš' in Pardubice, felt the weight of responsibility fall upon his shoulders.

#

I flicked through the album, trying to spot Oldřich Dvořák in pictures from this time period. One photo shows a group of eleven men sat around a table, all facing the camera; presenting almost like a Czechoslovakian version of the last supper. There are paper chains, decorations and a bottle here and there.

My best guess is that this is Christmas 1941, just three days before the dispatch of ANTHROPOID and SILVER A. My grandfather is in a festive white tunic, standing in the centre. Dvořák is at the far left of the picture, looking back towards him, his curly black hair and low forehead unmistakable. Another shows the young man undergoing radio training in a foggy parkland, his side cap perched at such an angle that it's only the radio headphones strapped over his head that are keeping it on. My grandfather is next to him, smiling with a cigarette clenched in his left hand and his sleeve pulled down for extra warmth.

I heard the toilet flush and closed the album, considering where to go next with my questioning. I looked out of the window and it was getting dark. I'd have to leave soon. I smiled as my grandfather lowered himself back into his seat.

"What happened to him…to Dvořák?"

THE RETURN

In April 1942, Josef Bublík found himself in the front line of parachutists to be dropped back in the heart of the Protectorate, with the young signaller Oldřich Dvořák right behind him. Despite Alfréd Bartoš' sharp warnings, these young men were to be thrown into an environment of terror and repression that none of them could ever have been prepared for.

Having followed his cousin into this kernel of intelligence operatives, Josef had been put through his core training at the second SOE run course in Arisaig in the Highlands of Scotland, which was held between August and September of 1941. In addition to Oldřich Dvořák, his training partners here had included Jan Kubiš, Alfréd Bartoš and his cousin Jaroslav's erstwhile tent companion, and would-be assassin Karel Svoboda.

The training school must have been a strange, frightening and thrilling environment for them all. Josef came into contact with a unique mix of characters: soldiers and civilians, sportsmen and criminals; anyone who was an expert in the new skills that would have to be built. He learned pistol shooting from an

Olympic champion and survival skills from well-known mountaineers and explorers. But this course was very much about 'ungentlemanly warfare.' He was taught lock-picking by convicted thieves and was instructed in close quarters fighting by two ex-members of the Shanghai Police.

Through detailed and explicit instruction, Josef was required to perfect a wide array of ruthless methods to kill a man quickly and – if necessary – silently, with his bare hands. He was also taught how to shoot and kill at close range in a cramped environment, using techniques that had been developed in the opium dens of China. These methods would be equally useful for fighting free of a hiding place in the Protectorate if discovered by the Gestapo during a radio transmission. This training was dangerous in itself; trainees were often injured and occasionally deaths occurred. The gravity of Josef's mission and the tests that would await him on his return home must certainly have become fully formed in his mind as he negotiated his way through the training. Despite their service in France, he and Dvořák were two of the least experienced men on the course and two of the few who were not professional soldiers. Josef was just twenty and Dvořák was only seventeen but as events were to show, they were made of considerably stronger stuff than the similarly youthful Gerik.

The group was led through its training by British Lieutenant Ernest Van Maurik, with a Czechoslovak officer as interpreter and liaison. Regardless of the challenges and the language difficulties, Joseph and his fellow soldiers excelled and impressed. They were happy to get away from regimental life and sucked up every morsel of knowledge they could whilst maintaining faultless discipline. At the end of the course, Josef and his fellow trainees presented Lieutenant Van Maurik with a gift of appreciation for his efforts. It was a copy of the book: 'Letters from England' by a well-known Czech writer named Karel Čapek, whose works had been blacklisted by the Nazis. All of the trainees signed it.

During the winter months, when ANTHROPOID, SILVER A and the other groups were dropped, Josef continued his training, now focusing on sabotage skills. His time was split between refresher training and spending time at the holding centre – Bellasis House: a fine country house in Box Hill, Surrey, built by the renowned architect Sir Edwin Lutyens. Records show that Josef's external training comprised of advanced demolitions, pistol and tommy gun shooting practice, grenade throwing, physical training and more unarmed combat. At Bellasis House, Captain Šustr continued to provide his best guess at appropriate operational advice for underground work.

The details of Josef's mission were planned as early as October 1941. Under the command of the wireless operator, Bohuslav Kouba, the mission - codenamed BIOSCOPE - was to be focused on sabotage in eastern Moravia. In addition to Josef, the group included another local to the area of operation, Jan Hrubý. For operational flexibility, two different targets were identified. The first was a bridge at Hranice, which was part of a key supply route. The second target was the transformer station at nearby Vsetín, which was critical to the supply of electricity in the region. For the latter, one approach would be to destroy the main power switches, meaning that the transformer would not be able to switch on. There were two other more permanent solutions which would cause the transformer to burn out: damaging the oil tanks or destroying the circuit breakers.

In those last months, Josef Bublík, Kouba and Hrubý undertook drill after drill, practising various approaches on a mock-up of the target. This included breaking into buildings, locating transformers by listening for their hum and firing blank charges into their target.

#

"So, were you parachuted in then?" I asked.

"With Oldřich Dvořák and Josef?"

'No…not then…I was parachuted later.'

"What was your mission?"

He paused momentarily, but when he spoke it was without reserve.

"It was an assassination mission."

My eyebrows raised. The statement was confidently made but having established his supporting role to the parachute missions at the time of ANTHRPOID, I was confused. I had done enough research to be pretty confident that if other assassination attempts were made in the Protectorate, I would have read something about it.

He looked at his watch and spoke with a sense of concern.

"You had better be getting home. The buses stop after six today."

I smiled at him. The spell was broken, and we were back in Chapel St Leonards again. And he was right – if I missed the bus there'd be no way home: neither he nor my grandmother were fit to drive, although they still had their car parked outside.

I stuffed my notebook in my coat pocket, stood and shook his hand, promising to be back soon. My grandmother appeared at the door and followed me down the corridor on my way out.

#

As his training duties eased, Jaroslav Bublík began to undertake work as a radio telegraphist at the VRÚ. The VRÚ was in the process of being moved from Woldingham to a more secluded base on a hill in a farmer's field in Hockliffe, a small village in Bedfordshire, just next to the town of Leighton Buzzard. This was close to the Czech government in exile's headquarters, allowing Beneš, Moravec and others to stay in close contact and control. It was also close to the SIS code breaking centre at Bletchley Park allowing the VRÚ to have access to its cutting edge equipment and technical expertise.

Oldřich Dvořák spent the winter in a similar fashion to Josef Bublík, alternating his time between periods at Bellasis House and further technical training. Military records say that he was formally trained in radio operations at the SOE school in Thame Oxfordshire from February to April of 1942. As the photographic record shows, Jaroslav Bublík was his chief mentor during this time.

This determined and able young teenager was entrusted with a very important mission all of his own. Operation STEEL was designed to add some strength and robustness to the fragile shine of SILVER A. Libuše was operating at such a pace that it was in danger of wearing out. Dvořák was to deliver a new radio transmitter and radio crystals to Bartoš in Pardubice and a spare radio for UVOD. He was also to take with him the items that Bartoš had requested in his earlier message to Moravec: smaller cyanide tablets, smaller pistols and the leather cases that were impossible for them to source. SILVER A provided a sound contact to use after his drop: a book printer who he would find in a town to the north of Pardubice. BIOSCOPE, STEEL and a third group, BIVOUAC – another sabotage mission – were to be dropped together.

\#

As Joseph Bublík and Oldřich Dvořák were undergoing their training, Jan Masaryk continued to broadcast to the people at home, who listened to their radios with the volume turned down and their curtains firmly closed. His Christmas message centred on hope and optimism.

"America is at war and this is another Christmas gift for you at home from those abroad. The American nation is today united and the defeat of Hitler is today much nearer. But we don't count on a German collapse. It will come anyway but we must make it quicker…I warn you again that it will not be easy – many trials are awaiting us still, and much blood will flow."

It would be some time before Masaryk would broadcast again, as he spent the early months of 1942 back in America, seeking the support that Czechoslovakia would need, come the end of this war.

#

"It's good that you came," my grandmother said.

"Of course. I like coming. I always do when I can."

"He's very tired at the moment. It will have really cheered him up that you came," she said as she reached the door. "What were you talking about for so long?

"We had a good chat…about the war and stuff."

Then, thinking out loud I mumbled, "…he said he had a parachute mission, but I can't find out anything about it."

"Oh yes. Foursquare…" she immediately responded in full voice.

"Sorry?..."

"Foursquare…That was his mission."

"What?" I responded, open mouthed. "What mission? What happened?"

"Something big," she grinned as she opened the door. "You know your grandfather – he never talked much about it. But he'd just returned to England when we met."

"Do you know anything about it?"

"He was based in Italy I think. Bari. That's where he went from. It was a big deal."

I glanced back to the sitting room where my grandfather was still sitting. I glanced at my watch.

"Someone from Czecho just wrote to us about it."

She let go of the door and darted back to her bedroom. I heard a draw open and she brought a letter out and handed it to me. It was type written and from a skim seemed to be a request for information about my grandfather.

"Do you want to respond to him?…I sent him some information already."

I took the letter, gave my grandmother a hug and strode out of the door into the cold.

#

In what had become a familiar routine, the parachutists dined with Moravec and Beneš before their departure, where amongst the ritual and ceremony they were reminded of the gravity and importance of their missions. Moravec's memoirs state that the men were made aware that there only a small chance of returning from their respective missions alive. But Beneš' sense of optimism seemed to be infectious to those who had a reason to buy into it. With the developments in the war and the assortment of forces now aligned against Hitler, the Allies were rightly confident of an ultimate victory. However, the appreciation of how long it would take to grind down the Nazi war machine was absent.

The parachutists themselves seemed to be of the view that upon dropping they might only have to wait a matter of months, or even weeks, before the regime collapsed and their homeland was freed. One thing was certain for Josef Bublík, Oldřich Dvořák and the others: there was no escape plan. They would be there until they were captured, killed or until the war itself ended.

#

Armed with the scribbles in my notebook spelling out the narrative of my grandfather's life from the time of Munich to the middle of the War, I began to research and deepen my knowledge. I needed a framework on which to understand his story and I would have to build it up at several levels. I already had a copy of a book by the author Callum MacDonald, which seemed to me to be the definitive story of ANTHROPOID. Through its reference list, I chased down further information and gradually things fell into place. For an overview of the narrative of the Second World War, I devoured all six volumes of Winston Churchill's war diaries. My search took me to the reading rooms of the Imperial War Museum, the British Museum and the British Library. As the weeks passed, I exhausted the knowledge available to me. I had come to understand Josef's story but I wanted to know more than the written word. As I sat at my desk one afternoon, with piles of books and magazines hemming me in, a compulsion came to me. I had to go to Prague. I had to see the places, engage with the people and really know the atmosphere. I would go as soon as I could.

#

The seven members of the three groups, BIOSCOPE, BIVOUAC and STEEL A, were to be despatched together. Their final practice session was photographed. It shows Šustr in front, in his full captain's garb in the full glare of the camera. Josef Bublík is stood tall behind him, clutching the parachute strapped to his body. Oldřich Dvořák is in front of them both, almost a full head shorter than Josef and ladened down with bags and pouches stuffed to bursting. Due to the fact that nights were short in the designated week, their drop zone was changed at the last moment to one requiring less flying time: the Křivoklát Forest between Prague and Pilsen.

The men took off at about 9pm on 27th April - just a day after the failed bombing of the Škoda works - and flew to Bohemia in a Halifax with Czech aircrew. By one thirty in the morning, they had arrived at their destination; the forest of densely packed trees, covering the undulating landscape like a virulent moss. All seven parachuted within fifteen minutes of each other. As they sailed to the ground, they would have been able to see the castle a few kilometres to their north west - towering above the forest canopy, a picture from a Brothers Grimm story made real.

On landing, the men of BIOSCOPE quickly found each other and the large container with their equipment which had slammed down within sighting distance. They silently gathered in their parachutes, buried them and then grappled with their equipment. With what demonstrated an alarming lack of foresight - and yet another mark against the planning of Captain Šustr - they found that it was too difficult for them to carry their equipment without drawing attention to themselves. In whispered discussions they made a new plan. Kouba would go to Prague to seek the support of Opálka and his men to help recover their hidden equipment. Josef and Hrubý would go ahead to Moravia immediately and start with the operational planning for the mission.

The two men slipped through the broad-leafed trees of the forest and immediately set off. Switching deftly from foot to road to rail, they scurried across the country to their contact addresses in Moravia. On arrival, like the missions before them, they found each of their contacts long since disappeared or imprisoned. Their final option was to try a railway fireman in Brno, named Jan Grim. This took Josef within touching distance of his family and friends in Banov. The irony must have struck him. He and his cousin Jaroslav had faced ordeal after ordeal – trekking across occupied Europe, the Middle East and crossing the Mediterranean to get away from here. He had fought with determination across France, walking almost its entire length in retreat and then fought his way on board a ship to find sanctuary in England. And now here he was - right back where he had started. It would be even more difficult to ever get out again. He must have known that this could be the last chance to see his mother and father. Hrubý, a fellow Moravian, was in an almost identical situation – his family in nearby Kunovice. The two men were in dire need of support, friends and succour. But as other events demonstrated – with Pechal of ZINC still haunting the forest near his parents' house, awaiting their inevitable fate – to return home would put their family and friends at risk. They decided not to.

Unable to find Grim in Brno, they had no option but to return to Prague where they met with Opálka. He passed them on to Jindra's landlord, Uncle Hajský, who found them refuge in Prague. In the embrace of the Jindra network, they found out what had happened to their fellow parachutists in those brief days since they had last seen them.

#

After scrutinising a patchwork of poorly constructed webpages for a couple of hours my eyes were sore and I felt a migraine stirring. But I had planned my trip. My main objective was to visit the Church of St Cyril and Methodius on Resslova Street, where the story of Josef and ANTHROPOID came to an end. But I had found a number of other places I wanted to go to and things I wanted to see. In particular, there was a military museum and archive in the Žižkov neighbourhood that piqued my interest. As I noted down the details, I came across an address for a researcher at the museum and had a flash of inspiration. Why don't I just write to them for my grandfather's military record? I immediately opened a letter template on my computer and started to type. It was worth a try.

#

After his arrival in Prague from the Křivoklát forest, BIOSCOPE's leader Kouba met up with Opálka. It was agreed that their hidden equipment should be retrieved on the night of May 1. Opálka embraced this opportunity to give the other parachutists some purpose. In particular, Arnošt Mikš, still distraught from the failure of ZINC, knew the area and was keen to play a role. They were to go to the forest in pairs: Mikš with Bohuslav Kouba and Josef Valčík with Auntie Marie's young son Ata. The explosives were to be moved to Prague and then both groups that had been dropped – BIOSCOPE and BIVOUAC - would start their missions. Kouba brought a map of where he'd hidden the explosives to a meeting with the men and copies were made for each group.

Unfortunately, luck continued to desert them. On the morning of 30th April, just a couple of days after the landing, a farm worker ploughed up the field in which the equipment had been buried. He came across the suitcase with the radio that Oldřich Dvořák had hidden. Despite initial resistance from the farm's leaseholder, who tried to play the discovery down, the local police were informed. Further inspection uncovered the other buried equipment in the vicinity and the police put the area under close and intensive watch.

Meanwhile, Mikš - eager to start his task - had set off to recover the equipment a day early with his temporary landlord: a local manual worker named Josef Kusý. Following Kouba's map, the couple approached the burial spot just before 10pm and skirting the forest around it, ran straight into two of the patrolling police officers. Mikš deftly drew his gun and shot one of them dead. The cluster of men then flung themselves behind the meagre cover of the tall, thin trees around them and began emptying their revolvers at each other. Mikš nicked another of the officers with one of his bullets but looking down, saw that his own blood was now watering the forest floor. He realised this was the end for him and shouted out to Kusý to run. He then put his gun to his head and squeezed the trigger with the vice-like grip of a stonemason.

Kouba arrived at Mikš' lodgings at the agreed time the next day and found only Kusý there. The news that he received sent him into despair. Mikš was dead and the material for BIOSCOPE was lost. Unbeknownst to the parachutists, Gerik had immediately been brought to the scene of the gunfight by his Gestapo handlers, where he identified the body of his former comrade in arms. Meanwhile, oblivious to events and still following the original plan, Valčík and young Ata Moravec made their way to the marked spot on Kouba's map. As they approached the forest clearing, their path was barred by a patrolling policeman. He realised who they were immediately, and a tense moment passed as he stared into the young men's eyes. But he didn't draw his gun. Instead he told them to turn around and go back to wherever they had come from.

Kouba was not so lucky. BIOSCOPE's leader headed east across country to Kutná Hora but on the morning of May 3 he was caught and put in a cell at the local police station, awaiting questioning. He knew how this would all end if left to follow its natural course; he would be tortured and his whole family would be used against him with threats of their murder. So Kouba bit down on the cyanide tablet he'd hidden about himself and ended his life.

As elements of this story were relayed to Josef Bublík and Jan Hrubý, it surely hit them like a mortar bomb. They had landed only days before, but already their leader was dead and they had no equipment to continue: their mission was over.

Dvořák's story was also one of failure. He had landed alone, buried his radio and then headed to a rendezvous with Bartoš at his flat in Pardubice. Dvořák had informed his commander that it was his intention to go straight back to get the radio and that he would need an additional pair of hands to do so. Bartoš and Potůček were fully engaged running Libuše so Dvořák contacted an uncle of his who lived nearby and set off with him back to the dropping point to retrieve his equipment. On staking out the location, they saw that it was being patrolled by police. Reluctantly, Dvořák realised the radio was lost. His uncle returned home and he headed back to Opálka and Jindra in Prague.

On landing, BIVOUAC went to the address of Karel Svoboda's family. Svoboda's father Jan owned a soda factory in Slaný, to the north west of Prague. The parachutists spent a night with them. Jan Svoboda had little to share with them but gave his supply of ration stamps as a parting gift. The men then set off for Moravia to find other safe houses but were all caught by the Gestapo within days.

#

I pulled out the letter that my grandmother had given me. It was curiously phrased:

"Excuse me please, that I trouble you without former announcing…"

It came from one Dr Martin Reichl. He was requesting information to produce a historical account of all Czechoslovak parachute missions and of the lives of the parachutists themselves. He asked a number of questions such as when and why my grandfather had decided to go into exile, when he and my grandmother had met and even questions about his political attitudes and whether he had been rehabilitated after the War. Looking beyond the broken English, I felt encouraged that someone besides myself was showing interest in these incredible stories. It seemed that Dr Reichl was a kindred spirit, trying to find the truth of this forgotten history.

#

The success of the whole set of parachute operations had nosedived after the high point of SILVER A. Half their number were dead or captured and none of their missions could proceed. Josef must have then considered: what next? The realities of life in the occupied Protectorate were now clear. Each day was a battle for survival and just their trips back and forth across country were a nightmare of inspections and questions from the police. The German occupation looked much more stable than he had hoped or had been led to believe.

It wasn't just Mikš, Kouba and the operational material that were lost in the various police raids. The Gestapo found a notepad on Mikš' body with the contact details of those in his native West Bohemia who had been supporting him. All of these people were now compromised and at risk. Josef Kusý was one of those who was immediately arrested and sentenced to execution at the Kobylisy shooting range in the north of Prague. Suspicions were also raised about Jan Svoboda and his family in Slaný.

It was at this point that disharmony broke out amongst the group of parachutists. From watching and listening to Kubiš and Gabčík, all came to realise that ANTHROPOID's mission was to assassinate Heydrich. Jindra and Bartoš were in furious opposition to the idea, knowing the harsh reprisals that would result and that the whole UVOD network was at risk. Bartoš therefore came to Prague and met with Jindra, Opálka and Gabčík. He told Gabčík that they knew what his mission was but that they had all agreed it was not the right time to conduct it. The fiery Slovak insisted that he would obey the orders he had been given.

Bartoš, who was still unwell, was furious. In desperation, he sat with Jindra and composed a note to go back to 'London' through Libuše, using Gabčík and Kubiš' codenames to identify them and identifying Heydrich only by his initial.

"Judging by the preparations which Ota and Zdeněk are making, and by the place where they are making these preparations, we assume, in spite of the silence they are maintaining that they are planning to assassinate 'H'. This assassination would in no way benefit the Allies, and might have incalculable consequences for our nation. It would not only endanger our hostages and political prisoners, but would also cost thousands of other lives. It would expose the nation to unparalleled consequences, while at the same time sweeping away the last remnants of organisation. As a result it would become impossible to do anything for the Allies in future. We therefore ask that you issue instructions through Silver for the assassination to be cancelled. Delay might prove dangerous. Send instructions immediately. Should an assassination nevertheless be desirable for considerations of foreign policy, let it be directed against someone else."

Their desire was to switch the focus of the mission back to Emanuel Moravec. Bartoš and Jindra waited impatiently for the urgent response they wanted but nothing came. Instead, on May 20, a message came for ANTHROPOID's attention, in a code known only to them. Bartoš delivered it and heard nothing further from them. From that point forward, there was no doubt that the mission would go ahead. Now returned to Pardubice, Bartoš became virtually bedridden with rheumatoid arthritis and Opálka assumed de facto leadership. Although he disagreed with the orders, he was not willing to resist them. If the men were to conduct the assassination, he would do all he could to ensure it was a success. He would complete it with them. And so would Valčík.

THE SIEGE

Having arrived at my small centrally located hotel, I very quickly made my way out with my hotel map to survey the city of Prague. Immediately, excitedly, I began to orientate myself to the city and its overlap onto the story I was uncovering. I walked down the banks of the River Vltava, that sweeps elegantly through central Prague and stopped to take a picture of the magnificent Hradčany castle with its sharply pointed spires pricking the white gray sky. Moving closer to it, I crossed the cobbled surface of the Charles Bridge – one of the historical gateways between Eastern and Western Europe - and looked up at this magnificent castle. How Heydrich must have loved positioning himself here at the prominent raised epicentre of this great city. How he must have loved looking down upon his new chattel, as their self-appointed king – with the satisfaction that wherever they went, they knew he was there; surveying them, dominating them.

#

With the loss of their equipment, Josef Bublík and Jan Hrubý were not sure what to do. As Bartoš had warned, the two men were of no operational use. They were surplus agents who were now a burden on the network. Uncle Hajský and Auntie Marie kept them moving around different safe houses, along with several others, including Oldřich Dvořák.

Dvořák, who had been nicknamed 'the gypsy' by some of his landladies, at least had skills that were immediately useful. He spent his time supporting UVOD with the makeshift radio they were operating. But for Josef there was nothing to occupy him except survival. At each address he would survey the escape routes and work out his plan, should a raid occur. He had to be ready at all times of day: one of his temporary landladies uncovered his gun under his pillow as she came in to make his bed.

Just days before ANTHROPOID went into action, Uncle Hajský took Josef and Hrubý to lodge at an address in Dejvice, at the north end of the city. It is likely they would have known something of ANTHROPOID at this stage. Josef had trained with Kubiš. He would most likely have inferred what was to happen, as the others had, even if he was not explicitly briefed. At the very least, Opálka would have informed Josef that a major incident was being planned and that for his own survival he would need to anticipate a significant ramping up of the already draconian police searches in Prague. Opálka probably assured him that detailed plans were underway for his evacuation too. But I suspect such words would have rung hollow and that Josef felt a knot of dread welling in his core. So in late May 1942 – as the men of ANTHROPOID made their final plans to kill Heydrich - there he was: sleeping with his gun clenched in his hand; full of readiness, fear and expectation.

#

Strolling back through the city, the streets of Prague felt oddly familiar to me. The atmosphere here felt brisk, business like, ordered and friendly, but not too friendly. I strolled to the old town square and stopped to look at the memorial to Jan Hus – the inspiration behind my grandfather's solo student protest all those years ago in still distant Banov. A crowd was building around the famous, astrological clock in the centre of the square, so I shuffled over to see it, fascinated by its ornate blue and gold dials. As the hour struck, the apostles appeared mechanically in procession through a small door at the top of the clock, as the watching people smiled and clapped. I dropped my gaze to take in the grotesque figures that flanked the clock face below, macabre and disturbing with their incessant shuddering movements. And there to the right, my eyes fixed on the skeleton of death ringing his bell calmly, his expression sculpted to be severe, mocking and confident. My mind wandered. How must the atmosphere here have been back in May 1942, as Josef and his Czech and Slovak brothers hid in the attics and basements of Prague sick to their stomachs with fear and foreboding? I swallowed hard and remembered the real purpose of my visit. I wasn't here for sightseeing. I was here on a pilgrimage.

#

On the morning of May 27, Opálka and Valčík took up positions along V Holešovičkách Street, an inconspicuous leg of Reinhard Heydrich's daily journey to Hradčany Castle. Gabčík and Kubiš waited anxiously, slightly further along the street, at a tram stop near the designated point of attack. At just after 10:30am, Valčík flashed a mirror towards them an alert, and seconds later Heydrich's open-topped, chauffeur-driven Mercedes came into

145

sight. As the car slowed for a hairpin bend in the road, Gabčík stepped forth, throwing his jacket from his shoulder to expose the sten gun he had just assembled. He lifted the nose of the gun towards the SS officer and pulled his trigger hard, but it jammed. He stood in panic, rooted to the spot, violently squeezing his finger in vain hope. Heydrich then rose from his seat and reached for his handgun, as Kubiš sprang into action, flinging his grenade forward. It hit the car with a metallic thud and a deafening bang and the young Moravian felt the hot sting of bomb fragments tearing into his face. The Butcher of Prague then stumbled from his car to the ground, shedding his own blood now, not the blood of others.

The assassins scattered, just ahead of the spreading news. Valčík heard it on his return to his lodgings, through a young neighbour, "…there's been an attempt on Heydrich's life…" By midday, less than two hours after the attempt, most of the city had heard. When news reached Josef Bublík, he would undoubtedly have asked the same question as Valčík did: "Is he dead?"

Josef laid low, wondering at the scale of the response and awaiting instructions. Radio Prague announced that Heydrich was alive and was in hospital receiving treatment. Announcements then came from Karl Hermann Frank, every half an hour on both the German and Czech radio stations:

"…an attempt on the life of acting-Reichsprotektor SS Obergruppefuhrer Heydrich, was perpetrated in Prague. A reward of 10 million crowns will be given for the arrest of the guilty men. Whoever shelters these criminals, provides them with help, or, knowing them does not denounce them, will be shot with his whole family…the state of siege is proclaimed by the reading of this ordinance on the radio…"

A curfew was to be put in place: anyone not obeying it would be shot after a single warning. Ten thousand Czechs were to be arrested and held hostage. All those already in prison for political reasons were to be executed immediately. The broadcast finished with a promise that this was just the beginning: "…Other measures are foreseen."

Then the sirens came. And the megaphones. Thousands of army troops and police, mobilised from all quarters of Bohemia, began to flood the streets of Prague and conduct house to house searches to find the guilty men. Josef would have gone to his predefined hiding place: a small cupboard, or a disguised room perhaps – and waited.

By 9:32pm, every route into Prague was sealed. Five hundred and forty-one people were arrested, of which one hundred and eleven were taken into custody for detailed questioning. Despite these efforts, by the time the curfew ended at 6am the next day, none of the Jindra network or the parachutists had been discovered. It had been close though. Karel Čurda of OUTDISTANCE had escaped detection only by dangling from a window over an airshaft. Opálka had stayed hidden in a small cupboard behind a sofa, while his lodgings were inspected by soldiers – just inches from him.

The next two days would have passed slowly for Josef, as the measures against the local populace steadily evolved. Everyone over fifteen was ordered to register with the police or they would be shot along with anyone harbouring them. Black and red posters were put up in Czech and German, providing details of the attack, descriptions of the men and repeating the reward for handing in the perpetrators. Josef would already have guessed the identity of the bomb thrower. Having undertaken explosives training with Jan Kubiš, he was well aware of his skill with a hand grenade. The poster also noted that a briefcase and a bicycle discarded by the perpetrators had been found. It was put on display prominently in the main window of the Bata shoe shop in central Prague.

With no culprits found, an air of desperation was already creeping into the hunt. These first days were critical for Oskar Fleischer and the Prague Gestapo. Karl Hermann Frank's brief tenure as ranking officer in Prague quickly ended as General Kurt Daluege was brought in from the Eastern Front - from where he could scarcely be spared. Emanuel Moravec, perhaps not realising how lucky he was to still be alive, came onto the airwaves to denounce Beneš and his 'criminal gang' in London. The exiles had been quickly identified as the sponsors of the operation, given the British origin of some of the equipment used. In London, Beneš took to the radio to record his satisfaction at this extreme flexing of the muscles of the Czech resistance.

Josef was being moved constantly from house to house. He needed to go somewhere more safe but it was unclear where this would be while the terror persisted. Public executions began, adding a growing tally of bodies to the ledger against that of Heydrich. On the last day of May, Uncle Hajský came to visit Josef and told him that a safe place had been found. He and Jan Hrubý were escorted to the Orthodox Church of St Cyril and St Methodius on Resslova Street in Prague, just on the east side of the river Vltava.

#

My map said that Resslova Street was only a brief walk from my hotel, so I set off on foot. It was a humdrum, low key day in

Prague, with people unexcitedly going about their business. I passed a kiosk selling flowers and bought a bunch.

I felt a flutter of anticipation as I saw the church, large and boxlike, dominating the corner of the road. As I gently opened the doors the familiar and expected smell of incense greeted me. That and the hushed, muted sounds, placed me firmly in a church setting. However, when I looked more closely at my surroundings, things were slightly alien. The church was in the Orthodox style, which gave it a flavour of the East.

#

The two parachutists were introduced to Father Petřek, a parish Priest for the church, who spirited them through a small hatch and down some narrow stairs. There they were reunited with three of the assassins: Kubiš, Valčík and Opálka. There was also another man, Jaroslav Švarc, who had discreetly parachuted into Bohemia two days after Josef with a highly secretive mission of his own. Josef would have seen immediately that Kubiš was injured; he was the grenade thrower alright. His face was pitted and freshly scarred by the shrapnel from his bomb.

#

I strode quickly to an unassuming door at the back of the church and entered a small room which served as the entranceway to the basement of the church. An elderly lady was sitting at a table which was laden with leaflets and pamphlets covering the events that unfolded here in 1942. I handed her my money and she passed me a green sugar paper ticket, wordlessly. I then stepped down onto the stone steps into the cellar, a chill seeping into the soles of my feet as I descended.

#

The next day, Gabčík arrived in the basement of the church. It would have been immediately obvious to Josef that he was unhappy. Arguably the most professional and capable soldier of them all, Gabčík set himself the highest of standards in his professional duties. This fiery, passionate Slovak was furious with himself for failing in his task: a bubbling cauldron of anger, fear and self-loathing. After all of these months of planning, he had found himself staring into Heydrich's pitiless eyes with a machine gun in his hands. Heydrich was at his mercy and he would take satisfaction on behalf of his enslaved countrymen. The obstinate refusal of his trigger to release was a point of transformation. In an instant, and in his own mind, he ceased being a crusading angel of vengeance and instead became his worst nightmare: an incompetent, bumbling amateur. Kubiš had come to his aid and salvaged something, but the Reichsprotektor was still alive. The mission had failed.

Auntie Marie was coming regularly to keep their spirits up, bringing messages from Pardubice. A congratulatory message soon arrived from Beneš.

"I can see that you and your friends are absolutely determined…the events over there have a great effect here and attract recognition for resistance of the Czech people".

This might have helped Gabčík a little. But it would have landed bitterly with the sick and despairing Bartoš when he had translated it. The murderous reprisals that were occurring were exactly the response that he had warned about and his view that the assassination order should have been countermanded can only have hardened.

As the days progressed, the furious pace of Nazis arrests and mass executions weighed ever more heavily on them all. Seven were now assembled in the ancient catacombs of this church. Josef and the other men would have looked to Opálka, the de-facto commanding officer, for support in this harsh environment. Unbeknownst to Opálka, one of his immediate team from OUTDISTANCE was struggling to cope with this claustrophobic pressure on his own. Following the house arrests that immediately followed the assassination, and his narrow escape from capture, Karel Čurda had fled Prague to stay with his mother and sister at their farm in Nová Hlína in Southern Bohemia. He was spending his days in increasing paranoia, sleeping in the family barn, wary of strangers, his only distraction news and radio reports from Prague that were increasingly horrifying.

#

The crypt was a rectangular chamber about fifteen metres long, with a number of deep square-shaped niches cut into the walls which had been the resting place of coffins. Discrete spotlights shone on pictures and exhibits describing ANTHROPOID and its actions, many elegantly nestled into coves in the carved stone walls.

I saw a picture of Josef. It was a familiar one by this stage. These young men had been photographed relatively rarely in their short lives and even less so in their military garb. He looked younger, more pensive, more uncertain and certainly more sad than I had seen him before. I looked away at a tattered pack of playing cards displayed nearby, poignantly telling their own story of those tense lost days.

#

At 4:30pm on June 4, after a final visit from Heinrich Himmler and with Karl Hermann Frank and Kurt Daluege hovering at the door, Heydrich died in agony from an acute infection of the pancreas caused by the bomb fragments and splinters from the car. Hitler ranted first at Heydrich's stupidity for allowing himself to be killed, before turning thoughts to cold, bitter revenge.

As word spread of Heydrich's death, Josef and his comrades would surely have enjoyed a grim celebration. Their most crucial mission had succeeded. Perhaps this feeling of satisfaction edged them closer to a recognition and acceptance that his death would most likely be in exchange for their own.

Klement Gottwald, the general secretary of the Communist Party of Czechoslovakia, came onto the radio from Moscow praising the 'as yet unknown' heroes for what they had achieved. The Communists were keen to associate themselves with this propaganda coup. Although the assassins were described as 'unknown,' Gottwald and Stalin both knew that the assassination had originated in London, not in Moscow.

On June 5, Heydrich's body was brought back out to the Hradčany Castle to lie in state. The Nazis created a grotesque period of mourning for him. As his lifeless remains passed through the streets of Prague, Czechs were compelled to line the streets to pay their respects. There his coffin sat in the Hradčany Castle for two days, shadowed gaudily by an SS standard and stone-faced troops. Heydrich's stolen castle was now his mausoleum. Many had heard a story that Heydrich, when he first came to Prague, had visited St Vitus' Cathedral, where the Bohemian Crown jewels were held, and had mockingly placed the crown of King Wenceslas on his head. Those same Czechs would also have known the legend that said anyone unjustly wearing the crown would die within the year. So it had come to pass.

Heydrich's funeral - on return of his body to Berlin - was like a Broadway production. Hitler, Himmler and the Nazi propaganda machine set about painting Heydrich as the ultimate Nazi martyr in a series of eulogies. The only accolade that bore any relation to truth was Hitler's description of the Prague hangman as the 'man with an iron heart.' With the funeral now passed, Hitler promised 'extreme measures' in the hunt for Heydrich's assassins.

#

As these events unfolded, the seven men continued to exist in their confined surroundings. The niches in the walls, where the mummified bodies of monks had only recently been stored, served as their bunks. Although it was June, Josef would have found the nights cold and damp. The only air came from a small barred slit high up in the crypt, which provided little ventilation and did nothing to disperse the smell of the lime and chlorine filled bucket that was their latrine. Auntie Marie baked fresh cakes for them, a kerosene heater and clothes for them to layer up to keep warm. But despite this help, it was inevitable that their minds would begin to turn inwards.

#

The crypt was still and calm. Preserved, as it was, it was almost as if the men had only recently been here. The handful of people that were also visiting treaded its floor carefully, speaking only in whispers. I drifted from one exhibit to the next, reading the English descriptions, paraphrased from their more generous Czech language versions, and with the odd spelling mistake. The crypt was a shrine to the parachutists, but, as I read a detailed account of the fate of the town of Lidice, I was reminded that it also symbolised the much wider horror that had been inflicted on the peoples of this country.

#

With tragic, cruel predictability and despite having had no involvement in the assassination, it was the Jews of the Czech

Republic that were made to suffer first and in the largest numbers. 'Operation Reinhard' was to take their lives as the first part of the Nazi revenge. Three thousand were sent on trains to Terezín, the Nazi ghetto and concentration camp in northern Bohemia, and then on to concentration camps in Poland. Hitler personally selected the next target: a small mining village named Lidice. A loose case was made that the people in the village had sons fighting for the Allies abroad and they had hidden ammunition and distributed anti-Nazi literature. It was also stated that they had not actively supported the hunt for the parachutists. Some of this might have held a grain of truth, but no evidence of a link with the parachutists has ever been clearly established. It didn't really matter. The important thing from Hitler's perspective was that an example must be made.

On the night of June 9, Lidice was surrounded by the Gestapo and SS troops. The families were simultaneously awoken by the smashing in of their windows. All men and boys over sixteen were separated from their families. The women and children were put into trucks and taken away immediately, wailing and despairing. The village was thoroughly stripped of all valuables and anything that might potentially be of use to the Nazi war effort. The men of Lidice must have spent those hours in stupefied terror, contemplating their certain death, as a group of Jewish slaves brought in from Terezín dug a large hole in front of them. As the sun broke over the calm meadows and gentle forests of Lidice's last day, the morning birdsong was rudely erupted by cacophonies of rifle fire, and the men of Lidice met their fate.

The whole village was then burnt, flattened with explosives and ploughed over. The women and children were taken that very night to a high school in Kladno. Two short days later, SS troops arrived and violently prised the mothers away from their children and babies. The distraught women were sent to their deaths in Terezín or other camps in the East. Their children were taken to hospital and subjected to batteries of pseudo-scientific eugenics tests. A small number were selected for Germanization and re-education with German families. Those that weren't faced the same fate as their mothers. Posters in Prague the next day notified everyone of what had transpired: Lidice and its people had been erased from the physical world.

These brutal and horrific events were designed to have a paralysing effect on the Czech population and in particular on the parachutists and those sheltering them. When news of Lidice reached the parachutists, it likely came as a hammer blow. As well as the threat of more executions to come, an amnesty was announced for anyone providing information on their whereabouts. The news also reached Karel Čurda at his mother's farm near the Austrian border. Isolated from his fellow parachutists, he was living his own hell of guilt, fear and uncertainty. He would have been aware of Mikš' death. Through the papers, he would also have known the fate of Oldřich Pechal and his family. Tricked into a rendezvous from his ghost-like existence in the forests near his parent's home, Pechal had been caught and tortured and his whole family murdered. Čurda's resolve slowly, steadily began to crack. He wrote an anonymous letter to the local police station at Benešov, naming the assassins as Jozef Gabčík and Jan Kubiš. There was no response. But Čurda began to torture himself with the idea that the letter would be traced back to him and that he had put the lives of his family at greater risk. The more he thought, the more he realised that he was committed now: there was no turning back.

#

Collectively, inexorably, Josef and his brothers were starting to lose their grip on reality. As men of action, they tried to make plans to stop this slaughter. Gabčík and Kubiš wanted to put placards around their necks and commit suicide on a park bench. At some point Jaroslav Švarc broke protocol and told them about his, as yet, incomplete mission: the assassination of Emanuel Moravec – the Minister of Propaganda. Huddled around their kerosene stove, the men hatched a plan to hand themselves in, saying that they had information that they would only share with him. On meeting this traitor, they would then kill him with their bare hands and commit suicide. It was a preposterous idea. But trapped like vermin and riddled with guilt and terror, they were not in their right minds. Their missions were all they had left to validate their very lives.

Auntie Marie made what would be her last visit to the boys on June 15. At about this time, Jindra - now firmly in the lead following the nervous collapse of Uncle Hajský - also came to the church. Father Petřek brought out Opálka to speak to him. The composed young officer explained the despair and terror that the boys down in the cellar were facing, and of their bizarre and desperate planning. "…they are finding it hard to keep a hold on themselves." he said soberly.

Jindra understood immediately and set about trying to introduce a dose of reality. Beneš had publicly announced that they must not give themselves up. They were soldiers and had to stay alive and fight. Suicide was not the answer, on grounds of its likely ineffectiveness at stopping any bloodshed and the propaganda coup it would give the Nazis. As a religious man, Father Petřek disapproved of the suicide plan on more basic and principled grounds. However, he noted that with the escalating measures, the Bishop of Prague himself – Bishop Gorazd - was now concerned that the presence of the parachutists threatened the Church. The men needed to leave before June 19.

They needed a plan urgently and Jindra provided it. He was to smuggle them all out of the church in coffins, in a funeral car that he would drive. Opálka was to stay in Prague as a key member of the remaining underground. The others were to go to a village just to the south of Prague to stay with a carpenter there. Josef, Švarc, Valčík and Hrubý would go to the mountains in Moravia, where they would join the partisans. Bartoš and Potůček were to take Libuše from Pardubice to a different quarry nearby. These plans sounded plausible, but the final proposals again verged on the fanciful: Opálka was to use a homing beacon to help a small plane land and Jindra, Kubiš and Gabčík would be flown to London. Regardless, these plans were all they had and most likely renewed their spirits.

#

Two days before the end of the amnesty and three days before the parachutists scheduled departure, Karel Čurda left his mother's farm, caught a train into Prague and walked to Gestapo Headquarters at the Petschek Palace. On telling that he knew the identities of the Heydrich's assassins, he was given a selection of briefcases and asked to identify the one used by them. He immediately selected the briefcase into which Gabčík had packed his disassembled sten gun. This got the Gestapo's attention.

They initially bluffed, saying that they had all of the information they needed from his old comrade, Gerik. Čurda told them all of the names he could remember, all of the safe houses and the names of those running them. When asked why he was giving up this information, he said that he wished to protect his family and claim the reward that was offered. He even gave up the names of his handlers and trainers in England and spelled out in detail the nature of the training they had received. One address he gave was that of the safe house at the centre of it all: the home of Marie Moravcová. Čurda was immediately dragged into a car with Oskar Fleischer, which soon arrived at Auntie Marie's flat in the Žižkov district of Prague. Fleischer bounded up the stairs and rang the doorbell, raising the family from their beds in their nightclothes; they were terrified. When Fleischer was briefly distracted searching the flat for any trace of the parachutists, Auntie Marie took the opportunity to ask the police interpreter if she could use the toilet and he excused her. She locked the door and bit into the cyanide tablet she had been carrying for just these circumstances. Spotting her gone, Fleischer broke down the bathroom door but it was too late: she had already been struck dumb by the poison. She was dragged out, and much to Fleischer's sadistic amusement, her husband, and sons watched in horror as her life seeped away in front of them. But, amused as he was, Fleischer still didn't know where the parachutists were.

Soon afterwards, Uncle Hajský's door was smashed in by the Gestapo. Before they could get to him, he too swallowed poison, taking all he knew with him. Fleischer had been thwarted again, but he still had his captives to work on. Witnessing the death of their matriarch was by no means the end of the Moravec family's ordeal. They were taken straight to the Petschek Palace and its notorious torture chambers, where Ata became the focus of the Gestapo's day. He was brutally beaten, stupefied with alcohol and subjected to the worst horrors of his interrogators' imaginations. At various times he was left with Čurda, who encouraged him to tell all. It is impossible to know exactly what he endured, but it is rumoured that he finally broke when shown the severed head of his mother, floating in a jar of alcohol.

#

I climbed out of the crypt and returned to the main atrium of the church. Then I stood and appraised the altar. It was magnificent, a structure of geometrically decorated tiles and pictures with the centrepiece, a sombre and dramatic statue of Christ dying on the cross.

Looking up, I saw the wooden balustrades of the choir loft flanked from my vantage point by striking frescos of angels and cherubs drifting through the sky. I glanced around that upper part of the church, linking what I saw with my now detailed knowledge of the events that occurred there on June 18, 1942.

#

On that fateful night, it had been the turn of Josef, Jan Kubiš and Adolf Opálka to keep watch above ground as the others slept in the crypt below. They had settled in behind the rood screen in front of the altar, seeking to take turns to get their own rest, in their more airy surroundings; it was a hot night and the crypt air would have been stagnant and stifling. Just after 4am, one of them might have sensed the shift in atmosphere and maybe heard noises outside, as two whole troops of SS men formed cordons around the church. Somehow they knew that the time for their inevitable ordeal had come as, by the time the soldiers arrived at the door they were in their defensive positions on the balcony of the choir loft.

The lead Gestapo officer, Heinz Pannwitz, rang the bell and the door to the church was opened by the janitor. As Pannwitz strode inside with a number of Gestapo agents, the parachutists' weapons were primed. From their covered positions, Josef, Opálka and Kubiš took aim without hesitation and the morning erupted with the crack of gunfire. A hand grenade was thrown towards the Gestapo agents, who began firing back indiscriminately. Within seconds, one of the Gestapo men was wounded. He was quickly dragged away, bleeding and screaming in agony while Pannwitz ran for cover. The SS troops had set up a machine gun post in the window of a school opposite. On hearing the shots, they fired a staccato burst of shells into the church windows. The first batch of stormtroopers then flooded in. But they found the Czechs had rehearsed this action well. Commanded to storm the spiral staircase to the loft, the troops were easy prey for the young men on the balcony.

#

The elderly lady in the museum foyer flagged my attention and offered me a seat in front of a television and video recorder. She fiddled with the buttons as I sat down and stared at the screen. An old black and white Czech movie about the Heydrich assassination began to play. The clip began with scenes of SS troops swarming into the church and the battle beginning. Men I assumed to be playing Opálka and Kubiš were prominent, diving for cover under flying bullets and debris, as wooden balustrades exploded under fire. The scene presented as a cacophony of noise and violence; the room gradually disintegrating into chaos as stormtroopers fell. The film also showed the other men in the cellar, awoken by the noise but unable to join the battle; frantically digging down into the cellar wall, looking for a route into sewers that might allow their escape. The film cut again to a younger man on the balcony. He had sandy hair and an earnest expression.

"That one must be Josef," I thought.

As I squinted at the screen I found myself blinking away tears.

#

With the steady accumulation of gunfire and grenades over a period of hours, the church became a shattered mess of wood and broken glass. Pannwitz and the SS were desperate. Time and time again, the troops had tried to storm the loft, and time and again they had been repulsed. Their dead were strewn across the church floor.

Josef and his comrades knew that their efforts would not save them. The objective was to take as many of the enemy with them as they could. An eye witness said that they fought like lions. They were calm and were excellent shots as you would expect from men trained by Olympic shooting champions. But defence couldn't last forever against this endless stream of opponents. Their ammunition ran low. The splinters from flying debris accumulated and then the first serious flesh wound from a bullet would have nicked one of them. The leather from Josef's shoe, recovered from the scene, was split violently; his foot was at some point torn apart. Still they carried on, and as Pannwitz in his panic began to lose sight of any attempt to take them alive, the shockwaves from hand grenades tore at their bruised bodies and the resistance was pummelled out of them.

The end came at around seven am, with an agonizing silence. A silence longer than the previous pauses for breath in the battle. Josef's body was embedded with sharp, painful shrapnel and riddled with leaking wounds. Noone could help him; certainly not his cousin, remote as he was, attached to proceedings only by the electrical buzz of coded messages. Josef put his gun to his head and firmly pulled the trigger.

The SS men climbed hesitantly up to the loft; the dead bodies of their fellow soldiers a reminder that fatal surprises were still possible. The bodies of Adolf Opálka and Josef Bublík were heaved out onto the pavement and laid out on the ground while a barely living Jan Kubiš was rushed to hospital. Karel Čurda and Ata Moravec were then dragged over to the bodies. Ata, fresh and raw from his gruesome torture, shook his head and refused to identify the men. Čurda peered over at his deceased comrades and gave Opálka's name but was unable to identify Josef. At some point, Gerik was also brought out to take part in this morbid game of 'guess who'.

It was clear that Gabčík was not amongst those found and there were indications amongst the possessions found that others were hiding in the church. Pannwitz turned his attention to Father Petřek, who had by now been brought to the scene. He soon confirmed that there were more men hiding in the crypt. Now that he knew this, Pannwitz desperately needed to capture these remaining men alive. Loudspeakers were set up in the street outside the crypt's narrow ventilation window and the men were called upon to surrender.

I descended into the cellar once again. A bright lozenge of light was shining through the ventilation slit which had been the focal point of the final battle on that momentous morning. That part of the crypt had been left exactly as it was; preserved, just like the bodies of the monks it had been built for.

#

The parachutists were desperately jabbing anything they could find into the inner wall of the cellar, attempting to break through into the Prague sewers. The stormtroopers began to fire bullets in through the narrow window of their hiding place, as the requests to give themselves up continued. But the bullets weren't a concern to the four parachutists who were lower down in the depths of the crypt. A stalemate ensued. Ata Moravec was asked to speak to his friends but again refused. Čurda was sent instead.

"Surrender boys. It will be alright."

His words were instantly met with a hail of bullets, causing him to dive for cover.

"We are Czechs," came the response. "We will never surrender."

#

I bent down and touched the scarred cellar wall, looking at the marks the men made on that morning. The hole in the brickwork was surrounded by mementos and gifts; notes left by visitors and small religious icons. The deep gash is a testament to their vigour and will to live. I could see them in my mind's eye, relentlessly hacking at it with improvised tools as the bullets ricocheted above them and the clamour and commotion outside steadily grew as the Prague morning awakened. But as I stepped back from it – looking afresh - it also seemed to me to be a testament to the inevitability of their fate.

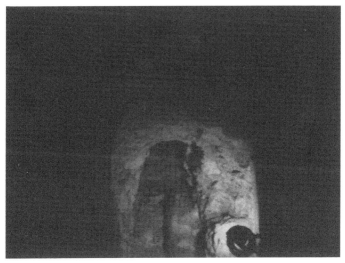

#

The fire brigade came and put a hose in through the opening to flood them out. Tear gas was thrown in, and promptly thrown back out again. Karl Hermann Frank finally arrived, stomping his feet at the public humiliation he and his forces were all suffering. Eight hundred SS troops had been sent hours earlier to capture seven men and they still couldn't do it. Finally, the main entrance to the crypt was found and dynamited open. SS troops were sent on suicide missions to capture the men, lowering themselves one by one into the crypt. The parachutists simply took pot shots at their dangling legs. Nearing the end of their ammunition and with the water steadily rising, the parachutists were forced into their inevitable last act. Four final shots rang out and then there was silence. Heads poked in through the detonated entranceway to confirm the situation.

'Fertig,' came the cry from inside the church: 'Finished.'

The four bodies were dragged out, dripping wet and laid side by side with Opálka and Josef's lifeless remains. Čurda and Gerik came again to confirm the dead.

#

I wandered out of the church and turned the corner to its side wall. The exterior of the ventilation window was a shrine now. Pockmarked with bullet holes from that day, it was a fitting memorial. A large plaque had been put above it. It shows a parachutist and a priest flanking the roll call of the men who lost their lives: Opálka, Gabčík, Kubiš, Valčík, Hrubý and Bublík, and the religious men who gave them sanctuary.

I looked down at the flowers I had placed as I passed earlier, fresh amongst older, dried and shrunken offerings, and felt a degree of closure in my understanding of Josef Bublík's story.

\#

It is hard to provide an exact tally of the direct cost of Heydrich's life. Certainly, three thousand Jewish men, women and children were deported to almost certain death in the East. Added to this are the three hundred and fifty victims of Lidice. In addition, making use of the names given by Čurda and Gerik, two hundred and fifty-two relatives and helpers of the parachutists were rounded up by the Gestapo and condemned in Prague. Čurda's failure to identify Josef Bublík was very fortunate for the Bublíks of Banov. They thankfully escaped this retribution, as did the family of Jozef Gabčík, based on his Slovak nationality.

The relatives of the other parachutists were interrogated and beaten and in some cases tormented with the severed heads of their relatives, hacked from the corpses left after the raid on the church. It is noted that their tormenters were surprised and grudgingly admiring of their defiance, particularly that of the women. Many were reported to have proclaimed that they were proud to die for their country. They were sentenced at Mauthausen concentration camp and shot or sent to the gas chambers. On September 3, in the Petschek Palace in Prague, the Nazis conducted a public trial of the members of the orthodox church: Jan Sonnevend, Václav Čikl, Bishop Gorazd and Vladimír Petřek. The men were executed and the church was abandoned, its property confiscated.

Less than a week after the siege, it was discovered that SILVER A's transmitter was being hidden in the hamlet of Ležáky. Soon afterwards, five hundred SS troops arrived and Ležáky suffered the same fate as Lidice, with the loss of fifty souls. And what of the other parachutists at large? The Pardubice Gestapo had been vigorously searching for Bartoš since his identity had become known. When eventually confronted by two SS men, he turned and fled through the crowded streets. The men grabbed bikes from passers-by and gave chase. He turned and exchanged fire but fell to the floor wounded. Before he could be captured he turned his gun on himself.

Jiří Potůček's reprieve was also short lived. He had escaped from Ležáky just before the Germans arrived. He had been making frantic contact with Jaroslav Bublík and his old colleagues in the VRÚ, sending them half a dozen messages and receiving nearly twenty in return. His last message was brief; 'Ležáky was levelled. I am the only one left.' Looking to survive and hoping to find Bartoš, he went to a succession of local villages he by now knew well and eventually to the address of a local family, using a rake as a walking stick to support his swollen legs. The lady of the house sent him to the woods to wait for some help. Overcome with exhaustion, Potůček fell asleep by a nearby brook only to be awakened a short time later by a policeman who shot him dead before he could grab his gun. So ended SILVER A: Bartoš, Potůček and Valčík were all now dead, and the princess Libuše was silenced with them.

\#

At this time Roy Tink, a teleprinter engineer from Bletchley, was regularly visiting the VRÚ at Hockliffe to help set it up and provide maintenance support. When recollecting that time many years later, he commented that none of the Czechs ever talked about 'business'. But he noted that one day he saw one of the men in floods of tears; he was told that this was because he'd just heard that some of his colleagues had been shot in Bohemia.

\#

In the aftermath of the assassination, Oldřich Dvořák had gotten as far away from Prague, and indeed from the Protectorate, as he could. His objective was to cross the border to the more benign atmosphere of his Slovakian homeland and seek the support of his family there. The accomplished young soldier managed to get as far as Skalica on the border, before the police finally caught up with him and he too was shot dead. Such was the fate of the man whose cherubic face is ubiquitous in my grandfather's photo album. He was barely a man - despite his resourcefulness and bravery, he was dead at the age of eighteen.

Of all of the parachutists sent, only four had survived: Vladimír Škacha and Jan Zemek of SILVER B, who had immediately gone to ground after losing their equipment, and those agents that had changed sides: Gerik and Čurda. The men's sacrifices and those of many others were lauded for the political achievement that was gained. The assassination was celebrated by the Russians, Americans and British who saw it (with Beneš' approval) as a spontaneous act by the home resistance and a demonstration that the Slavic peoples would never accept German domination. The fact that the actors were British trained parachutists was not publicised. British government figures noted that they were not in the business of publicly supporting political assassinations. Plausible deniability from all involved was necessary and for that reason, any heroes had to remain unsung.

#

I had my second trip planned for the next day: I was going to visit the Army Museum in Žižkov. As the Heydrich assassination was so central to Czech military history, I was certain I'd find more information about it there. I also had some crumbs of information on my grandfather's parachute mission to investigate further, in particular a name: 'FOURSQUARE.'

After asking advice in the small lobby of my city hotel, I hesitantly hopped on a bus, not entirely sure it was the right one, and took my seat. It wasn't a long journey but it was an interesting one. As the minutes passed, the picture postcard, fairy tale setting of central Prague changed. The ornate stone of the old town was replaced with simple, off-the-peg office blocks and flats. Žižkov was of course the area where Auntie Marie and her family lived. My mind drifted to thoughts of Josef and his fellow parachutists hiding out behind these walls. Scanning road names and looking back to my map, I started to hover over my seat, trying to work out what my best stop was. Eventually I picked one and soon after I left the bus the museum came into view. It was as I might have imagined it: boxy, post-war and with a tank sitting outside on a plinth.

I climbed a dozen or so stairs and passed through a wrought iron gate into the museum, approaching a woman in uniform at the entranceway. I asked her about the various exhibits and her patient but firm responses to my questions allowed me to infer quite quickly that strangers appearing unannounced and seeking obscure details about one of the most murky and emotive periods in the country's history would be treated with some suspicion and curiosity. Once I had been diagnosed as generally harmless, we finally connected on the topic of the Heydrich assassination and my interest in parachute missions from England. I was briskly escorted down a small corridor to a room full of glass cases and displays. At this point I forgot entirely about my guide and became mesmerised. The centrepiece of the display was a map of Czechoslovakia, showing the landing points of all parachute groups during World War Two. There were many more than I had uncovered from my research. Open mouthed, I drifted through the displays and saw to my surprise and delight that each mission had its own section and the photographs of all of the members were shown. I was certain that FOURSQUARE would be mentioned here. There was a section for BIOSCOPE showing headshots of Kouba, and Jan Hrubý, and the by now familiar picture of Josef Bublík, standing against a brick wall.

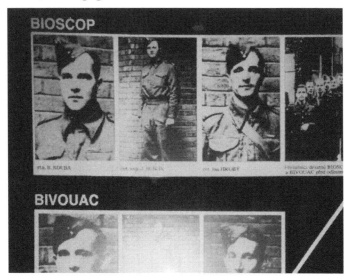

'ZINC' was there too, showing the faces of Pechal, Mikš and next to them, the young, callow face of the traitor Viliam Gerik. Checking instinctively to confirm that my guide had disappeared, I pulled my disposable camera from my pocket, wound the film on with my thumb and began to snap away.

I took a picture of 'STEEL': the solitary member of that group, Oldřich Dvořák, photographed at an angle but still unmistakeably the man from my grandfather's photo album with his high forehead, mop of black hair and cap perched on his head like an offset horn.

I was surely on the brink of a revelation here. I scanned the display for the missions that were new to me: CHALK, WOLFRAM and PLATINUM. Looking at the details of Operation WOLFRAM, I saw a familiar name: my grandfather's old tent mate Karel Svoboda.

"So he was dropped after all." I thought, making a note to make this an avenue of my research and hoping that I would find that the mission had gone well for him.

I stopped at the display for operation CLAY. There was a face that looked familiar to me there. I grabbed a photo for a later day. But it seemed that the face of Jaroslav Bublík was nowhere to be seen. I double checked, and triple checked. There was no mention of FOURSQUARE at all. Deflated, I carried on inspecting the displays.

There was a map of the key locations for the Czech exile army in England and behind a glass case a mannequin in a flying suit, with a portable radio transmitter. Another display showed some of the key members of the parachutists training team. Karel

Paleček - the man behind all the missions - was there of course: a middle-aged officer with a row of medals on his chest and arched eyebrows that gave him a quizzical look.

Below him was a picture of Šustr – the 'arrogant swine': a younger man in a suit and tie. I took a photograph and amused myself with the thought that I could now check whether he did indeed look like Nigel Patrick, whoever that was.

I left disappointed, but keen to share what I had seen with my grandfather; it seemed that only he could answer the central questions I had: What exactly was Operation FOURSQUARE and why was there no record of it?

AFTERMATH

The Nazis' openness about the atrocities of Lidice had significant unintended consequences. In their fury, they had allowed a window to be accidentally opened into their true mindset. Events gave a glimpse of the broader atrocities that were being committed undercover, lending strong support to the rumours and stories that were already being spread about the scale of genocide and murder at the heart of Hitler's regime. As the waves of shock, outrage and sympathy continued to emanate towards Prague and Lidice, the environment became ripe for change to the political standing of Beneš' Czechoslovakia. The Russians quickly expressed their support for complete restoration of Czechoslovakia within its pre-Munich borders. Jan Masaryk – still in America – found a strong response across the whole of that country too, not just from the expat community. He reported that one serious-minded American statesman told him he wasn't sure whether the determination of the American people had been more strengthened by Pearl Harbour or by Lidice. By August, there were developments in their standing with the British too. Masaryk was back on the airwaves in August with important news to his traumatised and damaged country:

"Today, as you know, I received an official letter from Foreign Secretary Eden, in which he informed me that the British Government does not recognise and never will recognise what happened in 1938 and 1939, i.e., that Munich does not exist for Britain…I represent this first republic, no other, and this republic will take its seat at the peace conference…determined to defend all its sovereign rights and prerogatives. Foreign secretary Eden in his speech made warm mention of you at home, and thanked you for your…courageous resistance."

#

I walked up my grandfather's path again, keen to talk with him about my trip. I also now had a sense of the world in which operation FOURSQUARE was planned. I would finally be able to ask him properly about this too, and to tease out the details I needed to know. I approached the door and pushed the doorbell but no sound came. I walked round to the living room window and tapped on it. I could see him sat in his usual spot and he raised his arm to acknowledge me. A minute passed and then I heard the creaking of the inner door and saw my grandmother fiddling with an impossibly large bunch of keys to open the door into the porchway. We greeted each other as we walked down the hallway. My grandfather took a while to get up when I greeted him; his handshake was weak and his hand spongy. He had recently suffered another small stoke. My Mum had warned me my grandparents were not coping well there and she was looking to alternative arrangements for them. As is always the case in these circumstances, when the elderly don't want to admit that they need more active support to live, it was proving complicated.

#

But even in the heart of a compassionate and principled man like Masaryk, the desire not just for justice, but for revenge, was taking hold.

"…there shall be retribution for Lidice," he continued. "No pardon, no mercy, no forgiveness."

The Munich agreement had been universally repudiated. But the events Beneš had triggered had a huge human cost. Whether he felt guilt about this one can only speculate. Beneš certainly felt that this was his chance to ensure that the Sudeten Germans would never again stab their fellow citizens in the back. He wished to agree their complete expulsion from Czechoslovakia: all three million of them. He had no compunction about this, seeing it as politically necessary and feeling no sympathy for the Sudetenlanders given their cynical embrace of Nazi Germany. Russia quickly gave its support. Keen not to be outflanked by Russia in the battle for public opinion, Britain followed suit.

#

I sat down, keen to show him my photos and talk about my trip to Prague. I talked of my visit to the church crypt and what I had learnt, asking him questions as I went. His eyes looked straight at me but there was a translucence to them that seemed to put a distance between us.

"Heydrich thought the Czechs were cowards – so he rode in an open car," I said at one point.

"Oh yes?" he replied sarcastically, his eyes bloodshot, and suddenly, briefly, awakened.

"We saw about that."

When I spoke about the death of the parachutists, including his cousin, he didn't say much. He knew this story well and I suspected it wasn't enjoyable for him to be reminded of it again; he had brought Josef out of Czechoslovakia and had led his way to intelligence work. He was more interested in little details of Prague; what it was like now and how I found the people. When he finally gave a view it was to speak about why the events should not have happened.

"I thought that Gerik was completely unsuitable for intelligence work," he said repeating his previous assertions, when I talked of Gerik and Čurda's treachery.

"I remember you saying that."

"Yes – absolutely. I said so in my report on him."

He paused for a moment.

"Bastard," he said finally. I was taken aback. I had never heard my grandfather swear before.

"I was over-ruled."

I had established in my mind that the fieldwork and intelligence training provided by Captain Šustr was poor. Being no fan of Šustr, I felt sure that my grandfather would have agreed with this. I had also formed a clear view in my mind that Gerik's situation had been gut-wrenchingly awful. In thinking about it, I'd applied the ultimate test: would I have done any differently in his situation? This thought was deeply uncomfortable.

\#

In the aftermath of the assassination, Gerik had been sent to investigate the activities of the family of Karel Svoboda. They had provided sanctuary and support to BIVOUAC when it landed.

Gerik approached the Svoboda house and introduced himself to Karel's father Jan as a parachutist looking for support. Forewarned of his arrival, they were guarded and they gave nothing away. Gerik would surely have sensed their nervousness but what he reported to his Gestapo handlers is not known. Regardless, some people needed to pay for what had been done. The whole Svoboda family were taken away and executed.

#

"What about Čurda?"

"He was an experienced soldier. He should have been able to follow his mission."

"What happened then?"

He thought for a while; a moment of reflection that seemed to free him briefly from the apparent discomfort of his body.

"He had complete change of personality. He was corrupted by the Nazis. He became different person."

I watched him recollecting again, his eyes glancing to the side.

#

Čurda, the professional soldier, was indeed more capable than his younger colleague and that capability was immediately turned to the task of hunting down the intelligence network and preventing its resurgence. There was a pressing task for him.

Much of the detail of what had happened at the time of Heydich's assassination was still not known by František Moravec and his team as 1943 approached. Confusion existed about who was still alive and what was actually left of the home resistance. Re-establishing communications with whoever had survived was thought to be the quickest way to rebuild. In particular, SILVER A had developed an extensive network and it was even thought that Alfréd Bartoš himself might still be alive. So it was agreed that a parachute team should be sent in to try and re-establish contact. It was called Operation ANTIMONY and it was dispatched at the end of October 1942. The group was formed of three skilled radio operators: František Závorka, Stanislav Srazil and Lubomír Jasínek. In the latter part of their training, Jasínek was seconded into the VRÚ. There, Jaroslav Bublík and the others coached this young man – still a teenager – in honing his practical wireless and telegraphy skills. ANTIMONY was despatched with close attention from Beneš and there were high expectations of it.

On landing, the group linked up with its designated contacts in the communist underground and began to send regular reports to London. However, over the weeks that followed, anti-partisan forces identified a number of ANTIMONY's radio broadcasts and began monitoring them. The Gestapo called in Karel Čurda, their secret weapon in the hunt that was now underway; with his insider knowledge their tracks were quickly uncovered. On January 13, 1943, some of the local underground were arrested and following interrogation the network was broken. One of the captured men – the partisan leader, Hlaváček - negotiated a deal with his captors. The partisans would be treated as prisoners of war and those helping them would be spared if they divulged all their information and handed over the parachutists. Soon afterwards, the members of ANTIMONY found the house that they shared with a group of partisans surrounded by armed agents. A bloodbath was imminent. Hlavacek approached and told them the agreement he had negotiated with the Gestapo. The response from Závorka - the commanding officer of ANTIMONY – was a clear-eyed one, "I'm not stupid enough to trust a treaty with the Gestapo."

Jasínek and Srazil readied their pistols for a gunfight with the fifteen Gestapo men dug in around their hiding place. Prepared for his fate, Jasínek asked Závorka for permission to engage but thinking of the lives of the partisans, Závorka refused. He called out to the agents besieging them with an offer that he and his team would hand themselves in, but only to Czech police. The offer was accepted and the three men came out, Jasínek humming the Czech national anthem as he walked. As they approached the car that was to take them away, Závorka called out, "You won't get us alive!" and pushed his cyanide tablet into his mouth. When the Gestapo saw what he'd done, they threw themselves on the other two men. They prevented Srazil from killing himself but in the melee, Jasínek swallowed his tablet whole.

Závorka sunk to the floor dead. Jasínek was thrown into the car and rushed to a nearby doctor's surgery where his stomach was pumped of its contents. But they were too late. The assembled policeman looked on astonished, as he rose and asked for a cigarette. The young radio operator then walked calmly around the doctor's office and studied the paintings on the wall as he smoked, until he suddenly lost consciousness and dropped to the floor. The Gestapo's efforts then turned fully to Srazil. Čurda had once again proved his usefulness to his new paymasters.

\#

He looked back to me, to share the memory that had come to him.

"We went, a few of us, to see Gerik and Čurda at their trial in Prague after the War."

I froze, eager to hear the rest. He wiped his dry lips slowly, before continuing.

"Gerik looked up at us in the gallery and waved to us, as they took him away."

He waved his own hand as he spoke, and a look of disbelief spread across his face.

" 'Cheerio boys'," he said, aping Gerik's youthful, friendly tone.

I swallowed and took a moment to try and imagine the motivation behind these final words. I had finally succeeded in moving him into an entirely open position regarding his war time secrets. I knew it was time to ask, so with some trepidation, I blurted out my question.

"What was Operation Foursquare? What did you do?"

I sensed the smallest flicker of reluctance before he spoke.

"It was an assassination mission," he said, fixing me with a stare.

"The mission was to assassinate German section leaders…"

"But, I couldn't find out anything about it anywhere. Even in the military museum in Prague. Were you dropped? Did it actually go ahead?

"It did go ahead," he said indignantly, and an undercurrent of frustration. "It most certainly did go ahead."

There was a pause as he thought before he spoke again, more calmly this time, and gazing to the side at his recollections.

"Before we went, we all had dinner with Beneš. We were in no doubt how important the mission was."

I could almost see him dusting the cobwebs from the vista of old memories that had opened.

"We were to initiate an uprising…Before the Red Army came in."

I was wrong footed; I couldn't formulate an incisive question so did the best I could in the circumstances.

"What happened?"

He halted for a moment, before the most succinct of responses.

"The mission was a success."

I absorbed this information, searching my memory for another question. I knew nothing about the politics and actions of this time. All that came to me was an awareness of the suicidal nature of all of the other parachute missions I had learnt about.

"How did you get out again?"

"It wasn't difficult. The war was over by then. The Americans were at the border. We came back through Europe. We made our own way back."

Out of questions, I sat back and absorbed what he had told me. I felt there was no way I would ever make sense of it. Then I looked into his tired eyes and wondered how deeply his strokes had affected him. These weren't the things he should be thinking about now. I felt guilty for coming here to gather information, rather than just to take an opportunity to spend time with him, while I still could.

Having opened up he had more to say. He spoke about post-war Czechoslovakia and how its democratic inheritance was ultimately lost. At this he became emotional in a way I hadn't seen before. These clearly weren't comfortable memories. So I gently

183

steered us back to more familiar topics, until eventually it was time to leave.

#

As part of their new duties, Gerik and Čurda disclosed the names of all those who they knew were working for Czechoslovakia's exiled intelligences services. Using these names, the Gestapo identified a selection of their family members for punishment. One of them certainly mentioned the name 'Jaroslav Bublík', as his older brother Jan was one of those that was taken from his home and imprisoned. Jan Masaryk came onto the airwaves to express his disapproval:

"I am making this declaration in the name of the Czechoslovak Government. We have taken note of the decision of the interlopers to imprison the relations of those working abroad to restore the Czechoslovak Republic...the disgusting Frank is making a great mistake if he imagines that he can intimidate you or us...The German Reich, as Hitler wishes it, will be destroyed... With all of the allies we have already resolved to punish the war criminals...In the name of the Czechoslovak Government and all the allied governments I repeat to you and your martyrs: We will judge severely, very severely."

#

A couple of months after my visit to my grandparents, I sifted through the mail in the shared entrance hall to my flat. There were a couple of letters for me but one caught my attention. I knew immediately that it was from the Association of Czechoslovak Exiles – a diaspora of Czechoslovak ex-soldiers who remained displaced from their homeland. I had sent a letter to the Association, having found the address on a newsletter I'd seen in my grandparent's house. I had written to its Chairman, František – 'Frank' - Kaplan, asking for any reminisces anyone might be able to share about my grandfather. I filleted the envelope with my thumb and slid out the type written note. It was indeed from Frank Kaplan:

"I must start by apologising for the delay in answering your touching letter. I was pleased to read about your recently developed interest in your grandfather's wartime activities. Unfortunately I did not serve with him in the same unit but worked with him after the war as [a] wireless operator in the communications and cipher department of the then Czechoslovak Foreign Office. He worked at the embassy in Berlin whilst I was at the Prague Office. So it was that we were in touch almost daily, tapping messages in Morse code to each other."

I smiled. This line of investigation offered the potential of new knowledge and new understanding. The letter continued:

"Not long after we came to Britain from France in 1940, he was transferred to the Central Wireless Exchange of the Czechoslovak Forces H.Q., (VRÚ are the Czechoslovak initials for it) which was responsible for keeping contact with the various groups which were parachuted into Czechoslovakia during the war.

"We have in our association one member who worked with your grandfather at the VRÚ whom I thought could help you, Miroslav Novák. When I rung him I found that you'd already been in touch."

Colonel Kaplan went on to describe how he was in the final stages of organising a major event with the Cholmondeley branch of the Czechoslovak Legionnaires. The 60th anniversary of the arrival of the Czech forces in England was just a few weeks away. The letter came with an invite to attend.

#

Cholmondeley Park was a forest of umbrellas rather than of tents on this typically British summer's day. Attendees were to congregate at the memorial to the arrival of Czechoslovak forces here in 1940, that had stood in this park since that time. A steady stream of elderly legionnaires were drifting towards it; a quite reasonable share of the three and a half thousand who had arrived here in 1940. The men were dressed in their military garb, many with medals spread generously across their breasts and berets carefully perched on their heads. Each was supported by their Czech, Slovak and Anglo families. I felt a hesitant affinity to all of them; here I might have found a secret tribe to which I belonged. Sheltering under my umbrella and listening to the steady, gentle patter of rain, I did an involuntary double take at someone who looked remarkably like my grandfather, with the same short, stocky build, and broad forehead. But as the man turned towards me, revealing a pirate eyepatch over his right eye, the illusion was dispelled. I was unusual in that my legionnaire was not here. He was now struggling through each day in a nursing home, near his home on the other side of the country.

A senior delegation from the Czech Republic and Slovakia was in attendance and proceedings were underway. I lifted my head to see a man stood sombrely amongst a display of national flags and red, white and blue bunting. He was introduced as Eduard Kukan, the Foreign Minister of the Slovak Republic. I listened intently as he began his speech.

"When the Czechoslovak supreme commander ordered his army, already deserted by all allies, to abandon the frontier defences, to bow to Nazi aggression, a terrible disappointment was all that the troops felt. These men had the determination, the clear resolve to fight for their country. And the bravest did not lay down arms. Thousands of them fled abroad. To Poland, shortly afterwards overrun by German forces, and from the defeated Poland to the East and West."

As he paused, a faint patter of raindrops was all that could be heard in the respectful silence of this calm green park. I found myself comparing the smart and stylish cut of the elderly soldiers with the more generic, chintzy looking military garb of the handful of younger Czech soldiers who flanked the lectern.

"The place where we are standing now is very precious to us Czechs, Moravians and Slovaks. In this wonderful park three and a half thousand Czechoslovak troops, just evacuated after the fall of France set up camp on July 7, 1940....thousands of bitterly disappointed men….the faith in a final, joint victory was reborn. How impatiently they – you – awaited the chance of liberating Europe and Czechoslovakia.…determination guided them to the Czechoslovak RAF squadrons, the Czechoslovak brigade and the paratroops whose task was to maintain contact with the resistance movement at home."

Eduard Kukan went on to speak of the ultimate victory but also of how, less than three years later, Czechoslovakia fell back under totalitarian rule. I knew that many of the men I'd seen in my grandfather's album were here; the lucky ones who had survived. But many had faced injustice after injustice even then. Yet here they were, in the late autumn of their lives, still standing tall and unbroken. And paying silent respect to their young comrades who had died all those years before.

Major General Kašpar was the next to speak. He spoke of the battle for France, the details of which were now very familiar to me: the brave stand of his troops, the withdrawal of the French and Moroccan forces, the ten days and nights of forced marches and their escape by sea to England. As he spoke of their arrival, it was with a palpable sense of gratitude and relief.

"Wallowing in the soft luxury of the train compartments, we started the last leg of our journey. We watched a German raider shot down over the harbour. We slept right through the night and woke up at the station called Beeston Castle. From there we marched, singing our Czech marching songs to reach our new temporary home, a tent town…After the sudden change of weather, we understood the meaning of the words of our Jan Masaryk, who came to welcome us saying: "As far as our British allies are concerned, you can rely on them one hundred percent. As for the weather – don't trust it.'"

A murmur of laughter spread through the damp crowd, relieving the tension momentarily.

I drove home in a sombre mood. I had debated with myself whether to come, particularly as my grandfather was so unwell, but I wanted to be there to represent him. I was glad I had been present, but any enjoyment of the occasion was bittersweet. I would have loved to see him in this environment: backslapping his old colleagues and refreshed with the energies of his youth. And just this car journey home with him would have provided an opportunity to show my deep interest and to really learn about his life and experiences. It occurred to me that, despite the family mantras, he was willing to share his stories, however difficult. It was more that I had never really shown enough interest in them.

#

Just three days after I returned home from Cholmondeley Park, my grandfather passed away. He received the last rites from the local Catholic priest – a final reconciliation with the doctrine that he'd struggled with for his whole life. The funeral was a small affair, attended by close family and a few dedicated parishioners. A bunch of flowers came from the Czech legionnaires. I called Frank Kaplan to thank him a few days later and he gave his heartfelt condolences. I said that it was a shame that we didn't get to meet up in person at the event - I had seen him there but had decided that I didn't want to disturb him. We had a final exchange before the call ended.

"How exactly were they related? Your grandfather and Joseph?

"Cousins of some sort. I'm not really sure."

"You know…I always assumed they were brothers."

THE SECOND PHASE

Time passed and initially I completely disengaged. Work and family came to the fore, and a world without my grandfather in it began to evolve. There was little or no time to continue my research into his story. But the unanswered questions continued to nag at me. I still had the sense that I would someday understand his full story. So after a while, in my rare free moments, I started to research once more. This wasn't easy; for the first part of my journey I had the support of some fantastic guides who had left a clear trail to follow. In particular, there was the work of Miroslav Ivanov, captured in his book 'Target Heydrich,' which provided the definitive story of the Heydrich assassination from first-hand accounts. For the broader political context, I had the work of Callum MacDonald – meticulously researched and thoroughly referenced. The next part of the story was a virgin forest by comparison and it would be hard work to hack and slash it into shape.

I decided I would follow the thread from those few people whose stories I knew carried over to this latter half of the

War. Their stories would set the context to understand the conclusion to this story. I put a request into the Newsletter of the Czechoslovak legionnaires for anyone who knew anything about the VRÚ radio station in Hockliffe, Bedfordshire. Unbelievably, a locally based researcher with an affinity for the Czech Republic and Slovakia, Neil Rees had put in a request for more information about the VRÚ in the very same newsletter. If there was such a thing as fate, this was it. I contacted him straight away.

#

Following Heydrich's death, the formal responsibilities of 'protector' fell first to Kurt Daluege and subsequently to the new Reichsprotecktor Willhelm Frick. In practice, a resurgent Karl Hermann Frank was the point of continuity in Nazi policy. Heydrich's brutal and cynical 'carrot and stick' policies were enhanced with vigour and remained effective. The Protectorate therefore continued seamlessly on its path as a key part of the Nazi war infrastructure.

Politically, the Heydrich assassination and the tragedies of Lidice and Ležáky gave a short period of grace for Beneš and his team. The outpourings of sympathy initially led not just to the achievement of strategic political objectives, but also lessened pressure on the Czechs to undertake overt acts of resistance. Beneš was happy with inaction. Purges of forces loyal to him would strengthen the Czech communists and would complicate his efforts to maintain political balance when the country was eventually re-established. His main action was therefore to continue to push unrealistic propaganda, heralding the efforts of his countrymen.

The war progressed quickly and with it the political dynamic changed and memory faded. Allied victories at El Alamein and Stalingrad as 1942 came to a close, had an important psychological boost for both the Allies and the occupied populations. Thoughts began to turn seriously to the retaking of continental Europe. Pressure on the Czechs to contribute materially to the war effort returned. In particular, the British began asking the exiles for specific details about the forces Beneš could muster in his homeland: How big is the home army? How confident was Beneš in calling it to action?

#

A batch of papers had arrived in the post from Neil Rees and I read them with interest. They included a list of the entire group of soldiers at the VRÚ in Hockliffe on its set up. The centre was led by Captain Zdeněk Gold, with support from that veteran of intelligence work – the code master - Václav Knotek. There were nine radio telegraph operators in all, including Jaroslav Bublík, Václav Modrák, and Miroslav Novák. To support them in their constant round the clock work, there were four radio mechanics led by Antonín Simandl. Simandl was the resident electronics master, who constantly innovated, creating bespoke designs and technology for transmitters and receivers. There was also a cook and a caretaker. Other than transient agents who came through on training duties like Gerik, Jasínek and later on Karel Svoboda, that was the entirety of the team. One of the radio mechanics, Jiří Louda, was still alive and living in Moravia. Neil Rees gave me his contact details.

#

When Jaroslav Bublík formally joined the VRÚ the nature of its work was already well established. It operated constantly, throughout day and night, the work requiring intense concentration. All knew that the price of errors was high. Stress had been a constant since the VRÚ's inception and members of the team had to be sent away to recuperate at times. The radio operators were fighting a constant battle with their Nazi counterparts. The enemy would not just track down those sending messages but would also from time to time successfully jam the radio signals. The technical experts, in particular Simandl and Modrák, constantly sought to stay ahead of the Nazis on the technical front: transmitting simultaneously on multiple frequencies and constantly seeking those that gave the clearest signal.

Modrák later described how on one occasion, as he vainly listened to static on his receiver, he watched one of his fellow operators at the VRÚ:

"…listening, writing, smoking and sweating, switching from sending to receiving and cursing aloud 'the German whore' who was interfering with his efforts. In utter desperation he opted for another frequency by pressing the key QRM5, and within seconds peace was restored to our place."

#

Just weeks before, Lubomír Jasínek had been sharing duties with the men of the VRÚ. Now, oblivious to the fate of ANTIMONY, frantic efforts were underway to contact him through constant monitoring of his designated frequencies. Just as they were close to losing all hope, familiar tones sprung into life on their equipment. The men strained their ears, jotting down the letters as the 'dits' and 'ders' accumulated. Listening intuitively to the style and signature of communications, they would have quickly discerned that this was indeed one of their own. Stanislav Srazil was in contact, as the only surviving member of ANTIMONY.

Information began to flow once more but any happiness at this new connection would have been tinged with doubt about whether or not he was broadcasting under duress.

Soon afterwards, under pressure to take action, Stankmuller and Paleček made preparations for two new parachute missions. Operations BRONZE and IRIDIUM would be focussed on sabotage, including another attempt at coordinating a bombing of the Škoda works. The missions were prepared and despatched together on the March 15, 1943. There was a brief feeling of optimism that they were engaging again and meeting the challenge set. But it didn't last the length of the flight. The plane was shot down by antiaircraft guns, killing the entire crew and both groups of parachutists.

#

The relationship between the Czechoslovak Government in Exile and the British SIS and SOE began to sour. Official files disparagingly refer to Beneš' approach as looking to "pull chestnuts from the fire [of war in Europe]". With Beneš continuing to cherry-pick the intelligence that he shared with his British hosts, the Czechs' independent communications at the VRÚ became an even sharper point of contention. Well aware of the political dynamic unfolding, the British began to feel uncomfortable about their lodgers from Czechoslovakia having secret communications with the other 'Big Powers,' in particular a resurgent Soviet Union.

At this time, the fate of ANTIMONY conspired to create a major disagreement between the British and the exiles. It had been sent into the Protectorate with a secret letter from Beneš to communicate to the home resistance. The letter implied strong British support for the restoration of Czechoslovakia's borders and the expulsion of the country's Sudeten German population. With the liquidation of ANTIMONY, the letter found its way into Karl Hermann Frank's hands and he referred to its contents in a public speech on February 26.

The British were furious. They worked out that the letter must have come from a member of ANTIMONY. As with all such parachute groups, SOE had performed a detailed check of each member prior to departure, to ensure that they had nothing incriminating about their person. The letter must therefore have been deliberately hidden from the British by one of the group. In private correspondence, the British Special Intelligence Services – led by Stewart Menzies - stated to the British Foreign Office in August that they had "completely lost confidence in the good faith of the Czech Intelligence Service."

SIS expressed grave concern about the Czechs' continued use of independent codes, the lack of public acknowledgement of the debt they owed to SIS and SOE, and the opaqueness and inconsistency of intelligence information provided to them by the Czechs.

#

I continued to review the copious material that Neil Rees had sent about the Hockliffe station. Of most interest were the notes from his discussions with Roy Tink, the British technician from the SIS centre at Bletchley who was a regular visitor to the VRÚ. Tink remembered the camp consisting of a number of huts by the side of College Farm; the radio station could be found through the farmer's gate at the top of a hill, near the accommodation and the mess. There were usually six to eight men there, always in uniform and always keen to chat and practice their English. He knew about

196

their work to remain in contact with parachute groups but they never spoke to him about it. I had also received diagrams that showed Hockliffe connected in a network of cables that stretched across the shires and down to London. Hockliffe had a teleprinter – the e-mail of its day – meaning they could communicate instantly with the experts at nearby Bletchley and other linked stations.

#

The Nazis and the Gestapo continued to fight a ruthless battle to eradicate what remained of the home resistance. As the war wore on Gerik was increasingly ineffective as an informant. In early 1943, again displaying his naivete, he tried to break free from cooperation with the Gestapo and establish contact with what remained of the home resistance. Having perhaps underestimated how difficult establishing his bona fides might be, his actions were unsuccessful and were quickly uncovered by Fleischer and the Gestapo. On April 6 1943, he was arrested and sent to solitary confinement in Pankrác Prison. After a short while, he was moved to Terezín and then finally to the Dachau concentration camp.

#

Neil Rees had arranged to show me around the key locations in Bedfordshire and Buckinghamshire where the Czechoslovak Government in Exile had been based. He knew every location in the area that had some link to the Czech exiles, from Beneš' long-term base at Aston Abbots to the VRÚ itself. It was the latter of these that was the main focus of the trip for me. As we got closer and closer to it, we eventually passed the industrial estate where I had worked for over two years. Thinking about this quite dazed me: yet another coincidence to spur on my investigation. I literally could not have found a job closer to my grandfather's wartime base.

Neil continued on and drove me up a rural road and a bumpy farm track to College Farm; the exact spot where the VRÚ had been based. It was a calm and unremarkable field. We climbed from the car and scanning the horizon I was reminded of some of the photos in my grandfather's collection. We met the farmer there who seemed happy at our interest and showed us a rusty, twisted pile of cabling with a mixture of pride and confusion. Apparently, he had recently ploughed it up, completely unaware of what it was or the nature of the many signals that had pulsed through it on this very spot some sixty years earlier.

#

In May 1943, British intelligence arranged a meeting with František Moravec. The purpose was to demand closer control of Czechoslovak communications and parachutists. The British planned to make a very strong demand to allow room for concessions. They therefore requested that Moravec place the whole of his communications network under their control, with British staff undertaking all coding and decoding work. Moravec, the wily intelligence man, played the game with aplomb and adopting a conspiring tone agreed on a lesser proposal that he felt he could take to his superiors. They would hand all codes to the British Secret Intelligence Service and give its head, 'C', all copies of their coded information. Moravec thanked them for their flexibility in the matter and the British spooks came away pleased with the apparent success of their strategy.

In fact, Moravec had no intention of making this request to his superiors. Jan Masaryk had briefed him in advance of the meeting that he must fully protect the interests of a sovereign Czechoslovakia. As Moravec feigned negotiations with British intelligence, Beneš was arriving in the US to strengthen his relations with that emergent superpower. His engagement with Russia was strengthening in parallel and so despite his preference for positive engagement with the British, he felt no need at this particular moment to sacrifice his hard-won independence to them.

#

I continued to hope that I might make direct contact with Miroslav Novák, my grandfather's firm wartime friend and confidante. I was sure he would be the magic key to unlock everything I needed to know about Operation FOURSQUARE. But I felt he was holding me at arm's length. After writing to him, he sent me a photocopy of some content from a book called 'Paths of Destiny," which outlined the careers of all known parachutists, including my grandfather. Its author was Dr Martin Reichl, the researcher who had written to my grandmother. The information provided was sparse, but scanning it I saw that it did mention Operation FOURSQUARE. It stated that the mission had been planned in Italy, but ultimately aborted after several failed attempts to land. I shook my head and threw the pages down on my desk. Both of my grandparents had said that the mission had been dropped. But the implication of this account and the absence of information in the military museum was that it had not. This was all very confusing. If FOURSQUARE did go ahead, Miroslav Novák did not appear to be privy to this information.

Amongst my grandfathers photos was a blurred photocopy from another photo album. One of the photos shows the men of the VRÚ standing together for a group shot at College

Farm. The names of each man are helpfully annotated. Jaroslav Bublík is there, in an open-necked short-sleeved shirt. Jiří Louda is in similarly casual dress: slender-faced with a short back and sides. Simandl – their technical guru - was there too and in another photo on the same album page is Václav Knotek.

#

Beneš and a few core members of his exile government spent May and June of 1943 in the USA for a range of meetings with Roosevelt and members of his administration.

The chief purpose of the visit was to get American support for the future borders of Czechoslovakia and also for the expulsion of the Sudeten Germans. Beneš felt that both of these objectives were achieved. Less overtly, he sought to encourage the USA to continue to adopt the friendly and collaborative attitude towards Russia that would be essential for the re-establishment of Czechoslovakia.

At the time, the US was providing huge volumes of military equipment and material to the Soviet Union. Beneš' positive views about Russia were therefore reassuring to American ears when others were vocal in their opposition. Beneš played on the fact that Roosevelt saw him as an expert on the politics of the area and trusted his views. Based on need and optimism, the Czechoslovak leader-in-exile was proving to be Stalin's chief diplomat for relations with the Allies. A quote in the US press at the time stated that:

"Co-operation between the United States and the Soviet Union is possible. Dr Beneš, more than anyone else, has proved it."

Another said:

"The example of Czechoslovakia proves that even a small country can carry out vis-a-vis Russia, a policy of friendship without sacrificing its political ideals, national interests and independence...big countries should do likewise."

Beneš had intended to go straight from the USA to Moscow to meet with Joseph Stalin to agree a treaty between Russia and the future Czechoslovakia. This was in spite of the fact that the British and the Russians already had a separate agreement that neither country would agree treaties with smaller countries until the end of the War. On learning of Beneš' planned visit to Moscow, the British were yet again extremely displeased. In a diplomatic dance - with Czechoslovakia and Russia each seeking to avoid the blame for this faux pas - the meeting was postponed until December.

#

I got a response from Jiří Louda.

"Thanks for your letter and the copies of photographs from your grandfather's album. I managed to identify some of the soldiers and places but unfortunately I served in the artillery regiment and your grandfather in the infantry, which meant different garrisons until we came to Hockliffe. The identified photos are in the small envelope."

Martin Reichl's book "Paths of Destiny" popped up again, with Jiří quoting its description of my grandfather's military career back at me in the letter, including the assertion that operation FOURSQUARE had been planned in Italy but ultimately aborted. I opened the envelope and the square pieces of paper I had cut from photocopies of my grandfather's album came fluttering out onto the table. Their backs were now annotated with Jiří's sharp, neat handwriting. He had pointed out Oldřich Dvořák on several of the pictures including the picture of him sitting with my grandfather in an intelligence briefing in late 1941. But Jiří's note expresses confusion about this.

"This can't be as 'Paths of Destiny' shows that your grandfather didn't enter the intelligence service until September 1942?" he had written, well aware as he was that Dvořák had died some months before then.

The picture was clearly of Dvořák, and there were many others. I also knew well that my grandfather had been working in intelligence since being recruited by Stankmuller in April 1941. This was a fundamental error that called into question the accuracy of the details provided by Dr Reichl; I reasoned that he was most likely wrong about FOURSQUARE too.

I flipped over another scrap of paper. It was a picture of a large group of signallers standing by a military bus wearing full communications kit. Jiří's notes identify one of the men as Ivan Kolařík, the young ex-medical student who committed suicide after parachuting in with Adolf Opálka as part of OUTDISTANCE. His face peers out from high above the back of the group, behind my grandfather.

Another, from the family of photos showing radio training in early 1942 is annotated:

"In the middle Lubomír Jasínek dropped 24/10/1942 (group ANTIMONY) committed suicide 16/1/1943".

Indeed. I stopped to look at these few brief words, knowing now the extraordinary circumstances of Jasínek's death and picturing this young man smoking his final cigarette as the acids in his stomach finally melted the casing of his cyanide tablet. I pondered how easily these stories had been lost. Jasínek, Dvořák, Kolařík and their colleagues and helpers had made the ultimate sacrifice. They were examples of what life could demand of anyone who listens to their conscience and surfaces in difficult political times. With a fluttering of fear and sadness in my stomach, I then flipped over another photo and read Jiří's annotations:

"The man in the centre is Čestmír Šikola, who was wireless operator in the group CLAY and was dropped on 13th April 1944 and still lives (born in 1919)."

I sat up. My mind flashed back to the display board in the army museum in Prague. I had of course seen his face there too. I delved into my box file and rummaged through the photos I'd taken and there he was; instantly recognisable with his high cheekbones: a handsome young man. Reaching for my grandfather's photo album, I quickly identified him in the 'last supper' picture with my grandfather, Oldřich Dvořák and others celebrating Christmas in 1941. Jiří had also identified him, standing tall, in a photo in Cholmondeley Park, taken so soon after their arrival that my grandfather is still wearing his French forage cap.

Šikola and my grandfather seem to have been together at various times throughout the war: Cholmondeley Park, Funny Neuk, Woldingham, where the VRÚ was initially based and Thame in Oxfordshire where wireless training was undertaken. Jiří's accompanying letter finished off sombrely:

"From all the people from our Woldingham station, only two are still alive, myself and Miroslav Novák, who lives in Dunstable with his English wife, being sadly ill."

He signed off with a P.S. somewhat more cheerfully. "I expect you know that you and I have the same Christian name, since Jiří means George."

I felt that I would like Jiří a great deal. Over the next few days, I set about looking into the activities of Čestmír Šikola. I discovered that his son had written a book about his wartime activities – albeit one that was out of print and in the Czech language. Nevertheless, I decided to try and source a copy.

#

Concerns about the fate of ANTIMONY and the veracity of the communication line to Stanislav Srazil were growing. It was now known that some members of the group were caught. The communications continued, but Moravec and Stankmuller treated the information with increasing caution. A 'danger' signal had been incorporated in the coding system devised by Václav Knotek, to allow operators to indicate when they were operating under duress. After some weeks of regular transmissions, Jaroslav Bublík and his fellow telegraphists noticed immediately when Srazil suddenly started to use this code. It was a desperate cry for help: he was caught by the Gestapo. The men would now need to continue the charade of communication just to protect Srazil's life.

#

At the end of November, the three big powers: Great Britain, the USA and the Soviet Union met in Tehran to discuss what would be the final stages of the war and to begin consideration of the postwar world order. Beneš' engagement with all three leaders – Churchill, Roosevelt and Stalin – in the run up to the conference had deliberately served to build a degree of trust between them that otherwise would not have existed. In effect, he had vouched for Stalin who, aware of this dynamic, had played his part with Beneš to perfection. The conference was dominated by the Soviet leader, who was in buoyant mood for his first meeting with a physically diminished Roosevelt, who had travelled the seven thousand miles from Washington in ill health. A number of key agreements were reached. Rather than continuing a push from Italy, as Churchill wanted, the Western Allies would retake France by sea on or before May 1944. Stalin would strengthen his attack from the east to draw the Nazi forces away from France. Roosevelt pushed for the Baltic states to have a democratic say in whether or not they would be reincorporated into the Soviet Union but Stalin resisted this, while giving his commitment to support the USA in the war against Japan. The borders of Poland were redrawn, with the country moved westwards into German territory in concession for the territory in the East taken by Stalin. The meeting was cordial and good mannered; the only really difficult exchange was around Stalin's proposals for retribution against the German Army. Roosevelt thought that the Soviet leader was making a crude joke when he suggested that fifty to a hundred thousand German officers should be executed immediately. Churchill, the former soldier, was violently affronted at the suggestion, stressing what should have been a self-evident point: that only convicted war criminals should face that fate.

#

"Hello. Is that Jiří?"

"Yes. Is that George? It is a pleasure to speak to you."

So began my call with my grandfather's old VRÚ colleague, who was as warm and friendly as his letters. He seemed very pleased to recollect their time working together in Hockliffe.

"Oh yes, I certainly knew your grandfather – Jarda to me."

"Yes – my grandmother called him that too."

His English accent was good – perhaps better than my grandfather's, despite him being a native of Olomouc in Moravia.

"We lived in this little Nissen hut in bunks. He used to sleep with his back to me across the corridor.

I worked with him from when I arrived in January 1943 until he left in early 1945. I never knew that he went to Italy for a parachute mission until I just read about it. There were a lot of comings and goings and then."

"So, you don't know anything else about his mission then? What it was?"

"No, I'm afraid I don't know anything about that other than what I read."

I felt a twinge of disappointment.

"The book said that he was to be sent to our country, with his team, from Italy. There were two unsuccessful attempts to drop them in West Bohemia. From Italy they went to France. By that time the war was almost over, so the mission was cancelled."

"Yes, I read that, but I'd like to know a bit more about it. About the purpose of the mission. He said he was sent on an assassination mission."

He paused for a moment.

"I wouldn't have known anything about that."

"Have you spoken to Novák"? He would be more likely to know I think, as he knew him longer?"

"No. I wrote to him and he sent me the information from the book as well."

"Ah well, I know he's having a tough time of it at the moment."

#

Over the summer, serious discussions began between SOE and the Czech exile army about the support that would be needed to organise an uprising in the Protectorate at the optimum time. General Miroslav, of General Ingr's exile army, wrote to Colonel Gubbins of SOE in July, with two specific requests. The first was for significant arms drops; enough for ten to fifty thousand men. The second was for support to drop five hundred Czech parachutists. The letter stressed that the timing of the uprising would be decided by the local leaders on the ground. SOE raised their eyebrows at the requests, stating:

"Usually the Czechs are an extremely logical people, but this letter shows a strange lack of reality."

The scale of material and people could not be practically delivered and the Czechoslovaks had nowhere near that number of trained parachutists. SOE immediately met with Miroslav to talk in more detail but private correspondence shows that this meeting only added to their scepticism and concern. The British responded formally to General Miroslav, stating that no support at all would be provided unless two conditions were clearly satisfied. Firstly, they would need to see a clear military plan and definite information about the strength and location of local resistance groups. Secondly, they would need absolute assurance that the resistance groups would rise only on receipt of a signal from London, in coordination with the broader allied strategy.

The trust needed to push forward on this endeavour was not being helped by the continued wrangling between Moravec and the British over the control of their codes. In June, just prior to Miroslav's request, Moravec had written to the British intelligence services apologising for the delay in his formal response to their previous requests and notifying them that having finally put the matter of control of codes to Beneš (referring to him pointedly as 'the President of the Republic') his boss would welcome a further discussion with them at an appropriate time. With Beneš engaged in shuttle diplomacy around the world, it was unclear when exactly this meeting would be.

#

On his latest BBC broadcast Jan Masaryk had a message for the people of Slovakia. Their collaborationist regime was becoming complicit in crimes against its Jewish people. It was time for each citizen to examine their conscience and decide which side they were on:

"And now a word to you, brother Slovaks. Your ridiculous government has the insolence to boast of how well it has solved the Jewish question...I solemnly warn every Slovak who supports this bestial attitude and helps to send our Jewish fellow citizens to certain death...The allied governments protest with horror against the unheard of anti-Jewish bestialities of the last few weeks. I appeal to the chivalry of the Slovak people. I am not prepared to admit that it is possible that the people of Jánošík should slay the defenceless, the wretched, the abandoned and persecuted."

Moravec had transferred Captain Šustr out of intelligence to work with General Miroslav in March of 1943. This was certainly a demotion and was consistent with the flaws in his work as liaison agent. Though he was not a 'big fish', soon after this in November 1943 he secured a visit to British Intelligence headquarters in London, to poke at various open wounds in the relationship between the exiles and their British hosts. He was in a particularly gossipy mood and ranted on a range of subjects, with the British drily noting that "all the points being put forward by Šustr without much prompting," and that he was "very ready to talk."

He proceeded to damn everybody but himself. Miroslav's team were 'incompetent and without initiative." František Moravec was disingenuous and was actively seeking to sow fear in Czech circles of the British exerting too much control. Beneš was exaggerating the scale and extent of Czech resistance activity and this was landing badly in the Protectorate itself. The kernel of Šustr's message was that the real power lay with Beneš and if the British wanted something from him they should be clear, direct and demanding: British politeness and reserve were not understood.

Šustr then went on to say that he felt that the real reason that the Czechoslovak exile government in London was ineffective was that it was 'filled with Jews'. He reserved special vitriol for Jan Masaryk, partly on the basis that his mother was a 'Jewess'. Although Šustr's credibility was fundamentally undermined by his bitterness and his clear anti-semitism, his contribution would certainly would not have helped the Czechoslovaks in their ongoing lobbying for help at this key point in the war.

To meet British demands a sizeable local resistance needed to be demonstrably in place in Czechoslovakia and primed for action. Another wave of parachute missions were planned to build communications with local partisans. The British were right in their scepticism about the numbers of parachutists available. Men from the first wave of trainees, like Karel Svoboda, Čestmír Šikola and Jaroslav Klemeš were approached again. But it was proving harder and harder to find new recruits. Younger men from later waves of exile to the UK were approached and cross examined to determine their suitability.

#

"I was supposed to be dropped on a parachute mission too," Jiří said, eagerly. "As the war came to an end, we all wanted to go back and liberate our country. I couldn't go in the end because of an injury to my knees which meant I wasn't fit to jump out of a plane."

He laughed lightly. I was reminded of the injury to my grandfather's nose and asked Jiří if he knew anything about it, but he didn't. He reminisced about a visit to Hockliffe in the 1970s and reflected that barely anyone even then, knew that the VRÚ had ever been there. He was clearly proud of their contribution.

"The radio station at Hockliffe had excellent radio operators – the absolute best – the peak ones. This was because making connections was very difficult so they needed to get the most out of them: get it right first time. The parachute groups and resistance networks lived under very difficult circumstances so we couldn't afford to get it wrong."

But the mood at the VRÚ was not always so serious.

"At Hockliffe we had a tame crow that we used to have around. We called it 'Katya.' Well your grandfather used to sleep with his watch – a nice watch it was – on the nightstand by his bed. One day, Katya took his wristwatch from the table while he was asleep and then she flew out and up to the top of a tree, holding the watch tightly in her beak."

He began laughing.

"Jarda was so mad. He was jumping up and down shouting.

"Katya…Give me back my watch you damn crow'".

He chuckled. This image still clearly tickled him all of these years later.

#

If the experience of Munich had taught Beneš one thing, it was that the future security of his country could not be left to Britain and France. Ignoring British concerns, Beneš pushed ahead with his 'Christmas' visit to Moscow, to cement relations with Russia, in December of 1943.

Beneš was fawned upon and flattered from the very start of his trip. Stalin and his foreign secretary Molotov welcomed him with a guard of honour and a banquet was held for him. Stalin greeted him cordially, having not seen him for eight years, and laid on the charm, smiling and joking with the Czechoslovak President. The Soviet leader's tone at their meetings was of down to earth pragmatist, concerned solely with defeating the Nazis and ending German aggression forever. A day after Beneš' arrival, the treaty of alliance - Beneš' key objective - was signed and all toasted it with Soviet-made champagne. The treaty enshrined economic and military co-operation between Czechoslovakia and the Soviet

213

Union but with Czechoslovakia as a fully independent democracy. The text had actually been settled in correspondence sometime before the meeting but a last-minute exchange lengthened its term from five years to twenty and removed the need for the Czechoslovak parliament to ratify it. If this caused Beneš concern he did not show it. Instead, he used every discussion to seek clarity on the practical detail of the agreement. Beneš pushed his case for the expulsion of the Sudeten Germans and found no reservations at all to his policy. He also stated that the worst war criminals should be dealt with in the first two months of retaking the country. Stalin indicated that he understood completely, readily accepting the need. Beneš could not have been more pleased with his progress, seemingly unaware that he risked creating an irresistible momentum towards punishment and revenge as core policies of the new state.

Beneš felt so empowered that he broached another difficult issue. Ultimately, he desired that any rising of the Czechoslovak population should have at its political core a group representative of his social democratic views. Any outside help would need to be on the basis that it was temporary and transitional until the normal business of his government and home rule could be resumed. However, the risk was that the Russians would seek to liberate the country and then take over all or part of it for themselves. He therefore came with an offer to test the limits of his new ally's recent expansionist policies. He told Stalin that he was prepared to cede the very eastern part of his pre-Munich territory - Sub-Carpathian Ukraine - to the Soviet Union. 'Uncle Joe' – as the Americans had by now nicknamed him – pondered this offer only briefly and his answer was clear: he would not hear of it. He had no territorial designs at all on Czechoslovakia.

Beneš next meeting in Moscow was with the Czech communists: Klement Gottwald and Rudolf Slánský. He was very keen to reach agreement with the men, as they would need to be engaged in and supportive of his new regime. They recognised Beneš' authority but were clear that they wanted strong influence in a new government. Beneš grudgingly agreed to a new National Front that would comprise of all parties but with the Czech Communist Party at its core. Even more grudgingly, he approved the setting up of 'peoples committees' which would give strong communist control of local decision-making.

#

Despite these difficult conversations, Beneš finished his visit the happiest and most optimistic he had been in his life. He immediately wrote to Jan Masaryk about his success; the new treaty enshrined all of the important principles that Beneš had wanted. He reported that Stalin's only real challenge to him had been on Czech passivity. He wanted Beneš to fully engage his men and resources in active war with the Nazi regime immediately. This report allowed Masaryk's optimism to briefly flourish too. In his radio broadcast he finally felt able to speak from the heart of the mission he had inherited from his father and his real hope that it might actually be achieved.

"Three weeks before his death he said to me: "How is it possible that the Germans buy millions of copies of this horrible book [mein kampf]…How low they have sunk…My father hated flag waving. Let us think hard and the petty little flags will disappear and all the sooner will there appear on the Hradčany again, and this time for good, the red, white and blue flag of the Czechoslovak Republic – free, democratic, socially just, belonging to Europe and the world."

#

Before Beneš went to Russia, he had spoken to František Moravec. He'd indicated that he was prepared to make compromises with Stalin, but that he had in his mind a limit he could not go beyond.

"He never specified to me what that limit was," Moravec commented in his post-war memoir. "…and his later activities made interpretation of those brave words very difficult."

Soon after Beneš' return, he came to see his intelligence chief again, in a buoyant mood. From their conversation, Moravec felt that Beneš was not being completely honest in what he had agreed with the Russians. He also formed a view that his boss was naïve about the threat posed by Klement Gottwald as a rival. Moravec understood instinctively that Stalin would never tolerate having an independent democracy on his border. But Beneš seemed to him to be hopelessly blind. A period of change was coming. He was deeply concerned that the messy practicalities of democracy would be no match for the Russian's tactics of infiltration and take-over. Moravec was right to be concerned. His niche as the controller of all of his county's intelligence, made him a key target. Unbeknownst to him the Communists were already spreading false rumours that he was in the pay of the British.

As a final aside, Beneš stressed that he had agreed to purge the 'fascist' element in the Czechoslovak army. Moravec was incredulous. He did not believe that there was such an element. The army was made up of men who'd left their homes and families to fight the fascists. Men like him. The implication was that the

Communists had already identified those who were in the way of their plans and who they were going to purge. As a man who carefully weighed trust in every daily exchange and movement, Moravec began - for the first time - to have serious doubts about his future and the robustness of his relationship with Beneš.

UPRISINGS

With sharp rebukes about the need for action from Britain and Russia ringing in his ears, Beneš knew it was time to go to work again. The way ahead was complex and if Czechoslovakia was to emerge sovereign and independent, he would need to weave a clever path. The timing and control of any uprising would be absolutely critical to the transition of power. The Russian army was closing in on Czechoslovakia, a development which was emboldening the communist underground in his homeland, who were readying themselves to take charge. To counter balance this Beneš would need strong support from the Americans and the British to strengthen his allies within the Protectorate.

Slovakia presented an even more complex picture than Bohemia and Moravia. The collaborationist and Catholic-dominated Tiso regime had started to teeter, as German influence and power had begun to wane. Democratic and communist underground factions began to work together and a 'Slovak National Council' – known as the SNC - was formed, with equal weight for each faction. Their stated mission was to re-establish Czechoslovakia as a democratic, secular state, whilst giving Slovakia more autonomy than in the pre-war arrangement. Beneš formed a marriage of convenience with the SNC. He would give them political weight and authority to act. In turn, this would validate his leadership credentials in Slovakia and their successful revolt would create an opportunity for the country's rehabilitation in the eyes of the Allies, who like Beneš, currently saw it as a reprehensible Nazi client state. The London exile government was therefore keen to support an early Slovakian uprising, despite still favouring a more cautious and nuanced approach in Bohemia and Moravia.

The most significant resistance group across both the Protectorate and Slovakia was known as R3, the 'council of three.' It was made up of the remnants of 'defence of the nation' (the Czech army group which the 'Three Kings' had been members of); the communist underground and the illegal trade union movement. This make-up ensured that it was well aligned to Beneš' political views and the group fully respected his leadership.

The R3 developed a guerrilla structure and began to prepare to assist the liberating armies when the time came. As the war had progressed its partisan groups, hidden in the mountains, had been bolstered by escaped Russian prisoners of war who brought valuable knowledge and skills. The R3 began to form reception committees for parachute groups from both the East and West.

So whilst resistance was growing across the breadth of Czechoslovakia, Nazi counter resistance continued to evolve in step. Many agent provocateurs from their prisoner population were sent to infiltrate the underground, motivated by threats to their lives and the lives of their families. So, it was in this paranoid and duplicitous environment that a succession of new parachute missions began in early 1944; to plan and prepare for the 'spontaneous uprising' that Beneš needed.

#

There was no easy way to navigate through this part of my research. As I delved further, all the available military information was hazy and lacking in transparency. There was no doubt that this was intentional when it came to the parachute missions. I had obtained Šikola's memoirs, but they were in Czech. I found a translator and, given the expense, tried to work out which excerpts from the book and other material I'd collected would be of most value. One of the first things I had translated was a letter that my grandfather had sent to Novák in his later years.

"Hi Mirek,

Thanks for your letter and the newspapers. You say that your daughter brought them from Bohemia. I suppose then, that she speaks Czech. I feel envy of it. None of my family speaks Czech. Only my wife can speak a little bit…"

The guilt of this sat heavily on me. He had actually tried to teach me Czech briefly but just glancing at the books he had handed me, I had decided that there was more chance of me perfecting all of his old gymnastics moves. After a while, selected excerpts of Šikola's memoir began to arrive by e-mail.

#

Čestmír Šikola's career exactly mirrored that of Jaroslav Bublík. The two were even promoted on the same day as each other on no less than three separate occasions.

Šikola's memoir describes how he was initially recruited into intelligence work. His commander sent him to see Captain Šustr and he was asked whether he wished to be dropped behind enemy lines for special missions. He was given three days to think it through but replied straightaway:

"Sir, you can count me in now, save you coming back in three days' time."

This was early in the days of intelligence recruitment. Oldřich Dvořák came into the room to see Šustr straight after him. Sworn to secrecy, the two were taken to the railway station at Leamington, near their base, where two other recruits were waiting, one of whom was Lubomír Jasínek. On arrival, they met with František Moravec and then set off for the SOE training school in Thame Park, Oxfordshire, where they went through telegraphy training with Jaroslav Bublík. The photograph I had seen from Christmas 1941 shows the three of them – Bublík, Dvořák and Šikola - together.

In another coincidence of names, Šikola's mission was - like SILVER A - led by a man named Bartoš. Antonín Bartoš, like his namesake Alfréd, had a military background from the pre-war days and had moved through the ranks to captain since his arrival from France. The third member was a Bohemian named Jiří Štokman, who had been a member of the underground resistance in Zlín prior to joining the army. The three men made a promising team, but they would have to wait two years for the opportunity to test that promise.

\#

In early 1944, the Gestapo finally discovered that Stanislav Srazil was signalling to 'London' that he was caught. By this time, the

Gestapo had many more informants and no shortage of leads to follow up on elsewhere. Realising the loss of his value, and angry at the waste of their resources Srazil was taken to Terezín, where after extraordinarily brutal treatment he was shot dead.

At this time the new parachute missions began. A two-man team codenamed operation SULPHUR was dropped just north of Prague on 8th April. A day later, operation CHALK, a four-man team, was dropped nearby. Both groups disappeared without a trace on landing, caught by the Gestapo and their double agents.

It was in this unpromising atmosphere that Šikola returned to his team to begin operation CLAY. CLAY was to establish a strong communications link in Moravia through the setting up of a new transmitter. The intent was to gather intelligence, organise partisans, and coordinate future reception committees in a new area of the country. Just four days after CHALK's unsuccessful drop, CLAY was despatched in a Halifax flown by a Canadian crew. Šikola's key equipment was a transceiver, some spares parts and one 'Simandl' receiver.

It was a clear night in Moravia when the members of CLAY made their run. Leaping from just two thousand feet, there was little time for their chutes to billow to their full size and little time for them to prepare themselves for their impact with the turf of their homeland. All landed deftly, hitting the ground within a few hundred yards of each other. Within twenty minutes, they had buried their parachutes and set off east, away from Zlín, together with their equipment. The team soon made contact with the bedraggled partisans of the R3, and efficiently set about their task. At eleven twenty-five pm on the thirtieth of April, less than two weeks after their drop, Šikola turned on the radio, tuned into the agreed night frequency and tapped out his call sign. After three attempts the men of Hockliffe replied with 'C-8-A' – their designated response. The small radio then burst into life in a staccato of buzzing and beeping, transmitting groups of five letters into which the content of the first telegrams was encrypted.

With Šikola now firmly in touch with Bublík and the team at the VRÚ, a firm link had been established between the R3 in Moravia and the exile government. Bartoš, Šikola and Štokman began to build a new underground movement. They each started by recruiting three local informants. These informants were then tasked with recruiting another three and so on, in a giant pyramid scheme of espionage. The beauty of this approach was that as the organisation grew, it left the men at the top of the pyramid with significant degrees of separation from the bulk of the organisation and therefore compartmentalised from infiltration by Gestapo agents.

#

General Čatloš, Slovakia's minister of war, was well aware that he was high on Beneš' list of war criminals; he would be amongst the first to face the gallows when allied victory came. With Russian troops amassing on Slovakia's border, Čatloš sent his emissaries to speak to the Soviets and offered to put the Slovakian military fully at the disposal of Stalin. Having weakly subordinated the country to the Nazis, he was now prepared to do exactly the same with the Soviet Union to save his neck. Beneš had contacts in Slovakia and he learned immediately that Čatloš' envoys were visiting Russia. His worst fears were realised when he received a copy of their memo to the Soviets, spelling out the offer that was being put on the table.

As well as proposing a Slovak military dictatorship after hostilities ended, it stated that Slovakia would become a Soviet satellite state and that "Slovak political matters might be solved in accordance with the interests of the USSR."

"Incredible, inconceivable…" Beneš muttered as he read the report he received on the matter. "So this is our reward for having so often stood up for the Russians!...this must be stopped."

Beneš protested directly to the Soviet government in the strongest terms and had discussions directly with Klement Gottwald. The Soviets backtracked and Beneš was pacified, against his better judgement. František Moravec continued to observe developments soberly from the side-lines.

#

Throughout the spring and summer, CLAY's network expanded and information started to flood back and forth between Moravia and Hockliffe. This included artillery garrison numbers, the movements of SS officers, the activities of officer training schools and details of the production of batteries for submarines. To cope with the volume of intelligence, Šikola and the VRÚ began to send messages in bulk at pre-agreed times, without immediate acknowledgment. This one-way traffic meant greater security and shorter transmission times.

The R3 military organisation also strengthened over the summer. Antonín Bartoš sent an urgent message to Beneš, requesting permission to ready a local military force. Despite his requests for action, Stalin in reality did not want Beneš to build a military capability with British and American arms and support. Either Beneš was aware of this, or he consulted with Stalin at this point; either way, his response to Bartoš was a clear 'no.' Frustrated at this answer, Bartoš explained that he had organised with leaders on the ground, who were ready to fight. Beneš still refused and instead, enquired about the political situation in Moravia. Bartoš rapidly despatched a note to the VRÚ.

"The anti-German sentiment has changed into hatred. This has been brought on by the Germans' arrogance and double standards of the Protectorate's authorities…Many cannot forget England's involvement in Munich. However, this is overshadowed by the fact that England then stood, alone, against Germany, saved our army in France and enabled political interaction with the world. Russia is gaining more and more respect in agricultural and industrial circles. It is generally accepted that Russia will play the biggest part in the reorganisation of Europe. The USA's task is considered to be one of economic help, its political influence is being disregarded."

This information would have only reaffirmed in Beneš mind, the importance of careful engagement with Stalin in the months ahead.

#

The work of the handful of radio telegraphists in Hockliffe continued to be gruelling. In their free moments, the men needed distractions to stay sane. They rigorously maintained their physical training and the Sokol members amongst them practiced their gymnastics. They needed other hobbies to replenish themselves and keep their minds steady. In his time in France, Jiří Louda had developed a fascination with heraldry and coats of arms. In his free moments in Hockliffe, he would sit in concentration, drawing out new designs. Jaroslav Bublík developed two hobbies at once. Unable to get hold of a chess set, he took a sharp knife and some offcuts of wood and whittled two sets of pieces. He then hand-painted them: one set black, the other white. His rare free time was then spent either playing chess with one of his colleagues or shaving other bits of wood into various shapes. It was a hobby he retained late into life, even carving toys for my brother, sister and I when we were children. These were what the brief pauses looked like at the VRÚ: the men engrossed in their pastimes about the farm, occasionally disturbed by the farmer's horse kicking out at the barn nearby, or by his dog barking when Katya their tame crow pulled at its tail as it ate. But even then, the silent invisible hum of the wireless station hung deafeningly over them, always ready to remind them that their turn at the Morse tapper would inevitably return, as the volume of communications approached its peak.

#

The Slovak National Council was mustering its forces to support an uprising under the command of General Ján Golian, a mid-ranking commander, who had been quietly building a coalition of anti-Nazi forces within the Slovak army. A careful survey of the political allegiance of officers had been undertaken and those willing to fight against the Nazi's identified. Golian's plan was for two divisions to rebel and fight for independence, with support from the Russian army. Significant supplies had been spirited away for the rebellion. Golian's army divisions would hold open the Dukla pass in the Carpathian Mountains and allow the Russians to enter Slovakia from the East. The action would be initiated by a signal from the Red Army, but if a German military occupation of Slovakia were to begin before this signal, the plan would have to be put into action immediately. In advance of an attack, the Soviets had been strengthening partisan forces in Slovakia via parachute groups. Despite pleas for restraint from General Golian, the overt threat to the Nazi-backed Tiso regime reached such a level that it made appeals to Germany for assistance. Golian's hand was therefore forced prematurely and on August 29 at 8pm he initiated the uprising.

Thirty thousand reservists joined Golian's rebellion. Initially things did not go to plan; German forces quickly captured and disarmed the two divisions holding the Dukla pass, and critical supplies of weaponry were lost. Nevertheless, Golian's forces managed to secure a significant part of Slovakian territory; Banská Bystrica, in the heart of the country, which became the de-facto rebel capital. Jan Masaryk contacted allied representatives in London, requesting support and that they clearly state that they viewed the rebel Slovak forces as legitimate combatants under the protections of the Geneva Convention. These statements came from Great Britain and the USA but no military support was provided. Moscow said nothing. The Slovak insurgents gritted their teeth and fought for the time needed for Soviet forces and allied supplies to arrive.

#

By September 1944, Karel Svoboda had long since recovered from his injury in the practice jump for ANTHROPOID and it was his turn to step forward once again. He would now risk sacrificing himself in order to seek some measure of revenge for the death of his family and to finally play the role destiny had planned for him. He was to be part of a six-man team – Operation WOLFRAM - to support the development of the partisan organisation in north eastern Moravia, near the Slovak border. He said a final war-time goodbye to his old comrade and tent-mate Bublík and disappeared for intensive refresher training.

When the time came, Svoboda was the first to jump. His lack of parachuting luck continued and as he plummeted through the air, he became entangled in the 'leg bag,' which carried his equipment. He managed to free himself before reaching the ground but then landed with his parachute draped across the corner of a house. For a time he dangled, unhurt, looking at his wireless and radio equipment lying exposed on the ground. Upon freeing himself, he gathered his chute and his equipment and made for the plentiful late-summer cover of the nearby woods. Unbeknownst to Svoboda, his teammates had hesitated before jumping, which left them widely scattered on the ground. Over a period of four days, he searched for them in an ever-widening circle. On the fifth day, he buried all of his equipment and tried to work out his next move.

#

The Slovak uprising remained delicately balanced. At Beneš' instruction, General Viest was sent from England by plane to Banská Bystrica, to take over command from Golian. By September 10, the rebels had gained control of large areas of the country. But forty thousand German troops steadily moved in to challenge them. The Slovak National Council and Beneš' government requested help from all quarters but nothing was forthcoming. Britain and the US were politically in support of the uprising, but it held little military gain for them. The Russian surge was still expected and they were implored to come in. But they appeared to have changed their mind. Stalin's real strategy was to let the fight play out, then flood the country with parachutists and orchestrate a communist-led uprising on the ground. Although

Stalin and Gottwald had to work through Beneš to an extent, they had no desire to see his 'bourgeois,' capitalist government at the head of a takeover. The Soviets made half-hearted promises to the Slovak National Council but no help came; not even weapons and ammunition from the air. The eastern part of the Slovak Air Force had by this time left to join Russia, but even that force was not allowed to help. In nearby Warsaw, the Russians were thought to be applying similar tactics by tactically withholding their forces to allow the nationalist rebellion to be crushed.

Despite the political risks, Masaryk turned once again to the USA and Britain for help in Slovakia. Finally, a handful of soldiers from the US Office of Strategic Services – its version of SOE - landed discreetly in Banská Bystrica. Through this team, twenty-four tons of arms were belatedly dropped from Southern Italy.

#

Across the border in Moravia, Karel Svoboda needed to make his next move. Unaware of his exact location, he approached a local civilian and asked for directions to the nearest village. Rather than going there, he settled into the woods nearby for the night. Despite his ruse, this interaction was his downfall; as Svoboda awoke to the chatter of birds swelling around him the next morning, he was immediately pounced on by two SS men who had tracked him down after a tip off from the same local. They searched him rapidly, stripping him of all he carried, including his poison capsule.

He was bundled into a car and taken to the police station. On arrival, he was blindfolded and tied to a chair for a cross examination by one male and one female officer. They immediately asked him about his mission: what was the purpose of 'Operation

WOLFRAM'? This tore away what little composure he had marshalled. If they knew what the mission was called, they had most likely already captured one or more of the team. Either that, or they had cracked the Czech codes and were listening in to their radio transmissions. Svoboda was evasive, saying that it had been a blind drop with no local addresses given. These answers did not please his interrogators, and still blindfolded and tied, he only heard the arrival of his torturers.

His ordeal began with a flurry of blows from fists and rubber bars, as questions were screamed at him. Betraying nothing, Svoboda soon felt a hosepipe violently forced into his mouth and twisted down his throat. Then water was switched on and as the terror of drowning overwhelmed him, he lost consciousness. When his awareness returned, the hosepipe was gone but the Gestapo had only just begun their interrogation. They repeatedly threw forward the chair on which he was sat, pitching him headfirst into the floor. With his hands bound, this forced him to twist his shoulders to brace his fall. Despite hours of this treatment, Svoboda divulged nothing. Eventually they hurled him to the ground and rained kicks and punches on him from all angles. Lifting his head defiantly, he screamed for them to kill him but his tormentors just laughed. They tore off his blood-encrusted hood, carelessly cut his bindings and slung him to the floor again.

After a brief respite, his captors tried a different tactic. An upholstered chair was put in the room and he was encouraged to seat his battered body on it. A local Gestapo leader proffered him a cigarette and after lighting it, began questioning him about life in England. Svoboda spoke honestly about the sense of community there, the efficiency and organisation of the British war effort and how he and his fellow Czechs had been welcomed into the homes and pubs of the British with generosity – as family. Flustered by this and dismissing his account as fantasy, Svoboda's interrogator then cut to the quick, telling him that the only way to save his life was to tell the truth. With both his life and his integrity hanging on every word, Svoboda did his best to present as a man whose will had been completely broken. Hesitantly he spoke, "My party and I were to go to Slovakia. Another uprising is planned any day." This had a grain of truth to it, like all the best lies, and seemed to land well with his interrogator. He was brusquely shuffled out of the room and led to a cell. Forced to strip naked, he lay his broken body down on the cold floor. Every half hour, his guard came in and each time swung an angry boot into him, wanting to hear a grunt of pain to double check that he was still alive. This is how time passed until the next day inevitably came.

#

Back in Hockliffe, at the top of the hill in College farm, Knotek, Bublík and the men at the VRÚ were nervously waiting for a message – any message - from WOLFRAM, tuning into the allocated frequencies regularly and with expectation.

They may not have been certain that Svoboda was the radio operator of this particular mission but they must at least have had suspicion. What seemed like mere days before, he had been sat in their midst, sharing the daily grind of tasks, chatting in the mess hut. Now no one knew where he was. The radio silence was ominous. It looked as if yet another man – and perhaps the whole group – was gone.

#

Svoboda was dressed, put into a car and driven back to where he had been found. His captors asked him to direct them to his dropping point and to where he had buried his equipment. Svoboda feigned confusion and they left empty-handed. He was taken on to Brno and cross-examined repeatedly on his story. His interrogators mentioned the names of people, places and training schools: Paleček, Šustr, Arisaig, Thame Park, Chicheley Hall, Funny Neuk. Over the next few days of interrogation, Svoboda came to understand that they had obtained cyphers to VRÚ and Russian radio transmissions and had a number of parachutists working on their side. The whole network was deeply compromised. He felt there were some things he need not keep silent about anymore.

#

CLAY's organisation had grown significantly in the increasingly fertile ground of Moravia. The network of agents was expanding exponentially and this was creating significant volumes of intelligence to go back to London and Moscow. On a doctor's advice, Bartoš had sent an exhausted Šikola on a brief break from his responsibilities at the end of the summer. This proved well-timed, as the late summer and early autumn proved to be the peak of his transmission of messages back to the VRÚ. Intelligence was sent back on the location of production plants of V1 and V2 rockets – the 'doodlebugs' that were raining terror on families like my grandmother's in London. Šikola also supplied the exact coordinates of a V1 and V2 launching site being built in southern Moravia. Armed with this information, American bombers destroyed these critical targets shortly afterwards.

#

At the start of October, Winston Churchill went to visit Joseph Stalin at the Kremlin in Moscow. On the evening of their arrival, the men met with just their foreign ministers and interpreters. A new Europe was dawning: one without the malign influence of Hitler. But mighty armies had been amassed and were drawing closer to each other by the day, as the Nazi machine was ground to dust. Each country had its own view of where it would seek political influence, and careful negotiation was needed. Churchill sought to remove any confusion that might lead to dangerous confrontations between the Allied armies. He grabbed a piece of paper and against a list of countries – Romania, Greece,

Yugoslavia, Hungary and Bulgaria - he wrote percentages indicating the degree of Anglo-American political influence and the degree of Soviet influence. Stalin took the piece of paper and after listening to the words of his interpreter, drew a large blue tick on it. Churchill described this exchange over future 'spheres of influence' in his memoirs; there has been much speculation about what each man meant and what each understood from this exchange. But regardless, and although Czechoslovakia was not listed, it was clear that - as at Munich – the major political decisions about smaller countries would be decided by the major powers in their own interests.

#

At this time, Stankmuller and Moravec were bombarding the SIS with requests for transmitters and new crystals. Crystals were needed to pull the message out of the incoming signal at the right frequency and were prone to wearing out. The VRÚ even got a sprucing up with new linoleum flooring, to combat the dust that was causing the need for the crystals to be constantly cleaned.

The messages were now flying into the VRÚ faster than the men could cope with. At one point during a particular tense and gruelling transmission, Modrák went temporarily blind. Trying to remain calm he continued, regardless. Jaroslav Bublík remained busy at his Morse tapper too. Researching this time, I was reminded of how he had once demonstrated to me how to transmit Morse code. He took a random piece of paper – a newsletter of some type - and laid it in front of him. Then he began to scan it and to repeatedly slap the index finger of his right hand onto the coffee table in front of him as he translated the words. He started quite hesitantly, screwing up his face as he concentrated, and then he came alive and began drumming out sharp staccato bursts of tapping.

#

Almost as soon as the American armaments began to arrive in Slovakia, they were stopped. It appeared that to continue the drops would be contrary to agreements between Roosevelt and Stalin. The US joint chiefs of staff's expressed view was that 'geography left only Soviet forces to do it.' The British lobbied the Soviets to provide support but all that transpired was their belated announcement of their support for the insurgents as a legitimate army. Finally, in early October, the Russian forces took the Dukla pass from the Germans. Some limited arms were sent and yet more Soviet parachutists, although these were spread across the country in a piecemeal fashion and not used to reinforce insurgent forces.

This all proved too little too late for Viest and Golian's forces. Having quelled a similar uprising in nearby Hungary, the Nazis became able to divert significant forces to the battle and Banská Bystrica fell on October 27. The next day – Czechoslovak Independence Day – Viest spoke on the radio: "The Czechoslovak Army command announces herewith that…an organised resistance of the army is no longer possible."

The Slovak army units reverted to guerrilla warfare, joining with partisan forces and awaiting the oncoming Red Army. Golian and Viest were captured, interrogated and executed. The Nazi forces were bewildered and infuriated by this attempted uprising as Slovakia had been considered a benign Nazi hinterland. In the Nazi mind, there could of course only be one reason for this revolt: the Slovaks had been too accommodating of their Jewish population, who were surely the masterminds behind it. Ignoring the Allies demands for restraint and compliance with international law, reprisals were initiated.

The whole turn of events had been both shocking and instructive to Beneš. He had been unaware of the degree to which there had been a carving up of 'spheres of influence' and it was now obvious to him that he had absolutely no option but to trust Stalin and the Soviets; he would win Czech autonomy only if Stalin allowed it. His relationship with Gottwald and the Czech and Slovak Communists was more critical than ever.

#

Soon after this, Moravec received a visit from a Soviet intelligence agent, Cicajev from the NKVD - the forerunner to the KGB - who had quite recently appeared in London. Moravec looked with a discerning eye on this man, who he had known well from the pre-war years as a disciplined diplomat, noting the changed opportunist he now saw in front of him. Cicajev cut to the quick. He stated that it was clear that the war had already been won by the Soviet Union and that provided Moravec co-operated, he would have a high post in the restored Czechoslovakian republic. He moved quickly on to a request for Moravec to collect all of the information that he could on British intelligence services and to provide it to him. For good measure, he added that Moravec would now also be required to provide information on Beneš' post-war political and military plans.

"When I regained my breath, I did not mince my words," Moravec later recollected. He stated very clearly that he had no intention of spying on either his president or his hosts and allies. Moravec went straight to Beneš to report this development. The President was initially shocked but to Moravec's dismay,

236

immediately began to rationalise events. Beneš reminded Moravec that the Russians could not be judged by western standards of morality and special allowances had to be made for their well-known suspiciousness.

With the Slovak uprising extinguished, a message from the exile government came through to Šikola. It asked urgently about the scale of military organisation in CLAY's network in eastern Moravia. Having pressed for earlier engagement to support the uprising, Antonín Bartoš was thoroughly exasperated at this sudden about-face.

"Have I not said that the 'lords' in London would suddenly one day decide that we should do this? And here it is and it can't wait."

He reported that he had three thousand men ready to take up arms and fight and had recruited two colonels to command the forces who were ready and keen to play their part. A response was received: arms would be dropped on October 7. Excited, the whole network went to work, making its preparations calmly and meticulously under the noses of the local Gestapo.

When the time came for the weapons drop, Bartoš, Šikola and Štokman listened for the agreed password that was to be broadcast on the BBC but there was nothing. For the next two nights they continued listening, but still nothing. Finally a message came through explaining that the drop had been abandoned. It was viewed that the war was most probably going to drag on through the winter months, so any decisions regarding weapon drops were now delayed until the spring. This was both a devastating blow to everyone involved and a huge challenge to the credibility of Bartoš and his team on the ground in Moravia. Disillusionment with the exile government in 'London' was at a peak. But there was little time for anger. Their recent activity to prepare for the drop meant that they were now ripe for Gestapo attention and infiltration. On November 18, Šikola moved his transmitter to a new location as a precaution.

#

The endgame was approaching for the war and for the Nazi occupation of Czechoslovakia. Jaroslav Bublík had sacrificed his opportunity to be dropped in his homeland at the start of the war. In some ways this had been fortunate, as he would now almost certainly be dead. But, five years after his exile from Banov, he still yearned for the opportunity to stand beside his countrymen in their fight. With the war coming to an end, there would soon be no need to train new radio operators; the need now was for active engagement. When Paleček and Stankmuller approached him in the winter of 1944 to ask if he was ready for his mission, the answer was a given.

#

Alarming news came to Beneš from his contacts in Sub-Carpathian Ukraine. The Soviet command was apparently drafting locals there into the Red Army. Beneš expressed his amazement at this development to the Soviet ambassador and demanded that he tell Moscow that the enrolment stop. An equally blunt response came back.

"Molotov asks you not to insist on the dismissal of the Subcarpathian Ukrainian volunteers from the Red Army and not to oppose further enrolments in the Soviet military units."

Beneš was flabbergasted. He had been willing to cede the territory to the Soviets in his discussions with Stalin but had been assured that they did not want it. Its integrity within Czechoslovakia had been formally agreed and assurances had been solemnly given as part of the broader agreement. If they were now going to break that agreement and take its sovereignty anyway, what could he believe? In fury and confusion, he wrote a detailed note to Moscow.

"Enrolment of our citizens into the Red Army must be stopped at once…They are Czechoslovaks and consequently their place is in the Czechoslovak army."
He pointed out that Czechoslovak citizens could fight with allied armies but only with explicit approval from himself, "Otherwise they would be considered deserters."

Stalin's response was that this was a misunderstanding. He had of course agreed he would have no dealings in internal Czechoslovak affairs but at the same time, if those in Sub-Carpathian Ukraine wished to seek independence that was for them to decide. This was clearly doublespeak, but Beneš took what reassurance he could from it. If he had known the detail of what was happening there, even this slim reassurance would have evaporated. communist agents were forcing village mayors to sign pre-made petitions asking to be 'reunited with their Ukrainian brothers on the other side of the Carpathians.' Soviet recruiters were simply rounding up men of military age and sending them under armed escort to Red Army depots.

These and other similar events drove Beneš to the view that he and his administration were now too remote from events in his homeland. He made plans to move his seat of government from London to the liberated territory in the east of Slovakia.

THE MISSION

As I turned the corner of this small residential road in Southsea, on the Hampshire coast, I looked through my windscreen and saw Píška standing in his front garden, peering at me quizzically. I knew it was him instantly. He was small, with the broad forehead of a Czech. I recognised his sharp angled eyes, even though I had only previously seen them in a sixty-year-old photo of him sitting in front of my grandfather on a camel. As I walked up his path and into his hallway, with a handful of files and maps at my side, we greeted each other and exchanged smiles. We had spoken on the phone a week or so before and he had agreed to help me in my research. He ushered me into his sitting room and we sat down. Before long his photo album appeared.

"This is nineteen thirty-two…thirty-three…this was our school…where we both went," he said. His voice was very much like my grandfather's – the same intonations and phrasing - but his tone was lighter and more high-pitched.

"I went there, he went five years earlier. I didn't know anything about him being in a labour camp like you said. I was still at school then."

I nodded, getting my first sense of the dynamic between the two of them.

"That was waiting for me. The summer of that year I would have been taken away...either that or I'd have had to become a Nazi or something."

Mrs Píška appeared at the edge of the room to inject some decorum into proceedings.

"Would you like some lunch?" she said, in a well-spoken English accent: clearly a local war time bride like my grandmother.

"I'm okay thank you ...I had a sandwich on the way."

"Well feel free to ask..." she continued, "...Czechs are very open with each other you know...don't be British."

I smiled and asked for a cup of tea. He told the story of his exile and it very closely mirrored my grandfather's. Following a path through the countryside, avoiding the police and soldiers but supported by mysterious 'guides,' who would point them in the right direction and then disappear again. He left Banov with his cousins about a week after the Bublíks, and the two groups even crossed paths just outside Belgrade. Píška then travelled through the Greek frontier, to Salonika, then by train across Greece into Turkey and Istanbul. After crossing the Bosphorpous on a boat, they went from Ankara to Syria and finally on to Beirut to join the Czech exile army that was to fight with the French.

I pulled out a document from one of the files I'd brought. It was a certificate of my grandfather's - signed by both him and the French consulate in Beirut - formally receiving him into the Czechoslovak exile army as a patriotic citizen.

"Do you speak French?"

"A little," I responded.

He began to read it, quietly speaking the words, clearly fascinated.

"I didn't get anything like that…" he mumbled softly. "I had no paper. Very interesting….it meant nothing politically of course."

It was dated the January 25, 1940.

"He was there a few days after me…"

I noticed that Mrs Píška was now sitting quietly next to us, and seemed to have been absorbed in our conversation for some time.

"This is very precious. I wish I had one," he threw me a look. "Don't lose it!"

Píška went on to describe their brief days in Beirut. They had stayed in tents, as it poured with rain, before moving into the lodging of the French Foreign Legion, staying in bunks in long wooden huts. The food was good: they had bananas and ate lamb. They could go to the cinema and walk freely around town.

Píška turned a page in his album and I saw a copy of the same picture I had, of he and my grandfather atop a camel, with Josef Bublík and a handful of other men.

"All of us here are from Banov," he said. "We didn't lodge together…We just gathered together and we used to walk around Beirut…We sang Czech songs…Four or five of us."

He peered closely at the picture, "Oh there he is… Bublík…he looked very young there."

He stopped for a moment and thought. "There were eighteen of us in all who ended up in the army in England. Once we worked out that, for the size of the each town, Banov had the most men that escaped and joined the army in all of Czechoslovakia."

He went on the explain how he was with my grandfather a handful of times as they were shipped out via Egypt and Algeria to Marseille. The last time they were together in the war was at the Foreign Legion camp in Marseille in early 1940.

"There we parted. I went into one section of the army and he went another. I don't know what he did for the rest of the war. We never spoke of it."

#

1945 had arrived. For the New Year and the final phase of the War, Bartoš moved CLAY to a village on the border with Slovakia. The courier network was still very active across Moravia. With that and so many parachutists now in Gestapo control, CLAY was ripe for infiltration. The Gestapo infiltrated the courier network and tracked Bartoš down to his new location: the family home of a patriot named Filip Poláček. A renegade courier called at the house and confirmed to his nearby handlers that Bartoš was there. Fortunately, Šikola and Štokman were elsewhere. Half a dozen Gestapo men then came to stake out the location, but judging that they needed better odds, hid outside awaiting reinforcements. In the early hours of the morning, unaware of the predicament, Filip Poláček went outside and was immediately caught by the Gestapo. Bartoš, now alerted, pondered the dire situation, as thirty new Gestapo men arrived. A firefight was inevitable; it was just a question of when it would begin. Before dawn came, Bartoš decided to take matters into his own hands. He leapt from a window and by firing his gun manically as he went, managed to kill the three Gestapo men blocking his route out. As he darted for freedom, the police opened fire with a machine gun and he flung himself to the ground, injuring his hand on the hard ice before scrambling back up and sprinting through the wilderness, his terror propelling him like rocket fuel. He had escaped but the Poláčeks were all caught and with them their knowledge of key personnel, codes and dropping plans. All would have to be planned again from scratch.

#

I opened a small brown envelope and the photocopies from my grandfather's photo album plopped onto the coffee table.

"What photographs are they?" asked Mrs Píška. She was sitting forward now with her elbows on her knees, fully engaged.

"These are my grandfather's photographs. I've been trying to identify who's in them and where and when they each were taken."

I handing them to Píška in turn. He carefully appraised them but without a flicker of recognition. These men were in a different part of the army, and many of the photos were taken while Píška was still stranded in France. Eventually, he flipped one over and read Louda's notes on the back, a grin slowly forming on his face.

"Šikola…Čestmír Šikola…I found the name," he chuckled to himself before flipping it over again. "That's him."

I smiled myself, awaiting an explanation.

"You remember when I said we were crossing and saw your grandfather and the policeman in the little house on the way to Komjatice?"

I nodded.

"As we went on, there was this 'Šikola' with us. He was coughing all the time." He put his hand to his mouth and forced out a hoarse bark to demonstrate.

"I said to him, 'God, be quiet…anybody can hear us and will wonder who is coming at this time of the day, and we are gone.'"

He smiled, looking at the photo again.

"A while ago, I saw his photograph in a Canadian newspaper someone sent me. I wrote to the paper as I wanted to know what this Šikola's Christian name was, but they never got back to me. Anyhow, I've got it now: Čestmír Šikola." He chuckled and clapped his hands lightly. "It's a godsend." He lifted the photocopy up again and brought it close to his eyes, reading Louda's notes. "So he was parachutist. Born 1919….a year older than me.?"

"Yes", I said. "He was the wireless operator for a parachute group: Operation CLAY. He's still alive according to the man who wrote that. The notes are from an old colleague of my granddad's: Jiří Louda."

Mrs Píška spoke softly, "So he was a wireless operator was he? Like Jarda?"

"Louda? Yes. He lives in Olomouc,"

"Olom-otz," said Píška, correcting my pronunciation. "And he's the one that marked these? So he knows that this fellow is still alive? That this Čestmír Šikola is still living?"

"Yes. I guess so."

#

Šikola and Štokman had been living separately in the next village to Bartoš. With Gestapo agents flooding into the area after Bartoš' desperate escape, they had to move on quickly and settled in a village called Prušánky, just to the west. Bartoš managed to find them again and Šikola transcribed the news of his near capture and tapped it out in Morse.

The code passed into the air as an electromagnetic vibration and instantly travelled far away to an antenna at the top of the hill on College Farm in Hockliffe. It arrived with a resonant shudder and the headphones of Bublík, Modrák and the others, began to hum with information.

#

Jaroslav Bublík's training began right at the start of 1945. He was to play his part in a final group of parachute missions composed of select members of the VRÚ, working with commanders from the 1st Czechoslovak Armoured Brigade. Moravec and Stankmuller were hoping that these new parachutists would replace the lost members of existing groups and extend the network into other parts of the country, particularly to eastern Bohemia. Success in transitioning to an independent peace still lay in their cooperation with the home resistance – the R3. The parachute groups were to be put under the command of the R3 on arrival.

Captain Václav Knotek, the codemaster who had been at the VRÚ from the very start, was to lead Operation CHROMIUM with another VRÚ alumni, Jan Štursa. In early planning, their mission was known to be about strengthening links with the democratic home resistance and encouraging the population to rise up. It was deeply focussed on intelligence and communications, and used men who were all proven in terms of their capability, reliability and trustworthiness. Operation MORTAR, under Václav Modrák, was to drop supplies to the resistance in eastern Bohemia and to strengthen communication links between London and the new government, which was to be set up temporarily in Košice in

Slovakia. Two further missions named ROTHMAN and CHURCHMAN were similarly concerned with communication, supplies and supporting the local forces.

Finally was Operation FOURSQUARE, which was to be dropped in south western Bohemia just ahead of the advance of US-led allied forces. The group comprised of Jaroslav Bublík, alongside three more recent recruits. Whilst Bublík provided the essential communications and leadership expertise, the use of these younger men suggested a more physical, combative aspect to the mission and some level of active engagement with the enemy.

Eighteen men were to be dropped in total. With Šustr no longer around, training for these missions was under the supervision of Captain Rudolf Krzák, who had experience working behind enemy lines in France. They were sent for a refresher in unarmed combat and then to attend sabotage training at the SOE training course in Market Harborough. From there, in mid-February 1945 was the obligatory trip to Ringway Airport for parachute training.

#

Píška produced a certificate which had caught his attention.

"This is a commendation. For the Czechoslovak War Cross."

I nodded.

PRESIDENT

REPUBLIKY ČESKOSLOVENSKÉ

UDĚLIL

V UZNÁNÍ BOJOVÝCH ZÁSLUH, KTERÉ ZÍSKAL V BOJI

ZA OSVOBOZENÍ REPUBLIKY ČESKOSLOVENSKÉ

Z NEPŘÁTELSKÉHO OBSAZENÍ

POR.PĚCH.V ZÁL. B U B L Í K JAROSLAV

přísl.čs.zahr.arm.

ČESKOSLOVENSKÝ VÁLEČNÝ KŘÍŽ 1939

V Praze dne 27. dubna 1946

Číslo matriky: 26.587

"Do you have the medal?"

"Well, no. I think at some point he threw the medal away."

"Did he?"

"Yes…He threw all of his medals away." I shuffled in my seat at this admission, and quickly moved the conversation on. "Is that a high medal?"

"It's a 'high medal', yes." Píška paused. "Do you want to see one?"

"Well...Yes please."

He rose from his seat and disappeared into the corridor.

"He was the youngest captain in the Air Force," Mrs Píška said, with a satisfied nod. I smiled and we sat for a moment, alone together for the first time, waiting out the natural pause together.

"How is your grandmother now?"

"She's not too..." I began hesitantly, before changing my angle of approach with an involuntary frown.

"...Physically she's very good. Very sturdy. She never sits down. But she's not...well...she's not really the same anymore."

"Not with us?"

I shook my head.

"Not with us...no. She cuts in and out. She's a bit like the radio. Sometimes she's there, sometimes she's not. She seems happy."

#

The men – Modrák, Bublík and the others – all arrived at Ringway airport for what was expected to be a routine set of practice jumps. Virtually all of them had received parachute training at various points in the previous three years, as at all times circumstances could have demanded their return to the homeland. Bublík's turn came and, laden with his equipment and rubber jump helmet, he leapt from the plane on Krzák's command and plunged through the wet Mancunian air. Mere seconds later, his line taughtened at speed and with a violent tug, his parachute was freed and his descent was slowed from a terrifying plummet to a more survivable fall to the ground. Looking down at his landing site, he saw immediately that he was hurtling towards a large tree. As he sailed towards it, there was nothing he could do to change his trajectory. He grimaced for impact and then felt the branches stabbing viciously into him as he shuddered to a halting stop in the trees' embrace. There he hung, shouting in pain, hopelessly tangled up. Unfortunately, his nose had been stabbed with an unforgiving shard of wood and it was completely ripped at the bridge, dark red blood pouring from the flapping skin. A flurry of men arrived and he was cut free, disentangled and taken to a medic. He had no broken bones and judged as fit to proceed, he was quickly patched up to resume his training.

#

I felt the weight of Píška's war cross in the palm of my hand. It was on a red, white and blue striped ribbon: the colours of the national flag. The medal itself showed crossed swords and the Czechoslovak emblem: a double tailed lion.

"I don't have the papers. I guess I would have had some at some point but I must have misplaced them."

Turning the medal over, I didn't initially notice Píška's attention being diverted to one of the other papers I had brought.

"This is a workbook. From the Protectorate…nineteen forty-two. Was your grandfather there then?"

He had picked up a brown and grey passport sized document. It was seemingly Nazi issued, with words in German first and then the Czech translation underneath.

"Oh, those are to do with his parachute mission I think."

He opened it and began scrutinising its words.

"Jablonec…was he born in Jablonec?…or is it a false paper. He wouldn't have been born in Jablonec.

"No".

"So, this is false paper." He looked up with a beaming smile. "You see…it can be made."

Píška continued to scan the contents, clearly fascinated.

"His profession here…it says 'baker'. So, he was *baker* there." His eyebrows arched.

"It says here Holešov …which is near Zlín in Moravia. No special education…just baker."

He dragged his finger across the paper translating as he spoke: "What practice has he got in labour?…helping during harvest times…some farm labour experience…"

"It sounds like it's trying to be as inconspicuous as possible," I proposed.

"Yes…dated the fourteenth of March nineteen forty two….So he's called Ludvik Zeman…this is the first time I've seen something like this. And he was *specialist in cakes.*" His eyes glinted as he turned to me. "Did he ever make cake?"

I shook my head with a grin. "He never made a cake for me."

"This is excellent…don't get rid of it."

#

Ignoring his aching bones and sore nose Jaroslav Bublík led his team through their next exercise: the successful navigation of an aircraft to a designated landing area using a Eureka radio beacon. Their final stop was then the SOE intelligence finishing school: 'the house in the woods' in Beaulieu, Hampshire. Since Šustr's departure, there was greater recognition that SOE support was vital for this final briefing and training. Under Rudolf Krzák's guidance, this part of the training was now much improved. Making full use of recent experience of parachute missions in the Protectorate, and his own experience as an undercover agent in France, Krzák had significantly increased the difficulty of the 'conspiracy training,' to reduce the possibility of failure and infiltration. The parachutists used aliases throughout their training and these were replaced with another 'on the ground' alias, the moment the operation started.

#

I pulled out one of the other photocopies that Louda had annotated. It showed my grandfather stood with three other men in a park: almost certainly Hyde Park, a stone's throw from Beneš' office at Porchester Gate in central London. He has a wide smile, wearing a side cap, with his team beside him in their berets.

"Jiří Louda identified these as being of the members of operation FOURSQUARE – my grandfather's parachute mission."

I fished out another similar picture of the same men in the same location. This time my grandfather is reclining on the grass, smiling again, with his cap off, and his team surrounding him. The men look young, happy, fresh and keen for their mission.

Píška inspected the first picture with interest but had nothing to add. I flipped over the note and was reminded that Louda had included the names of team members, with an extra annotation for each.

"Josef Špinka – died 1988. Josef Krist – died 1985. Karel Hubl – still living in Prague."

I was reminded of the happiness I had felt at first seeing this note. Whatever their mission was they had survived it. My grandfather had got them home.

#

On February 11, 1945, the big allied powers met at the resort city of Yalta, on the Black Sea. Broadly, they were concerned with agreeing the partition of Germany but each man had his own private objectives. With Great Britain having entered the war in defence of Poland, Churchill was fighting for that country's post-war borders, now being redrawn under Soviet demands. Roosevelt, with his health declining, was most concerned about the war that was still raging in the Pacific. He wanted and needed Russia's support in winning in that theatre. Stalin was interested in political influence after the end of hostilities. With the Red Army sweeping across Europe and on collision course with the western advance in Berlin and Prague, he was in a stronger and stronger position to expand his territory and influence. No one at the table was strongly motivated to consider Czechoslovakia's independent democratic future.

#

Píška continued rifling through the papers I had brought and found another of interest.

"So he must have been in Italy," he said, as he continued to peruse the words.

"I think he was in Bari," I replied.

"This says that he was in Brindisi and that he was supposed to start the operation from there," Píška continued.

"Really?"

I sensed the mental effort of reviewing this text was wearying my host.

"Please translate this all and look after it," he said, putting the papers down. "A lot of records were lost in the war, between the exiles and the new country."

"I will. I have a lot of stuff to get through. Even if it's my retirement project, I'm going to join the dots."

"Good...This has been interesting."

I thanked Mr and Mrs Píška for their help. I had recorded hours of conversation on my dictaphone, which I knew would be of immense value in my research. I said goodbye with a hearty shake of hands and was unexpectedly sad to go. On my drive home, I reflected that I should have felt a little awkward imposing myself on them as I had. But I had actually felt completely at home. With a tweak here and there I could have been back in Lincolnshire listening to my granddad hold court, as my grandma flitted in and out of the room. It had been a gift to be able to relive those moments.

#

On March 17, Beneš and most of his cabinet left his presidential accommodation in Aston Abbots, to head to the Kremlin. There he was to meet the Czech Communists to agree on the makeup of the post-war government. The venue for discussions, under Stalin's watchful eye, was a considerable psychological advantage for Beneš' communist rivals. A plan for Czechoslovakia had already been worked out secretly between the Soviets and Czech Communists, with the ultimate objective of the complete communisation of the country. Their strategy was to keep the Czech lands and Slovakia separate and autonomous. A 'divide and conquer' approach was sought, marginalising non-communist Slovaks. They would push ahead with the setting up of 'national committees' made up of 'representatives of the people' to undertake local administration. Punishment of collaborationists, traitors and fascists would be embraced with zeal and subverted to suppress political adversaries. In matters of the economy - banks, farming, unions - Czechoslovakia would become fully aligned and dominated by the USSR. These measures were all to be couched in the language of nationalism and presented to be democratic. Even the Sokol and Boy Scouts were to be communised.

A key area for agreement in Moscow was the distribution of cabinet portfolios. Six separate parties would be represented in the new government, each with its own vice President. Beneš' ambassador to Moscow - Zdeněk Fierlinger - was to be made prime minister. Having been in post since the early days of the war, he was now completely aligned to the Communists. Beneš charged Fierlinger with the formation of the cabinet. Jan Masaryk was assigned the Foreign Ministry, but Vlado Clementis, the communist politician who had shared a tent with Jaroslav Bublík in Cholmondeley Park, was given an overlapping role as Secretary of State for Foreign Affairs. Their other tent mate, and another Communist, Václav Majer was made Minister for Food. The Communists cherry picked the posts that were most important for their plan, taking the departments of the Interior, Agriculture, Information, National Education and Social Welfare. Beneš achieved only one notable victory. His close ally Jaroslav Stránský was made Minister of Justice. This provided some ability to fight attempts to undermine democratic principles. With only the eastern part of the country liberated, and Prague still in German hands, the government was to be set up temporarily in Košice, in eastern Slovakia.

The new government programme was published on April 5th. On the same day, Klement Gottwald – happy to bide his time as a Vice President awaiting the moment to challenge Beneš - made a grandiose speech, speaking of Slovak autonomy and of the government's plans as the 'Magna Carta of the Slovak Nation'.

From that moment, Czechoslovakia was a divided state, with the very foundations of its national existence under mortal threat. Beneš and the forces aligned to him were hanging by a thread against the direct threat of a communist totalitarian regime swiftly and seamlessly replacing the Nazi one.

#

Arriving at the tube station in Kew, I felt like a child waking on Christmas morning. The SOE's records on Czechoslovak operations in the Second World War had just been declassified. From a search of the catalogue, I had seen that there was a file specifically on Operation FOURSQUARE. So here I now was, striding towards the Public Records Office. I would finally get the answers I needed to understand Operation FOURSQUARE and how my grandfather's war had ended.

Although the building was large, with sharp angles of concrete and glass, it rested peacefully in its unruffled surroundings. After the brief bureaucracy of obtaining an identity card, I was allocated a desk and an accompanying numbered pigeonhole. I requested the files I wanted: one on FOURSQUARE and one on another mission - Operation PLATINUM - which was dispatched just before it. When I saw an administrator drop a paper file into my pigeon hole, I rose immediately.

It was the file for PLATINUM. The radio telegraphist for this group was Jaroslav Klemeš, who Louda had identified in a picture from 1940, stood next to my grandfather and Čestmír Šikola in Cholmondeley Park. I pulled the file out with reverence and took it back to my seat at one side of an octagonal set of desks. The file was tightly bound, with treasury tags biting into it. I began gingerly turning the papers and found myself glancing around, fearful that I was breaking some rule or procedure. But no one was paying any attention to me in the sparsely populated room. Each was lost in their own passion – some wearing white gloves as they gently leafed through old manuscripts and papers to explore the echoes of other long-forgotten stories.

The papers were in reverse order, so I turned the file over on its front and began reading the memos and reports from the back. I quickly understood that PLATINUM had been dropped in February 1945, on a mission to organise the reception of stores and agents and to prepare landing grounds for planes. PLATINUM was laying the groundwork for the flurry of missions that were to follow. It was a four-man team led by Captain Jaromír Nechanský. The group had two wireless operators: Klemeš and a sergeant major named Vyhňák. In the file there was a memo from the SOE, which pointed out that the success of the mission would lay in the 'tiny details'. But the first telegrams I came to referred to a very large blunder. A bizarre situation arose where an officer from the US Office of Strategic Services turned up at the last moment to share PLATINUM's plane. The man arrived ready to board dressed in a US officer's uniform and apparently with no reception committee planned for the crates of material he had brought with him. The members of PLATINUM were reportedly horrified and informed him that he would have no hope of recovering them on the ground. This incident seemed from the correspondence to have sparked much confusion and mistrust in the intelligence services; from skimming through the file I could see no satisfactory explanation. Next was a summary of PLATINUM's mission and drop.

#

After flying from Italy in a Halifax aircraft with a Polish crew, the men of PLATINUM arrived at their dropping point near the border between Moravia and Bohemia. The drop was a disaster. Three of the men saw their leg bags detach and their kit crash to the ground ahead of them as they sailed downwards. On landing, they discovered that the only piece of technical equipment that remained unbroken was one Eureka device for the navigation of incoming planes. The men gathered what they could and headed to the addresses they had. Their contact at the second house they tried had run from the Gestapo just ten days before, leaving his wife alone. The house had been staked out by the Gestapo until literally hours before their arrival. After some convincing from Nechanský, the wife accepted them in and through her they linked up with the R3 in western Moravia. It was at this point that Vyhňák's technical skills became critical. He patched two radios together to create a device which was able to send signals to the VRÚ, but not receive them. On February 25, he sent a message requesting a supply mission with replacement kit and asking for acknowledgement of the request through a coded message on the BBC. The confirmation came and the replacement stores were quickly sent with a parachutist called Hromek. This was unwelcome news for Klemeš. Hromek had originally been earmarked to be a member of PLATINUM but he and Klemeš had a difficult relationship, which culminated in a punch-up between them. Hromek had been removed for the morale of the team.

On landing, Hromek was rattled and pulled his pistol on the partisans that came to receive him. Nechanský calmed the situation but grew frustrated with Hromek when it became apparent that he did not know which containers were dropped for

PLATINUM and which were for his own separate mission. Nechanský eventually found PLATINUM's equipment and Hromek then disappeared with a group of partisans, who had already opened his stores and were helping themselves to them. It had been an inauspicious start, but the men of PLATINUM now had their equipment. As they now had two radios, they split into two separate groups and began their work, planning for the batch of missions that was to come.

#

Putting the file back, I went to the cafeteria to grab a cup of tea and did my best to be patient. When I returned, the next file had just been placed in my pigeonhole. I slid it out and headed back to my designated desk. Turning the file to the back again, I scanned the notes. My first priority was to find out what the purpose of the mission was. In the file for PLATINUM the mission objective was clearly set out but I could find nothing similar for FOURSQUARE. Pondering this, it occurred to me that if it had been an assassination mission, as my grandfather had claimed, I should expect that the purpose of the mission would be obscured. The early notes instead focused on the group's movements. The first, headed 'top secret' and sent from London on March 7, notified the US Army in Italy that four men were heading their way on March 12, led by Cadet Officer 'Bednář.' I noted the date carefully, remembering that my grandfather received his commission as a lieutenant at exactly that time. He would be accompanied by privates Švec, Hejda and Kovář. Reaching into my carrier bag, I fished out the photocopy I had made of the picture of the members of FOURSQUARE. Louda's spindly writing confirmed the men's names: Špinka, Hubl and Krist. I looked back at the names in the file and noted that the initials all matched up.

After arrival in Italy, the four headed to Brindisi, getting clearance in Naples and Bari as they went. The next note of interest was on March 27, from a US Army captain, stating that the four men left Brindisi the day before, on a Dakota 311, with 1000lbs of baggage.

"During the stay at Brindisi certain small points were raised, but owing to the uncertainty as to the date of their departure I left them to be dealt with on their arrival north. They are as follows:-

1. The operators would like to exchange their pipe tobacco for cigarette tobacco.

2. One member of the party has an operational watch that is not reliable. He wants to change it.

3. The party would like to take a small quantity of pepper into the field to discourage dogs from following them (in England "Renardine" was employed for this)."

I wondered to myself whether the broken watch was the fault of 'Katya' the crow, but this levity was dismissed when I read the next note: "Enclosed you will find the translation of instructions for the use and maintenance of a silenced sten gun."

This was the first indication of what they might be doing, and it provided some validation of what my grandfather had told me. Surely, the gun being silenced supported the claim that they were to undertake an assassination.

#

At this exact time, Beneš set off from Moscow on the final leg of his journey home. He was troubled by developments, but ever the optimist, he had no option but to present a confident view that he could lead his country to a balanced political situation once he was there. The trip began with a three-day ride across Ukraine, and on April 3rd, Beneš and his entourage - flanked by a guard of Russian soldiers - crossed the border into Slovakia. Beneš decided to do the final journey by road as a chance to gauge the mood of the people. The response was beyond his expectations. Patriots lined the streets in vast numbers to thank him for what he had done to liberate the country. He was overcome, surprised at how he, the dry technocrat, had come to mean so much to his people over the course of the War. Just as his doubts about the future had started to solidify, he had an epiphany: the people would, of course, be his greatest asset in restoring a democratic Czechoslovakia. The strength of his reception found its way back to Russia and the communist Czechoslovaks very quickly. The message was clear. Beneš could not easily be marginalised; certainly not on a short time horizon. In a similar vein, neither could Jan Masaryk, the spiritual heir to the country.

On arrival in Košice, Beneš set up the new government. His first act, as a concession to the Communists, was to formally fire František Moravec from his post. The man who had done so much for the cause of a free and independent Czechoslovakia was now surplus to requirements and was discarded. This might be seen as brutal enough, but the Communists would not forget how well Moravec had done his job through the War. They would seek further revenge at their own leisure. Karel Paleček made his way out to Košice from Italy, to replace Moravec.

Prague was emerging as the fulcrum at which the balance between East and West would be decided. The Red Army was now racing west towards Bohemia. Were it to take Prague, this would be a propaganda victory and would give them the practical control to exert communist and Soviet influence over the future centre of government. This would forever kill Beneš' ambitions of an independent democratic Czechoslovakia. But thoughts of a home army liberating the country were long forgotten. At this time, the Czechoslovak Brigade were still heading across Europe from Dunkirk. They would take time to reach Prague. The native resistance was broadly aligned to Beneš objectives and the shared purpose of expelling the Germans. But this resistance was under-supported and the Soviets had assiduously infiltrated it with partisans and local communists. Beneš key hope rested with FOURSQUARE and the other parachute groups that were readying themselves for their missions. With American support, perhaps they could tip the balance.

The US Army was already on the south western border of Czechoslovakia, their advance sped by the German's surrendering to them rather than to the Russians. But they were holding back from entering the country. It had been agreed that Czechoslovakia was in the Russian 'sphere of influence.' Roosevelt was very ill and he and his deputy Truman were instructing the US-led allied army to respect Stalin's wishes. With the Nazis on the verge of destruction and irrelevance, two massive armies were soon to be looking into each other's eyes. Sober judgement and calm were needed on all sides to ensure that a new war was not begun through accident or misunderstanding.

#

Meanwhile, CLAY had ended up in a small village to the south of Brno. On the twelfth of April, exactly a year after they were dropped, Soviet forces arrived there and the group's mission was complete. Despite the Gestapo's repeated attempts at infiltration Šikola, Bartoš and the other members had maintained their vital communications links without interruption right up until that moment.

On this same day, following the death of President Roosevelt, Harry Truman became the 33rd president of the United States, tasked with winning the war in Europe but also with shifting US focus to the now more significant war in the Pacific.

#

The next paper of interest was from 12th April. It was a despatch from the London Czechs containing passwords, contacts and dropping points for FOURSQUARE, obtained from Nechanský and his teams on the ground. The dropping point was to be somewhere in a triangle between the southwestern border of Bohemia and Pilsen. They were to be parachuted near the position of US Third Army on the border. There was real urgency to the message:

"Please carry out mission immediately. Please supply foursquare with twelve thousand Reichsmarks and 200 pounds in gold dollars or diamonds. Foursquare NOT repeat NOT to be sent to field without this money. Confirm soonest."

Then there was a message for Captain 'Bednář': should a reception committee be in place for the drop, sixteen containers and parcels would be thrown out with them. If there was no reception committee they would be dropped blind without supplies. From this it was clear to me that whatever FOURSQUARE's core mission was, it was not simply the supply of arms to partisans.

The plan was to rendezvous with a post office worker named Joseph Tauber. Passwords were given for the introduction. Having established their bona fides, Tauber would formally introduce them to the local resistance. I read the next line carefully:

"Please obtain Lt Bednář's signature on one copy and return to this HQ as an acknowledgement."

I glanced to the bottom of the message and saw the signature:

"Jaroslav Bednář, 23· IV· 1945."

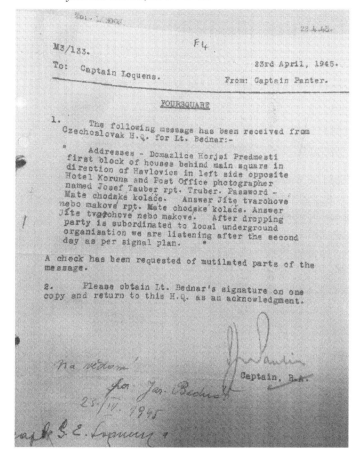

The handwriting was intimately familiar to me. It was the same writing that signed off the cheques I received at the start of each and every month, to help pay my way through university. I touched the marks on the page, the royal blue fountain pen smooth and elegant next to the brutal typewriter text of the rest of the note, and bit down on my tears. It felt like a message he had left specifically for me, waiting patiently in these old papers; we were connected across time. And as that fleeting feeling melted away I realised that in reality I was now more remote from him than I had ever been.

#

Nechanský and Klemeš arrived in Prague. They immediately made contact with the emerging National Council there and installed their wireless set for direct communications with the VRÚ and the remaining London exiles. Nechanský toured the city, seeking recruits for the uprising and Klemeš began sending desperate requests to Britain for arms to be dropped. An initial promise to send twenty-four bombers laden with equipment did not materialise, to the understandable disillusionment of all. But the populace was nevertheless beginning to feel bold. Uprisings had begun to occur, starting in Přerov in Moravia. These uprisings threatened the lines of communications of the retreating German army. Rumours were rife that the Americans were planning to enter Prague. Prague was getting ready to fall.

#

FOURSQUARE was equipped and ready to take off from Rosignano airport in Italy on April 24. However, it was hard to know exactly what happened next. The file was a jumbled mess of telegrams and memos continually talking about delays, changed codes and weather problems. The men arrived at the airport on four consecutive days but due to bad weather the operation was continually postponed. On April 28, they were transferred to Dijon, to depart from there instead. One typed note outlines the instructions for Captain Panter, FOURSQUARE's liaison with the US military, from a US Major Klauber. It describes the lodgings, equipment and support Panter must provide. I could see no details of the mission but there was at least clarity that the mission did have a specific purpose:

"When operation FOURSQUARE has been completed you will return to H.Q. at the earliest opportunity."

In fountain pen, Klauber has added a final instruction for Captain Panter.

"You will under no circumstances accompany FOURSQUARE on the final stage of this journey, onwards from Dijon."

#

At the very end of April, Adolf Hitler committed suicide in his bunker in Berlin. The empire of the Third Reich was collapsing by the day, assailed on all sides by allied forces and disrupted from within by partisan uprisings and resistance activity. At this time, US-led allied forces were concentrating on the drive east through Austria into Hungary and were skirting along the south west of Bohemia's border. This was consistent with agreements about Czechoslovakia being in the Soviet 'sphere of influence.' But at lower levels of the army command structure, there was a strong desire to liberate Bohemia. Under pressure from his own officers and with intense lobbying from the Czech exile government, General Dwight D Eisenhower made the decision to send the US

Third Army into Czechoslovakia. He sent a message to the Soviets that he was going to drive towards the line of Karlsbad-Pilsen-Budweis. After this, his intent was to push on further to the banks of the Vltava. In other words, the Americans were going to move quickly to occupy the west of Prague.

#

On May 3, FOURSQUARE apparently still had not been dropped. They were notified that, with the US Third Army moving into Bohemia, their landing site was now right on the German defence line to the south west of Pilsen. Captain Panter asked Captain Bednář if he still insisted on carrying out the operation and if so under which conditions. His response was clear and categorical. The mission would go ahead. He and his team would all parachute during the same run. If they could not find the assigned landing point, they would drop at any place nearby which appeared safe. They would only abort if it was clear that there was fire on the ground, as this would mean parachuting to a likely and immediate death.

#

On learning that US forces had entered Bohemia, Beneš was ecstatic.

"Thank God, Thank God," he said to his aide Edward Táborský, before rising in excitement and pacing the room. If General Patton and the forces of the Third Army could get all of the way to Prague, then the political impact would be immense. In particular, he could negotiate a mutual withdrawal of Eastern and western troops, leaving him in control at the centre of government. He called out to Madame Beneš, his voice trembling with emotion, "Patton is across the border!"

Word was also spreading through the Protectorate itself, as the populace readied itself for its liberation.

#

On May 4 at 21:40, Captain Bednář and the other men of FOURSQUARE took off from Dijon airport. At around midnight, the plane's navigator announced that they were above the target, just to the south west of Pilsen. FOURSQUARE readied themselves for the jump. They were completely prepared. Their leg bags had been thoroughly checked and they were equipped with everything they needed: their gold, diamonds, false papers, silenced sten guns and cyanide tablets.

As the men made the final checks of their parachutes, the plane's navigator beckoned Captain Bednář over to confer. The dropping point was under very heavy fire: he asked him to have a look for himself. He looked out. There was no moonlight, so the land could not be seen, but the fire and explosions on the ground were clear. Patton's Third Army was engaging the crumbling German forces right below his feet. Bednář looked to his young team and grappled with his decision. Would they survive the jump? For twenty minutes, the plane circled above the dropping area, as he calmly considered what to do: weighing their lives and his own in the palm of his hand. As the time for deliberation came to an end and looking at the persistent white hot sparks and bursts of fire below them, he made the only call he felt he could. The files were clear. FOURSQUARE had been aborted.

#

Pilsen was quiet on the dawn of May 5. But slowly flags began to appear in the windows of houses, like the first buds of a sudden spring after the cold six-year long winter of occupation. Then the heat of summer suddenly erupted, as partisan activity exploded across the city. Bullets began to fly through the streets, as the population rose. Emboldened by what they saw, young Czechs disarmed the Hitler Youth. The headquarters of German forces were quickly besieged by partisans and civilians and an uneasy standoff ensued, as all awaited the coming of the Americans.

On that same morning, plans were also in place for the uprising of the population of nearby Prague. As dawn came, the uprising began there too with radio broadcasts instructing the population to rise. The resistance organisations and Czech civilians began pitched battles with the occupying Germans. Having been solicited with messages from Beneš, a battalion of Russians who had been conscripted to fight for the Germans, defected to the Czechoslovak side.

The occupiers counter-attacked but were fought back by Czech resistance and citizens. Pleas came on the radio for support:

"Calling all allied armies. We need urgent help. Send your planes and tanks. The Germans are advancing on Prague."

#

On May 6, the US 16th Armoured Division arrived in Pilsen to a rapturous reception, as the German forces there surrendered. The Americans were handed food and Pilsner beer and their vehicles were covered with flowers. The Czech partisans sent out a radio broadcast:

"This is Pilsen, the free Pilsen calling. Long live our freedom, long live our allies! Hereby I announce that the tanks of the 16th Division are on Republic Square in Pilsen. I am an eye witness of their arrival from the West."

It was announced that the American armoured vehicles were leaving straight away for Prague. But, the Prague populaces hopes for salvation were short-lived. The Russians had now responded to the American announcement that the Third Army intended to advance into the western half of Prague. Eisenhower's Russian counterpart Aleksei Antonov reminded him that they had agreed that Soviet forces would halt short of the Lower Elbe river, in the northern theatre of operations, and that he expected the similar agreement regarding Bohemia to be honoured in the south. Eisenhower therefore halted the US 3rd Army's advance. As in Slovakia, the native population would have to fight to liberate their city alone until the Russian army eventually came.

#

With the support of Nechanský, Klemeš and the other men of Operation PLATINUM, partisan forces fought to gain control of Prague as quickly as they could. On May 8, Czech and German leaders signed a ceasefire but skirmishes and fighting continued. Beneš and Stalin saw eye to eye on one thing: the Germans must be punished viciously for what they had done, and messages to the people on this theme came through the radio. With revenge and retribution on the minds of the Czech populace and with a state of lawlessness in place, Prague became a brutal firepit of bloody revenge. Its humiliated and brutalised citizens were now free to express their outrage. The evil of Fleischer, Frank and Heydrich was to be paid back in kind. Make no mistake, any German, Nazi collaborator or Sudetenlander needed to get out and get out quickly. By the time the Red Army finally arrived on May 9, the local populace had established control.

#

Seeing in black and white that my grandfather's mission had been aborted left me deflated as I continued to read through the file. I traced his next steps dutifully but without excitement. My interest perked up again a little when I read a message from the London Czechs on May 7:

'Feel most strongly in view of continued fighting in the area that operations should continue.'

Despite the failure to execute FOURSQUARE on May 4, it seemed that the mission was not immediately cancelled. The team stayed in Dijon, awaiting further instructions with the other groups, CHURCHMAN and ROTHMAN. Then came a memo from May 11 indicating that operations to Czechoslovakia had finally been fully cancelled. It seemed that my grandfather and his team had arrived in the UK with Captain Panter soon afterwards, on May 12.

#

Beneš quickly sought to establish control of the liberated country. The new government arrived in Prague from Košice on May 10 and Beneš followed, again by road. Throughout his trip, people lined the streets to show their appreciation. Even his Russian guards could not stop the well-wishers from approaching him to shake his hand, hug him or offer their sincere thanks. Men lined the streets in their Sokol uniforms, as a show of loyalty and patriotism; just owning these clothes would have been a punishable offence mere days before. Beneš eventually arrived in the capital on May 16, amid rapturous appreciation and celebration.

#

As I continued flicking through memos and notes, I found a report of the state of post-war Prague, sent to SOE from the Third Army on May 26.

"Civil affairs and government definitely in hands of Czechs. No apparent Russian control. Very few Red Army troops in city. No evidence of occupation by Russians…Beneš popularity greater than ever…photo in almost every window"

So it seemed that the timing of the uprising had been helpful in ensuring that Prague maintained a degree of self-determination. Another note to the SOE, which tied up some loose ends of my previous research, caught my eye as I skimmed the memos.

"Have contacted WOLFRAM leader. He reports Svoboda safe and working with him for Paleček (sic)."

"Thank God for that." I thought, feeling a wave of relief for him.

The file contained a personal letter from Colonel Perkins of SOE to a colleague in England, describing his observations on entering Prague and of the growing presence of the Russian army. He was unimpressed by the examples of revenge-taking that he saw form the local populace, and his view was that much of the bloodletting was at the hands of members of the population who had previously been too fearful to do anything. He was disturbed by the chaos and lawlessness on the streets: two German women paraded through the streets covered in their own blood; a German soldier summarily executed by a Russian soldier for not walking quickly enough, and the Czech standing behind him accidentally killed too by the same bullet. He also noted that the Russians, who were by now flooding in, were immediately seeking to dominate.

There were reports of rape and looting. Perkins noted that there were no Union Jacks on the streets anywhere, except in the American occupied part of Bohemia; just Russian and Czech flags, and the odd fluttering of the stars and stripes.

#

For Beneš, the war was over. Munich and its consequences had been annulled and the big three powers had agreed on Czechoslovakia returning to its pre-war borders. Beneš also considered it a major victory that he had obtained consent to the massive transfer of Sudeten Germans to Germany, which he viewed as essential to ensuring that Czechoslovakia would not be conquered from within again. He had failed to realise a Polish-Czechoslovak confederation, but he had secured an alliance with the Soviet Union that provided protection against future German aggression and another Munich. He was at the head of the Czechoslovak government and felt he had reached a reasonable compromise with the Czechoslovak Communists. Importantly, he now had control of the capital and seat of government.

But in his more sober, honest moments, Beneš should and must have been deeply concerned. There was no balance in the influence of East and West in his country. All political and military power was now in the hands of the Soviet Union.

#

As I sat on the District line train home from Kew I felt embarrassed. Hoping that my grandfather had led an assassination mission was shameful on my part. This wasn't some children's war comic. This was real life. I pondered why he had said what he did. Why had he been so insistent that this mission actually went ahead? He had certainly been unwell; his mind wasn't what it had been. He had always been a touch vainglorious and despite all the secrecy, he never underplayed himself or his capabilities. Maybe it was too much to admit to himself that he never got his opportunity? Maybe he convinced himself that the mission went ahead? Time can hinder recollection and stories can evolve in the act of continual recall. Perhaps the truth was more subjective than I had ever really understood.

#

By the time Jaroslav Bublík and his fellow members of FOURSQUARE had returned to England, the VRÚ was no more. The remaining men had been flown back to their country to set up the radio and communications network there, taking much of the equipment that the British had loaned with them. After a short stay in London, Jaroslav Bublík would return to Prague to help them. The nissen huts in the fields of College Farm were abandoned, the signalling equipment ripped from them. Only dangling wires and a lonely, wandering crow served as evidence that the men had ever been there.

The contribution of the VRÚ and its members and of the complementary operators at the UVOD, was explicitly recognised by Beneš:

"Let us remember their exemplary and successful effort that provided our side with a steady flow of information about the various states of our country's resistance to German occupation…This enabled us to pass to our allies quick and accurate information on German military moves and often even about their intentions and plans for the future…in the autumn of 1940, I paid a visit to the wireless station in Great Britain and watched the Operators at work, expressing my admiration for their efforts. Within minutes I received their pledge of loyalty and devotion to the cause of Czechoslovakia. Many of these wireless operators fell as brave soldiers in the struggle shared by both Czechs and Slovaks. In their courage, resolution and dedication to serve they are forever a shining example for us."

#

The letter from the military institute finally arrived.

"Enclosed are the copies of archive materials with the information about the service of Mr Jaroslav Bublík in Great Britain as requested. Regarding his participation in the parachute mission 'Four Square' we inform you as follows:

The mission consisted of four Czech radio operators, which should have been deplaned in the south western region of Bohemia at the beginning of May 1945. On 1 May the mission had been above its target but wasn't parachuted because the fighting took place on the landing site. The SOE Headquarters quickly found a substitute landing site but before the mission took off once again, this site was occupied by the German troops.

The Prague uprising broke out on May 5, but the mission from Italy with help and supplies didn't materialize due to the bad weather. When the weather conditions improved on May 8, the capitulation of Germany had been signed and no further help was needed. Because of this the operation 'Four Square' didn't take place. Also, we would like to inform you that no archive documents about this unrealized operation are found in the…Central Military Archive."

There I had it. Paths of Destiny, the SOE files and the Czech Military Institute all agreed. The details did not quite line up but the broad message was the same. And they had no more information for me. My work was done.

#

A note my grandfather sent to Novák in his final years, paints a picture of the late winter of that generation's lives. Mentioning the names of those who had left them, he laments "…most of our group have already crossed the river Acheron."

Soon after my visit to Kew, my grandmother 'put on her slippers,' as the Czechs say and joined my grandfather in the peace of the next life. She had suffered with dementia, perhaps mercifully, since my grandfather had passed and it was reassuring to think that they were now together again, in a calm, unexcitable spot in the Lincolnshire countryside, with just the chirping birds for company.

For many years I moved on, busy with my young family, career and completing my PhD – to become an academic as my grandfather had wanted. There were many reasons to ignore all of the notes I'd collected and the nagging compulsion to keep on with what I'd started. In those lost months and years, the last witnesses I could have spoken to finally went over the river too: Karel Hubl of FOURSQUARE; Čestmír Šikola; Jaroslav Klemeš of PLATINUM and the Píškas. All of them drifted into the land of memory, destined to be forgotten as generation moved to generation. But I knew they were still there waiting for me in the box file under my desk, and when the right time came their stories would come to life again.

THE COUP

The quiet hiss of the dictaphone stopped with a gentle thud as the tape rewound to a stop and I fumbled with my thumb to press the play button. Holding the small speaker to my ear with the volume up, I was reminded of Píška's hushed but still piercing voice.

"Back home we used to have political discussions. Everybody talks about politics there. Czechs talk about politics everywhere. In the pub…in the café. People here don't like it. I like it. I do it here…"

"He does," came Mrs Píška's distant voice, somewhat grimly.

I heard the uncomfortable sound of my own laughter and then my voice, familiar and strange at the same time.

"It was the same with my grandma and granddad. He used to talk politics a lot. It was a touchy subject. He was Labour and my grandma was Conservative."

"He was Labour?" came Píška's voice.

"Yes…Oh yes."

"Good grief!"

I noted the time it took for Píška to process this information.

"He was a socialist," I heard myself mumbling, to fill the gap in conversation.

A loud clanking noise caused my eardrum to throb and I moved the dictaphone away from my ear.

"Do you take milk?" I heard Píška ask.

"Yes, I take milk and sugar," came my response, followed by the banging of a seemingly giant spoon against a hulking piece of china.

"So anyhow, in forty-five I came back…"

#

I had taken some time away from work and started to write. To fully describe my grandfather's journey would be a momentous effort but I was finally prepared to make it. I wanted my children to know who he was and I wanted our family memories not to be tainted by those final months when he fell apart in front of our eyes. I put up a picture of him up in my study as inspiration, pulled out my files and immersed myself in the rest of the story, still unsure of what the ending would be.

#

On his return to Prague, Beneš had taken temporary hold of the levers of power. The Moscow 'Christmas' agreement allowed him to issue laws under government request, until a new national assembly was formed. These powers were used to assert government authority across the country. In fact, there was a full year's delay before elections were held. In the meantime, a temporary assembly was put in place and radical decisions affecting the future structure of the country were taken swiftly. The public, keen to move forward and embrace change in the name of national unity, was broadly in support of these proposals. Popular public support also quickly swung to the expulsion of the Sudetenlanders. Beneš made a decree on June 21 for the expropriation without compensation of the property of all Germans and Hungarians on Czech soil, and also the property of all Czechs and Slovaks found guilty of collaboration.

#

"The army came earlier in May. Soon after the war…because we were in Dunkirk it took time to get back. When the Americans invaded the Czech army followed. Your grandfather was lucky. He got good job for instance. He could probably get a flat or something. The local army took all of the flats and houses from the Germans. When we came there was nothing. It was all gone. Eventually I got a flat with my wife…"

"I have a name Louie."

"Madame Píškova," came Píška's voice, introducing his wife to me afresh with a sarcastic flourish.

I heard Mrs Píška's stern response as a muffled echo. When intelligible words came, she had moved her attention to me.

"When did Jarda return after the war?"

"He came back in '48 with my mum, from Germany to England."

"So, he never went back? He didn't go back to Czecho?" she continued.

"He did!" piped up Píška, "He had a job with the United Nations or something,"

I had paused to collect my thoughts before I had answered.

"He was in England for most of the War, then he was in various places in Europe for a parachute mission, and then he came back to Prague briefly in 1945. When he returned to Prague he worked at the Foreign Ministry at Czernin Palace in Prague. He was working for Jan Masaryk."

Píška had then rifled through the files and found one of my grandfather's certificates and traced his finger across the signature at the bottom, translating the text.

"Oh, so it is Jan Masaryk."

"What's that?"

"It's about a promotion. It says he was named actuary – some high office in 7th or 8th grade in higher service in the Ministry of Foreign Affairs."

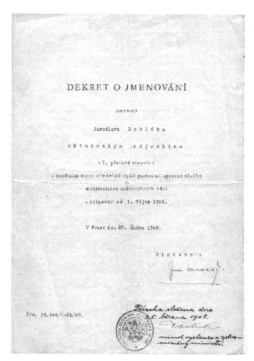

Jan Masaryk's neat signature was at the bottom of the certificate.

"After that he went across to…I think…a couple of places…maybe Yugoslavia…and then he ended up in Berlin."

#

The first elections were held on May 26, 1946. The Communists were bullish about their chances of securing a majority. Such a result would facilitate the rapid communisation of the country that they desired. But the people of Czechoslovakia, with their commitment to democracy, intuitively knew that this was not the way forward. The Communists finished with thirty eight percent of the vote: the biggest party but not the majority. The coalition of parties would continue. Czechoslovakia lived to fight another day.

284

However Klement Gottwald was now the Premier, supported by his new number two, Rudolf Slánský.

#

I had searched hard for information about the Czechoslovak post-war government. But for such a central story in the birth of the Cold War, there seemed to be surprisingly little written about it. Beneš' memoirs were a key source, but they were never fully completed. A couple of out of print books by Hubert Ripka and Edward Táborský - members of the exile government - formed my core reading. It felt like this part of Czechoslovakian history had been deliberately forgotten. Perhaps it really was, as Orwell said, that "History is written by the winners."

From my grandfather's records, I could see that he took a job with the new government and was based in Prague for a time. I was also aware that he had spent some time in Belgrade. Wracking my brains for anything that he had said about this time, only one memory came to me. I was sitting in his front room at some point in the mid-nineties, with the TV news on. One of the news items was about the civil war in Rwanda and the desperate situation that had resulted there. The report cut to Madeline Albright, who was at the time the US ambassador to the United Nations, sitting in a committee room of some sort.

"She is Czech you know?"

"Who?"

"Madeline Albright."

"I thought she was American?"

"She is American citizen, but she is Czech."

As we watched the television, he carried on absent-mindedly, "…I remember her as little girl…"

I had laughed thinking this was some strange joke. But after a small pause it was clear that it was not.

"As a little girl?" I repeated.

"I worked with her father…after the war. He was friend of mine."

"Where?"

"In Czech government."

I had found this all slightly bizarre. I turned back to the TV and then back to my grandfather. The gap between the UN headquarters in New York and a handmade bungalow in Chapel St Leonards seemed an impossibly large one. I was intrigued. Looking back, that was a key moment in me deciding that I would one day seek to fully understand his story.

Armed with this memory, I subsequently discovered that Madeline Albright's father was a Czechoslovakian diplomat named Josef Korbel. He had served as ambassador to Yugoslavia in the post-war government. Like so many of his peers, Korbel had eventually become a Professor in the USA. He had mentored two eventual US Secretaries of State; both his daughter and Condoleeza Rice. I ordered a copy of a book he'd written and another by Madeline Albright to add to my reading list.

#

Jaroslav Bublík relocated to Berlin at the very start of 1946. He was stationed in the US occupied zone, as part of the Czechoslovak Military Mission to the Allied Control Council for Germany.

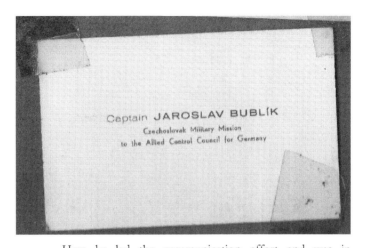

Captain JAROSLAV BUBLÍK

Czechoslovak Military Mission
to the Allied Control Council for Germany

Here he led the communication effort and was in constant touch with embassies across Europe, tapping out messages to Frank Kaplan in Prague and Miroslav Novák in Switzerland. He progressed quickly through the ranks to become a major. With a senior and trusted place in the recognised government, his life was good, with a swish apartment in Berlin and servants to help with domestic life. His English wife Marjorie had joined him there and was beside herself with the glamour of it all. Unlike some of his former colleagues, who were already being investigated overtly by the Communists, his seniority and closeness to ministers left him relatively untouched for a period. The Allied Control Council was the governing body for the occupation of Germany. It dealt initially with the abolition of German laws, then demilitarisation and denazification, but also with more routine matters – any practical problems associated with the running of the now dismembered country.

In his role he was involved with arrangements for the acceptance of those expelled from Czechoslovakia who were being received into Germany. Expulsions of the Sudeten Germans to the

American and Soviet zones of occupation began in January 1946 without significant planning or care. The Czechoslovaks found common cause with the Soviets in the punishment inflicted by this blunt process. Over six million hectares of farmland were taken from the displaced population. Given the Communist centre of gravity in the Czechoslovak government, this new inheritance became a handy source of wealth to distribute and instil the value of party membership.

Another key point of discussion for the Allied Control Council was the prosecution of war criminals, an emotive subject on which the reaching of a consensus amongst the Allies ultimately proved impossible. At the close of the Nuremburg trials in October 1946, and with the great powers having fundamentally different conceptions of justice, all cooperation on war crimes trials ceased.

#

At the end of 1946, Čestmír Šikola was transferred to Prague and given a task to analyse the activities of parachutists who had been caught by the Nazi's during the war; in particular how they had come to be captured. In March 1947, he asked if he could interview his old comrades in arms, Gerik and Čurda. The two men were in Pankrác Prison awaiting trial. As a result of Gerik's poor performance as an informer for the Gestapo and his ultimate attempt to break away from them, he had been arrested in the autumn of 1942 and imprisoned in Dachau concentration camp for the remainder of the war. Unlike many who were desperate to see the men hanged for their treasonous crimes, Šikola understood deeply - from his time as a member of CLAY - the practical challenge of working as an agent inside the Nazi controlled

Protectorate. He did not come to judge but to seek to understand their motives.

Despite his open mind, Šikola did not form a favourable view of Čurda. When asked why he had betrayed his colleagues, he stated that he was worried about his mother, at whose place he was hiding and who had suffered a nervous breakdown. He also said he was under extraordinary pressure due to the hundreds of daily executions under martial law. Although these were rational explanations, they did not leave Šikola with any greater appreciation of Čurda or justify his systematic betrayals. He felt that Čurda was fully aware of his guilt and what awaited him.

His meeting with Gerik was entirely different. He had been fond of him during their training days and had noted that he had been somewhat insecure, something he tried to hide by being a joker. In Šikola's view, he had been an excellent radio operator with a technical mind. Šikola noted that Gerik's eyes had their familiar spark when they met. They spoke for three quarters of an hour and Šikola felt that Gerik responded to all questions openly and fluently. Šikola sensed Gerik's naivety and formed a view that he had not collaborated wholeheartedly with his captors. It was also apparent that since the end of the war Gerik had maintained faith that he would secure leniency when he eventually had the chance to explain what had happened. The only question that caused him discomfort was when he was asked how he could accept a reward for the capture of his friends at the church on Resslova Street. His face reddened when he attempted an explanation.

"I swear I didn't play any part in their capture. I didn't have a clue where the boys were hiding. I was taken to the church after they died to identify them. I recognized and identified some of them. I couldn't hurt them anymore by doing that."

When their conversation ended, Šikola gave Gerik the rest of his cigarettes and said goodbye. He felt sad, knowing as he did, that at Gerik's trial his explanations would find a less sympathetic audience.

Just a month later, Jaroslav Bublík made a special trip to Prague from Berlin to see the trials of Gerik and Čurda with his own eyes. The official photos taken indicate what he saw. One shows the two men sat on a wooden bench seat, separated by a military guard. Čurda is in a suit and tie, legs crossed, turned away from the others. He looks urbane with his slicked hair and bristly moustache but he is clearly tense, with a fixed stare. Gerik paints a more tragic picture. His curly black hair is overgrown and his arms are folded with resignation. His open-necked shirt and wide collars are splayed over an ill-fitting jacket and he is wearing gigantic striped pantaloons that are tucked into his socks. He had done his best to look presentable - a handkerchief placed in the breast pocket of his jacket.

Bublík would also have seen when 'Jindra' – Ladislav Vaněk - was brought out to testify. Captured in the arrests following the Heydrich assassination, Vaněk swallowed his poison capsule, but the Gestapo had managed to purge it from his stomach before he succumbed to it. Unlike Čurda or Gerik, he said nothing, even under intense interrogation. Consequently, the Gestapo did not understand how significant he had been to the whole affair. He had managed to survive the war and his testimony was key to condemning the two traitors.

Proceedings were being overseen by the Minister of Justice and former exile, Prokop Drtina, one of the few members of the exile government who had been given a portfolio. His oversight of trials was being closely scrutinised from all sides, with the Communists ready to level accusations of leniency on the flimsiest of evidence. Given this and Čurda and Gerik's unquestioned guilt, their death sentences were inevitable.

So it was that upon sentencing, Gerik spoke out to Bublík, Šikola and his other old friends in the gallery of the court, with a wave and a final goodbye.

"Cheerio Boys."

I had a different picture of the scene now. I had initially envisaged his final words as something akin to a grotesque joke. I now saw them as final attempt to rekindle memories of when he had last been at ease in his short life – almost a lament. Šikola's view was that Gerik's sentence was a harsh one, that he accepted with courage:

"There is no excuse for treason but one must take circumstances into account. In my view Gerik didn't deserve a death penalty. I am convinced that had he been in amongst his friends, in a battle with a gun in his hand and a soldier's uniform on he would have shown bravery. Instead, he came home as a civilian, thrown at the mercy of a heartless enemy but also human apathy and unfavourable circumstances. He fell naked into brambles and was not ready for it."

Gerik was executed by hanging at the Pankrác prison at 11:45am on April 30, 1947. This too is recorded. The photograph taken in the courthouse shows his small lifeless body dangling from a pole, hanged by the method of the old Austro-Hungarian overlords; a grotesque marionette. Karel Čurda's execution followed just twelve minutes later.

Less than a month afterwards, Karl Hermann Frank's turn came. Big crowds had gathered in the courtyard of the Pankrác prison to see justice done for the vast array of crimes he had committed. The scourge of the 'Protectorate' looked old and frail as he was led up the steps and lifted up to the top of the hangman's pole by a sling. The sling was removed and Frank's body was dropped a short distance to yank tight the noose that had been placed around his neck. Frank's left hand briefly rose, seemingly more in acceptance of his fate than protest, before falling loose at his side. He had suffered far less than his many victims.

#

Karel Svoboda was also investigated by the Czech military court. Following his ordeal at the hands of the Prague Gestapo, he had ended up in a concentration camp before being found by Paleček on the liberation of Prague. When the investigators came to see him, he was half his weight and in a dreadful state of anxiety. When investigated, the view was formed that he probably said more than he should have under interrogation. He begged the investigator to take into account that the torture inflicted on him was more than any human being could withstand and that he was not ashamed to say so. Despite continued pressure not to be lenient, the investigators found him truthful and recognised that the alibis he gave most likely saved the lives of the other members of the group. He was spared.

#

With Europe financially exhausted, the US stood as the strongest power, and the Marshall Plan for the US to invest in the rebuilding of Europe was reaching its conclusion. A conference was planned for Paris, at which the plan would be discussed with each of the beneficiaries.

The non-communist elements of the Czech government, led by Jan Masaryk, viewed the participation of Czechoslovakia in the Marshall Plan as absolutely essential. As well as rebuilding the economy, it would help Czechoslovakia to develop a trading relationship with key partners and help it to maintain its desired place as a bridge between East and West. On July 4, Jan Masaryk, noting that the Poles were also attending, outlined a very clear proposal for participation. He argued that he would not accept any conditions incompatible with his country's political and economic independence. No view about Czechoslovak participation had been expressed by the USSR, so the Communists in the government had no objections to participation. The proposal was accepted without debate.

Two days later after Masaryk's proposal had been accepted, a delegation headed by Klement Gottwald, Jan Masaryk and Prokop Drtina headed to Moscow, ostensibly to speak with Stalin on an intended treaty between France and Czechoslovakia. While Masaryk slept - before what he thought would be the key meeting - Gottwald had a private audience with Stalin and was informed that he did not approve of Czechoslovak participation in the Marshall Plan, which he felt would breach the country's alliance with the Soviet Union. Upon awaking and convening with Gottwald, the news hit Masaryk like a thunderbolt. Here he was, the heir of Tomáš Masaryk, the country's founding father, utterly humiliated by the certain knowledge that his country was in fact not sovereign. The message was clear: the USSR was in complete charge and Gottwald and the Czech Communists would be Stalin's unquestioning instrument of control. The proposed treaty with France was similarly vetoed. Appeals to Beneš were fruitless. They had to bend to Stalin's will.

Jaroslav Bublík watched these events from Berlin with alarm. Like Beneš and many other Czechs, he had a natural affinity with the Russian people, who were his kin, and who had at that point always been strategic supporters of his country. But Czech sovereignty had been the essential objective. This objective was clearly faltering, and his political protection was faltering with it. On August 18 1947, Marjorie Bublík gave birth to a daughter – my mother - in the American Hospital in Berlin. With a young family, he was now in a phase of his life where he had others to think of besides himself.

#

František Moravec had been under constant attack from the Communists since his firing from his intelligence post. However, he remained a regular visitor to Beneš and with his old mentor's support, he was given a post as commander of an army division in Mladá Bolesav, a city well outside Prague. Beneš was pleased with this outcome, but Moravec was more sanguine, recognising it as a slap in the face for someone of his rank and only a temporary reprieve from his enemies' more drastic plans for him. The army was led by General Svoboda, who Moravec felt was a more than willing tool of the Communists.

In July of 1947, Beneš suffered a serious stroke. As the conscience of the fragile National Front, and as the only guarantor of the liberty of Moravec and many others like him, this was a very worrying development. The bulk of the former London exiles were affiliated to the National Socialist party, Beneš' historic party, and they in particular became deeply concerned. Beneš survived, and was forced by circumstances to continue his duties but for Jan Masaryk this was a warning. As Beneš' nominated deputy, his responsibilities looked likely to mature at the gravest of times for his country.

At this time, the economic redevelopment of Czechoslovakia stalled because of a severe drought which damaged the harvest. This hurt the popularity of the Communists as the leading party in government. Their standing was further undermined by the totalitarian behaviour of the police, which to many Czechoslovaks was far too reminiscent of the tactics of their previous Nazi overlords. The National Socialists and Slovak Democrats saw their long-awaited opportunity and pushed for elections in the Spring. May 1948 was eventually decided as the preferred date. A degree of optimism flowered; they were confident that the Communists would haemorrhage votes. Gottwald was aware of this too and launched an open war on the democratic members of the government. The Minister of the Interior, who ran the police force, was a Communist Party member called Václav Nosek. Under his leadership, clear abuses of power began: the use of agents provocateurs and extraction of false confessions to marginalise opponents. As Minister of Justice, Prokop Drtina had been put in post by Beneš specifically to fight such abuses; a violent clash with the Communists was therefore inevitable.

In September 1947, letter bombs were sent to Drtina, Jan Masaryk and another pro-democracy minister, Zenkl. The assassination attempt caused great concern to the public. Evidence indicated that communist members of the police force had planned and executed the attack. But the police created a false narrative implicating a number of Slovak Democrat leaders. This created a pretext for a major purge of pro-democracy leaders. By the autumn, the police - supported by coordinated mass demonstrations of trade unions and other pro-Soviet forces - had managed to contrive a situation where the local ruling body in Slovakia, the Slovak National Front, had been reconstituted to deprive the democrats of their majority. The success of these tactics emboldened the Communists. Given the timing and likely result of elections, they needed more subversive actions of this type and they needed them quickly. Gottwald and Slánský led the planning for a final seizure of power.

#

Amongst the many documents that were translated for me were a handful of communications between my grandfather in Berlin and the Ministry of Foreign Affairs in Prague. They were brief, typed memos, on yellowed ministry headed paper. Reviewing them, I found one of particular interest. At face value it was fairly mundane and innocuous. It was a memo accepting his request to defer unused leave from 1947 into 1948. It was the date that caught my attention: January 1948, when vicious infighting was underway between the Communists and the democratic exile camp. I wondered if he was carrying it over to provide some contingency against events? His country's future was in the balance, and if the democratic faction were to lose, he would need some time to plan and execute his families departure.

#

For his next move, Nosek demoted eight of the highest-ranking non-communist police officers. In desperation, the pro-democracy ministers put a motion to the government to reinstate them. The motion was approved without the support of the Communists, but the officers were not reinstated. On February 20 1948, twelve democratic ministers resigned in protest that Nosek had not obeyed the motion. The ministers, who included Prokop Drtina and a number of Slovak Democrats, firmly believed that Beneš would side with them. One of the men – Hubert Ripka – later reported that the President had privately assured them that he would do so.

Beneš was initially adamant that he would not accept their resignations. There was therefore an impasse and Gottwald and Slánský decided it was their turn to raise the stakes. The Soviet Deputy Minister of Foreign affairs arrived in Prague on a supposedly unrelated visit. With the Red Army sitting at the border, this served to remind the enfeebled and indecisive Beneš of the potential consequences of not making the right decision. Gottwald threatened a general strike and pressed Beneš to accept the resignations. Communist agents then occupied the offices of the ministers who had resigned. Beneš ultimately did not have the nerve to stand his ground and on February 25 he accepted the resignations and reconstituted the government according to the wishes of Gottwald and Slánský. It was Munich all over again but worse. He had legally sanctioned the new coalition government which was now completely made up of ministers who had sold their souls to the USSR. Beneš had rubber stamped a communist coup d'état. The world took note of this shocking development, which was one of the key events that solidified the Cold War world for the next fifty years.

#

I sped the tape forward a little and heard Píška's accelerated tones in high pitch, before sliding the button back to its neutral position.

"I lost my job because I was in England during the War. The Communists didn't need people like me. In fact, I could show you a book of how many people the Communists have hanged and shot. Somehow I anticipated that there may be trouble later…you had to be prepared."

Reflecting on the stakes for all of these men at this critical juncture, I stopped the tape and reached for the notice of my grandfather's promotion that had attracted Píška's attention. I looked at the date of the signature. Jan Masaryk had personally appointed him to a higher rank in the civil service on February 20, 1948. That was one day before the resignation of the democratic ministers. This was surely not a coincidence. Masaryk had of course known what was about to happen and this promotion would have given my grandfather more authority and autonomy in the period that was about to unfold. It seemed that Masaryk was trying to protect him, just as Beneš was doing his best to protect Moravec.

#

The Foreign Ministry was immediately taken over by a Communist 'committee of action' under the pretence of a sham vote by show of hands. A US intelligence report, based on first-hand accounts, states that there was a "dumbfounded acceptance" of the takeover. Jan Masaryk should have been the one to take a stand at the Foreign Ministry but instead he took himself off to bed in despair.

On the day of the coup, Moravec was called to see the Chief of the General Staff of the Army, Colonel Boček. The Colonel had been a wartime friend of his but had since become an ardent communist. Moravec was told that he was relieved of active service. On his way out, he saw the commanders of the Air Force and War College go in. Both were veterans of the war in the West and therefore were no longer trusted. Twenty-five other generals were relieved of duties in those first days. Moravec knew he was living on borrowed time. With a sensible degree of foresight, his daughters were being schooled in England, but he needed to plan for his and his wife's exit.

Beneš was a broken man. At the end of February he left the Hradčany Castle, taking down the presidential flag and its motto 'Truth Prevails,' seeking to resign. Even in this, he showed weakness and accommodation to those who had maliciously used him. Gottwald wished to maintain the charade of legitimacy in the transition of power. He lobbied Beneš to stay in power for a time and to cite health reasons for his stepping down. Beneš conceded this but as a condition he gave a list of names of people that should not be persecuted. One of the names was František Moravec. It's likely that another was Jaroslav Bublík.

On hearing of Beneš' refusal to accept his and the other cabinet members' resignations, Prokop Drtina had fallen into a deep malaise. Since his resignation, he and the other democratic former ministers had been constantly shadowed and guarded by police. Their letters were intercepted and their phone lines tapped. Only the most loyal and brave of friends continued to visit them. The press – now fully communised – derided them as traitors and 'putschists' who had sold out to the West. At the end of February 1948, Drtina opened the window of his third floor apartment and leapt from it. He had only brief words to those brave enough to visit him in his hospital bed later, where he was taken with a badly damaged hip and fractured skull.

"I hope that everyone will understand my gesture of protest: The only thing that I regret is that I did not succeed."

Jan Masaryk had not resigned. Like Beneš, he was publicly staying neutral and above politics but his commitment to honesty and decency were making every minute in his role untenable. On March 7 the Communists noisily and clumsily celebrated the birthday of Tomáš Masaryk, even posing as supporters of democracy in his name. How Jan Masaryk felt about this one can only speculate. However, three days later he was found dead, dressed only in his pyjamas, three floors below his bathroom window in the courtyard of the Czernin Palace. The communist press immediately stated that it was a suicide; spreading the somewhat ludicrous explanation that Masaryk was driven to his actions by telegrams from reactionaries, furious at his support for the 'popular democracy.' The verdict of suicide was supported by the Ministry of the Interior, after a speedy investigation. Many suspected foul play and the circumstances of his death were by no means transparent. Those who knew Masaryk felt that he would never contemplate suicide and that in the coming parliamentary sessions he was likely to make a stand against what was happening in his country. But suicide was a plausible explanation. Everyone knew of Masaryk's delicate and emotional disposition, and that there was a history of mental illness in his family. Another of the ministers who had resigned, Hubert Ripka, summed up the emotions at Masaryk's funeral, which was attended by 200,000 people from across the republic.

"One felt the impression, at once sorrowful and painful, of a horrible discord: Communists and democrats were bewailing the same man – a man whose death had widened still more the abyss that separated them. The most cynical hypocrisy mingled with the most moving sincerity, the coldest political calculation with the most pathetic sadness."

#

I remembered part of my final conversation with my grandfather on these topics and pulled out my brief handwritten notes. I had shown him photos I had taken of the Czernin Palace on my trip to Prague.

"That's where I worked for a time," he had said, softly.

I had nodded and mentioned that I knew that Jan Masaryk had fallen to his death there. He had immediately, visibly, become moved.

"I knew him personally. I knew him well. He was very nice man."

I had looked at my grandfather's eyes and they were reddening.

"We used to speak together," he gestured at the small gap between us. "Like you and I are speaking now."

I had never seen him this emotional before. He was not a sentimental man.

"I remember when we were in England," he had continued "he would come into the pub, and say, 'Now, which one of you 'blokes' is going to buy me a pint.'"

With the final words he had become choked up, and tears had welled in his eyes.

"…I was very sad about his death."

#

On March 19, František Moravec went out to get his newspaper from the local station as usual; a daily routine to reassure watching eyes. Mrs Moravec accompanied him, carrying a non-descript shopping bag which contained the meagre possessions she would take out of the country. He had planned separate routes out for each of them. So after buying his paper, he kissed her goodbye and she went to rendezvous with her guides. Moravec mingled into the crowd and shuffled towards a train on which he had booked a one-way ticket out of the country. In his small travelling case, after a lifetime of service to his country, he had only toiletries, handkerchiefs, socks, a citation for the American Legion of Merit, the Medal of the Order of the British Empire, and a loaded pistol with twenty-four spare cartridges.

A few weeks later, the communist forces had reached Jaroslav Bublík in Berlin. At the start of May, he received a letter from the Ministry of Foreign affairs. He was to be transferred back to the Foreign Ministry in Prague with effect from June 1, 1945. He would be working at the same building from which Jan Masaryk had just fallen to his death. Two special agents immediately arrived at the Military Mission on business from the new government to see how everything was proceeding there. One of them became friendly with him and taking him aside, discreetly explained to him that the reason he was to be recalled to Prague was to be investigated by the Special Military Police for his activities in the war. The agent advised him that he would be facing a capital charge. He thanked this man for having the conscience of a good Czech, took the leave that was owed to him and began to plan his escape.

#

Beneš formally resigned on June 7, 1948, to be replaced as president by Klement Gottwald, the prime minister. In his confusion he actually went so far as to send Gottwald a congratulatory telegram. After this, he became a virtual prisoner under house arrest. After a while, in order to feel closer to events, Beneš and Madame Beneš were allowed to move to an apartment close to the Ministry of Foreign Affairs at the Czernin Palace. As he declined to his eventual death, Beneš finally came to understand his chief error.

"For a long time I believed that Gottwald at least didn't lie to me but now I see that all of them, without exception, do it. It is a common matter with all communists, especially the Russian ones. My greatest mistake was that I refused to believe to the very last that even Stalin lied to me, cold bloodedly and cynically, both in 1935 and later, and that his assurances to me and to [Jan] Masaryk were an intentional deceit."

#

Prague was lost and the epicentre of the Cold War had now moved fully to Berlin. Stalin was blocking railway and road access to the international quarters of West Berlin, including the US administered section where Jaroslav Bublík, his wife Marjorie and his baby daughter Anna were living. The 'Berlin Airlift' was now in place, with all goods and supplies entering and leaving the city in a convoy of allied aircraft. Fortunately Major Bublík had good relations with the US authorities, from his latter days in the war and with their support he contrived a plan to get him and his family out of Berlin to England.

#

"…then when the coup came, he got out pretty sharpish back to England in 1948. That was lucky for him."

Although I hadn't really engaged with it in our original conversation, listening back I was getting slightly annoyed with Píška's insistence on my grandfather's good fortune. All these years later, he clearly still had some anger about the indignities he had suffered in his home country, while his old friend from Banov was elsewhere, enjoying the material comforts of a member of the government.

"Well…no…it was quite touch and go I think. He had to go separately from my mother and…"

"Oh yes?" I heard Mrs Píška say with a supportive tone, but Píška had carried on regardless, seemingly ignorant of the mortal danger my grandfather was actually in.

"…'48 came and the Communists took over and they didn't need us, so I had to start running away. That was where he was safe with all his goodies that's what I'm saying. He didn't have to…"

Mrs Píška's voice cut him dead, "You should be careful what words you use, Louie."

"Which one is that?" I heard Píška replying defensively, "…the goodies?"

The pause that then came indicated a hint of shame at the rebuke.

Mrs Píška's voice disappeared in the hiss of the background noise and I could only hear a few muffled syllables.

"…I'm sarcastic now?" came Píška's defensive reply.

"George has only just met you…"

"I know."

"…and your peculiar sense of humour."

"He wasn't being funny," she said, the words now directed at me.

I paused to think about Píška's situation. He had been in the vanguard of those ostracised by the new regime at a time when my grandfather was still in government; hoping that a compromise could be reached with the Communists. This did leave the men in very different positions for a brief time. Píška had continued.

"I had to send two small children to England with my wife…I was then smuggled out of Prague on a coach going to the frontier. But I was caught by Germans on the border. They could lose me somewhere in the forest – shoot me; in 1948 anything was possible."

"Anyhow, fortunately they were quite friendly. They took me to the Americans in Frankfurt. I flew to England and came here…after that, it wasn't bad was it?"

He had directed his final question at Mrs Píška, who had smiled in return.

#

As I scoured my grandfather's documents for some relevant information about his flight from Berlin, I remembered a discussion from long ago.

"How did you get out of Berlin then Grandma?"

"Oh that's a story," she had responded, with a cheerful smile. "It was all very mysterious. Things had gone bad in Czecho and I knew your grandfather was very unhappy. These men came to see him at work and told him that whatever he did he shouldn't go back to Prague. So one day, he came to me and said - very shifty he was: 'Look Marge, someone is going to come and get you and Anna.'"

She had aped his furtive tone and body language.

" 'They're going to take you back to England on a plane.' He spoke very calmly about it all. 'Don't worry,' he said. 'Just pack some things and go about your business. Don't draw any attention to yourself or do anything differently. Just be ready to go when they come for you. I need to go separately. I'll see you there a few days afterwards, when I know you've got there okay.'"

So they boarded separate planes, days apart, each destined for Croydon airport; the same airport where František Moravec and his team had arrived in exile in 1939.

#

In the years immediately following the coup, the prisons of Czechoslovakia became a common meeting ground for the Czech parachutists and soldiers who had been based in England, as they were purged and humiliated. These men were freedom fighters in a genuine sense: a practical and a symbolic threat to the new regime.

Čestmír Šikola married in autumn 1948 and was thrown out of the army at the same time. He had saved up some money and decided to finish the chemistry degree he started before the war. However, in April 1949 he was arrested during mass arrests of western officers. With tragic irony, he was imprisoned in the Pankrác prison, where he had visited Gerik and Čurda just two years earlier. In an echo of the brutal Nazi interrogations undertaken here in 1942, Šikola was taken to have a confession extracted from him. Despite having one of his teeth punched out, he refused to sign a statement saying that he had been preparing bomb attacks. The proof presented was one of his study books entitled, "The technology of explosives." He was interrogated again a week later on a different charge. Despite having a barrister, there was no chance of success at his subsequent trial. The sentence of two and a half year's imprisonment had been prepared in advance.

Between 1949 and 1950, all of the men who had fought with the Allies were similarly dismissed. Jiří Louda ended up serving a year in Moravia's infamous Mírov prison. He had company there. Amongst the people he met on the inside was his old commanding officer from the VRÚ, Zdeněk Gold. Jaroslav Klemeš was imprisoned in Hradčany Castle, where he was interrogated regularly over a period of fifteen months.

Karel Paleček had been transferred to the Eastern Front in 1945 and after the war he was put in charge of the build-up of paratrooper units, becoming their first commander in 1948. But in November 1949, he and Rudolf Krzák, who had trained FOURSQUARE and the other aborted parachute missions, were sentenced to nine years in prison. Emil Stankmuller was retired from the military in October 1948 and was later arrested and put into a labour camp. After initially finding work in the Czechoslovak airlines, Václav Modrák was dismissed in 1950 and sent to do hard labour in the Kladno mines. These are just a few of their stories; all suffered persecution as a reward for their efforts.

In 1952, a further, deeper purge of the country's leadership came and many of the Czech and Slovak Communists who were active in the subversion of the country found themselves accused in the most political of show trials, which became known as the 'Slánský trials.' Twelve high ranking Communists, ten of whom were Jewish, were executed. Chief amongst them was Rudolf Slánský, and their number also included my grandfather's old friend Vlado Clementis. They had finally come to understand that no one can be immune in a culture of lies.

FOURSQUARE

Two different things had come into my possession when my grandmother passed away. The first was my grandfather's gold and diamond 'gypsy' ring, which she had taken to wearing in those last years. The second was a light blue cardboard document wallet stuffed with old paperwork. I stowed the wallet in my attic. The ring was far too flamboyant for me to wear, so my sister bought me a chain to put it on as a present; after a week or so I put it away too. Both had lain abandoned for many years when I decided to fish them out as inspiration for the completion of my work.

As I rolled the ring heavily between my fingers and studied its shape - snakes swallowing their tails, plaited around the three stones at its centre – I remembered my grandmother's story about this ring. It had been a gift to my grandfather. He was on a plane manned by a Polish crew, flying above enemy territory for a parachute mission. He had been playing poker with the Poles the night before and one of them owed him some money. Just as he was about to jump from the plane, the man, thinking he would never see him again, took the ring off his finger and gave it to him.

With what I now knew, this incident could only have happened as part of the jump for Operation FOURSQUARE. But if the jump didn't happen the story didn't make sense. I grabbed the blue wallet. It seemed to mostly contain old bills, medical cards and the similar bits of random paperwork one accrues through a lifetime. But in the middle was a wedge of more interesting papers. There were certificates, identity cards and letters: a virtually complete audit trail of his life and the story he had told me. And everything checked out perfectly. One note that instantly drew my attention was signed by my grandfather in his own name on April 25, 1945. It was a receipt note for Reichsmarks, US dollars and gold sovereigns, mirroring the request that I had seen at the Public Records Office in Kew. Then I found the most striking thing of all: a typed and signed mission report for Operation FOURSQUARE, its yellowed pages stained with rust from the ancient staple that still held them together.

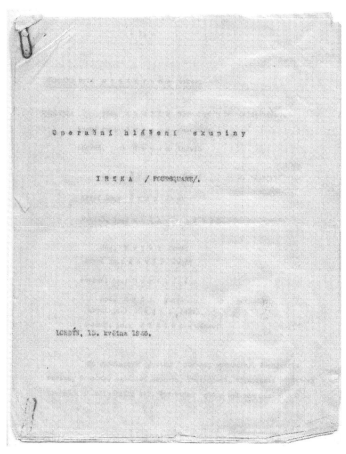

On the first page I could see the names of the FOURSQUARE team. Lieutenant Jaroslav Bublík was named as commander and first radio operator. His code name - Jaroslav Bednář - and his operational name - Ludvik Zeman – tallied with the other information I'd seen. The other members of FOURSQUARE were identified too, by the same names given to me by Jiří Louda. I sent the report away for translation, certain that it would provide new insight. But when it came back this was not the case. It told the official story I knew - the group took off and flew to their target on May 4, but were not dropped. The mission had then been cancelled after a succession of delays. I expected, at the very least, that this top secret report would provide clarity as to the intended purpose of the mission, but the entry in it for 'mission goal' contained only three vague and meaningless words: 'connecting, organisation, receiving.'

Something didn't fit. Why would he have a personal copy of this report - a report describing a mission that didn't happen? And why did he so forcefully insist to me that it did? Might it in fact be the case that this parachute report was his alibi? Might it be there to obscure the truth rather than to present it? This would hardly be unusual. I thought about the Heydrich assassination. In the SOE files that action was formally considered a spontaneous act of resistance until well after the war. The details only emerged when all of those directly involved were dead or in safe exile.

What had Bismarck said? Who rules Bohemia rules Europe. And in May 1945, the battle for Bohemia was reaching its climax. The Nazis were defeated. Only two great powers remained: the United States and the Soviet Union. And they were each eyeing Prague with interest, considering their next move. Beneš was standing right at the crux – one leg on the eastern communist jetty, the other leg on the western democratic boat that was gradually but unwaveringly drifting away. He knew that publicly he had to show trust in Russia and hope for the best. But he also knew the extreme risks of the Russians being allowed a free hand in Czechoslovakia. It was completely contrary to his philosophy of balance between East and West. The Czech Communists were planning to move in and smoothly assume control with their new 'national committees.' But Beneš wanted a local uprising, as General Miroslav had stressed to SOE. Support had been requested and rejected for five hundred Czechoslovak parachutists. But the German troops were by this point leaving en-masse. National control might now be achieved with less effort. I speculated: was a decision taken to trigger an uprising with a smaller, more targeted parachute force supported by those already on the ground?

Beneš had been ecstatic when he heard that General Patton's Third Army was entering Bohemia and advancing on Pilsen. FOURSQUARE was to be dropped exactly there a day before the Third Army were due, and just before the Prague uprising 'spontaneously' began. But the United States army had then been prevented from advancing towards Prague on the direct orders of General Dwight D Eisenhower, who was anxious to maintain cooperation with the Red Army. If a final batch of parachutists were to ensure that an uprising did happen, the dilemma would then have been whether or not to proceed without formal US support. If they did this, the Russians could never know about it: the liberty and life of all of those involved - even Beneš - would be forfeit. All needed plausible deniability.

As soon as the American army arrived in Pilsen, the acting US Secretary of State, Joseph Grew, had lobbied hard for an American advance into Prague to 'make the Russians negotiate on equal terms.' Eisenhower's order was a bitter one for many to follow. I looked for evidence of the US continuing its collaboration with the London Czechoslovaks in secret. If this was the case, then most likely that support would be provided by the Office of Strategic Services – the OSS - America's version of SOE.

Records show that an OSS team had landed in Banská Bystrica in September 1944 to support the Slovak uprising. They had been instrumental in delivering the few supplies that the uprising received. I then went back to the story of how an OSS agent had apparently turned up to join 'PLATINUM' of his own accord, with no dropping plans, at the last moment. British intelligence expressed extreme scepticism about this.

"The story was that when they got into the plane to take off they found included in their party an American officer, complete with stars and stripes, with a couple of colts slung at his hip."

It was clear from the report that the British were not convinced that either the OSS or the Czechs were being straight with them.

"I think you will admit that if the above story is true, or, if you will, only half true, not only have PLATINUM good cause to complain to their folks, but I, myself, have cause to wonder who is responsible for these operations."

The note continues, with classic British understatement, "I can well imagine that there is some simple explanation which has escaped me. Hence my request…for a report in order that I can reassure the Czechs…to say nothing of my own wonderment."

Captain Nechanský and the men of PLATINUM denied knowing this man and they were quick to proclaim his stupidity. Their witness statements were all taken by one Captain Panter. I knew that name. He was the liaison agent between the US military and operation FOURSQUARE. Other accounts in the SOE files at the Public Records Office imply that the renegade parachutist was in fact known to them and had spent time living with them in advance of the drop, as was custom for groups going out together in the field.

I also re-examined the role of the parachutist Pavel Hromek, who had brought replacement equipment for PLATINUM following their botched drop. British intelligence expressed confusion around his work and scepticism as to the veracity of his account of his time in the Protectorate. Throughout the Prague uprising, Hromek's radio to London mysteriously went silent. A note from May 11, just after Prague was taken, indicates that Hromek claimed that he had used the wrong signal plan. Would a VRÚ trained agent make such an error? It seemed much more likely to me that he was actually engaged with the rebellion, and that his wireless was instead tuned to the frequencies of PLATINUM, CHROME and those of the OSS agents on the ground in Bohemia.

It seemed that contrary to the official agreements reached by the big powers, the OSS were secretly working with the London Czechs on this final flurry of missions, from their base in Italy. The missions were tasked with initiating the Prague uprising to Beneš' timetable and they were dropped in secret. They received some support from SOE, but more broadly the British Intelligence Services were kept in the dark, as they always had been.

I requested a translation of a newspaper clipping from a Czech newspaper I had been sent by Jiří Louda. I had lost interest in it after seeing the mission files at Kew but now was the time to look again. It concerned those final missions and mentioned them all: PLATINUM, CHROME, MORTAR and FOURSQUARE.

Skupina FOSQUARE před ukončením výcviku v Anglii

When I carefully scanned and digested each word, I was stunned to note that it actually presented my hypothesis right back at me.

"[CHROME's] original task was set at the turn of 1944 and 1945. According to some sources the group were to carry out special political tasks set by President Beneš. This most likely meant trying to establish direct contact with the remaining members of UVOD and ON (National Defence) and contribute to the setting up of a representative leadership of the Bohemian and Moravian resistance...If in fact it went ahead, and Václav Knotek did suggest that it did so several times after the war, it was limited to the speeding up of the uprising in Bohemia and Moravia, or rather to making sure that it would actually happen. The remaining members of the Czechoslovak administration in London showed...impatience in this respect (Hubert Ripka and Jan Masaryk), which was evident in their radio communications with the homeland."

With Beneš in Košice, under the watchful eye of the Communists, Masaryk and the London Czechs had overseen the parachute missions themselves, providing the plausible deniability that was essential for all. Knotek had said after the war that the missions did in fact go ahead. Finally, I had found evidence corroborating my grandfather's version of events.

#

I reviewed his mission report and the events leading up to the crucial date of May 4:

"Equipped with all necessary material we were morally and physically prepared for the operation," he states.

"If the receiving group did not arrive, we were to be deplaned blindly without supplies. If they did sixteen containers and parcels would also be thrown out."

"We arrived at the airport in full operational gear, but at the last moment the operation was postponed due to the deterioration in the weather. The following day Captain Panter notified us on behalf of the aircraft commander that the American Army was twelve kilometres from our landing site and the chances were that the German defence line went through this location. He asked us if we still insisted on continuing…Our reply was that we categorically insisted on carrying out the operation."

#

Most of the Czech parachute missions were named after chemical elements, but the names of those that were not, often contained a message. 'ANTHROPOID' had been about a man: Heydrich. What did 'FOURSQUARE' mean? I went to the dictionary and there were a few descriptions: Solid and strong; forthright; honest; marked by boldness and conviction.

Skimming through the files I noted a comment from the SOE: "We consider leader of FOURSQUARE very reliable." The photographs of Jaroslav Bublík and his team, outside Beneš' office at Porchester Gate after their briefing, show a man comfortable with his role and his mission.

Since the battle for France, duty had kept him from the front line but the electrical buzz of his wireless receiver had left him painfully connected to the tragic deaths of his cousin and friends. On May 4 1945, as his plane flew over Bohemia, the battle to take back his country and to gain a measure of justice was there under his feet. The mission files for FOURSQUARE all acknowledge that the decision about whether to jump was his and his alone. Of course he jumped. Why would I not take him at his word?

In my mind's eye I could picture the events clearly. I could see him standing up in the dark and crowded plane interior and gripping the frame of the plane to steady himself for his leap. At the aircraft's low elevation, he would have seen the shadowy ground racing past. I could see the plane's navigator rushing to him to delay his exit and pushing a heavy golden ring into his palm. Their brief words would have been exchanged then – the levity easing the tension like an anaesthetist's quip before oblivion comes. I knew what had happened next; he had slipped the ring onto his finger and dropped into the air.

He would have seen the open countryside racing towards him, and the crates of supplies and armaments sailing through the air behind him. Thudding to the ground he would have rushed to help his team mates gather in their parachutes and secure their vital equipment with a desperate, forced calm.

#

US forces in Italy sent a 'top secret' note to British Intelligence on 4th May, stating the official position that FOURSQUARE's drop could not be completed because of bad weather and troop movements. The note makes clear that the men would stay under US authority for the foreseeable future.

"Pending further instructions FOURSQUARE should remain in Dijon as there is a possibility we may use them for operations this end."

Already, the group's tracks were being covered by the Americans.

#

The SOE files noted that on landing, the group was to be received by local partisans. When Jaroslav Bublík, posing as the baker 'Ludvik Zeman,' met the partisan leader 'Josef Tauber,' the two men would have used the agreed words to establish their identities. On seeing the rugged partisan, Bublík most likely cried out with a smile of relief:

"Do you have Bohemian Kolaches?"

Tauber would perhaps have replied with his own smile, at the shared ruse: "Do you like the ones with sweet cheese or poppy seed filling?"

A cluster of bedraggled militiamen helped them secure their supplies in preparation for their distribution to the emerging rebellion. Josef Tauber would then have provided Bublík with the help FOURSQUARE needed to complete the central purpose of its mission, perhaps even conveying him to the key location: the field posting of the German Army in Pilsen, where a number of its officers would have been asleep, oblivious to the mortal danger they were now in.

#

As regards what happened next, I only knew what I had been told.

"It was an assassination mission. The mission was to assassinate German section leaders...We were to initiate an uprising before the Red Army came in...The mission was a success."

Somehow, with the support of Josef Tauber and local partisans, the men of FOURSQUARE launched a violent and unexpected ambush on the leadership of the local German forces at their barracks. Using intelligence gathered by the local resistance, Bublík and his team would have positioned themselves for a surprise attack. Their mission would have been executed by squeezing the triggers of their machine guns, the satisfying bursts of fire strangely muted to a smooth mechanical chug, as the hot bullet cases were spat to the side. Two or more of the German officers were killed, throwing the occupying force into complete disarray at this crucial moment.

This was the most overt act of war by the exiles. FOURSQUARE had forced the local populations hand; the uprising would certainly now occur, as Beneš, Jan Masaryk and the London-based Czechs had desperately wanted.

#

Czechoslovak flags rose in Pilsen on the morning of the May 5; the moment of defiance and relief that had been awaited for six long years. Late in the morning, a group of partisans in a truck attempted to storm the Kommandantaur building in Pilsen, where the German General Major Majewski had his headquarters. They were repulsed and three of them were killed by a German soldier firing an anti-tank rocket. But it was clear that fear of the Germans had waned. An angry crowd assembled around the headquarters. The General Major sought to calm tempers, making a personal address but the citizens would no longer be pacified. Emboldened, they stormed into City Hall and took it over. Majewski refused to surrender but informed his men to stay in their barracks. He would only surrender to the US Army.

#

I pulled another of the items from the blue wallet file. It was a segment of pages from a Czech-German pocket dictionary, plucked from its spine. I had found it with my grandfather's mission documents. I reasoned that these pages were the key he used to code and decode the messages he sent and received in those few frantic days. Like the false papers I had seen, this relic was a first-hand witness to events and I rubbed it gently between my fingers as I sought to piece the events of those days together in my mind.

It would have been FOURSQUARE's radio that sent the message to the US 16th Armoured Division that Majewski was ready to surrender to them and prompting it to come into Pilsen immediately. All four of the group were skilled in radio operation and one of the team - Krist, Hubl, Špinka or Bublík himself - would have set up the transmitter. Placing down the small mechanical arm of the tapping device, one of the them would have frantically begun an intricate finger drumbeat on its rounded end.

#

American forces arrived in Pilsen on the morning of the May 6. Resistance was reportedly light, with only some token fire from a guard tower, as the US 16th Armoured Division approached the Škoda works. As ranking allied officer Colonel Perkins of British SOE was the first senior officer to make it to General Major Majewski's headquarters and he accepted Majewski's unconditional surrender of the forces under his command. The defeated commander swiftly pulled a pistol from his desk drawer, put it to his right temple and shot himself dead. Skirmishes with German troops persisted for some hours but by the end of the day, American forces were firmly in control of the city.

The Americans had two armoured divisions and four infantry divisions poised to strike at Prague. Expectations were high, but what actually came was crushing disappointment. PLATINUM had been despatched to Prague at the end of April. Captain Nechanský had been 'buoyant and full of resolve.' He was to coordinate the insurrection. However, Russian requests to the Americans had now averted that plan. Records indicate that the Americans were awaiting a formal request to enter Prague from the Czech National Council there. But it also indicates that the Czechs were not happy to publicly make this request, given their understanding of how the Russians would perceive it. Nechanský therefore had to oversee the Prague uprising without any formal support from the US Army. Knotek and Modrák's teams had been despatched there to supplement the small patchwork of resistance fighters on their ground. But that wasn't enough. He needed all of the men he could get.

#

On arrival in Pilsen the American forces would have informed FOURSQUARE that they were halting there. This news would have left Bublík and his team deeply concerned. The next step of their mission had been to become embedded with the US Third Army as it liberated Prague and to link up with Nechanský's small cadre of soldiers there to secure and prepare Prague ready for Beneš' arrival. They did not now have the protection of the US Army. Their mission had suddenly become much more risky. Bublík would have radioed Klemeš in Prague to receive his orders from Nechanský. It is clear what they must have been. The men would have received orders to make their way to Prague immediately.

Records show that the US Army sent some OSS reconnaissance forces into Prague at this time, and it's likely that they went with FOURSQUARE. This was the furthest to Europe's east that any western forces would get in the Second World War.

#

SS forces had been despatched to Prague by Field Mashall Schörner, the last Commander-in-Chief of the German Army, to bolster the area as occupying forces had started to melt away. The German forces had howitzers, 88mm guns and seventy tanks at their disposal. The scene was chaotic, with the local population tearing up the streets and creating barricades to seek to stop the German tanks.

Nechanský's chief concern was the absence of weapons for the forces he had to command. While Klemeš sent out sober but urgent radio requests for weapons to the allied forces, a group of policeman and civilians stormed the radio station to make their own broadcast:

"Calling all allied armies. We need urgent help. Send your planes and tanks. The Germans are advancing on Prague. For the Lord's sake send help."

The soldiers of the US Army were desperate to respond, but their orders to stay in Pilsen held firm. Nechanský organised the ragtag forces under his command into small resistance groups. Their cause was helped by some Poles and a unit of Cossacks who, having collaborated with Germany during the war, had now belatedly changed sides as the Russian forces approached. The well-armed and well-trained soldiers of FOURSQUARE would have formed a key plank of these efforts. Nechansky's men seized a number of key locations over those next few days, as the German forces gradually departed the city. Prague descended into lawless chaos and bloodletting as messages from Beneš and other exiles encouraged the population to viciously avenge themselves against their occupiers and the ethnic Germans who had supported them.

One typical account of the battle from the home resistance tells a story of unremitting heroism on the part of the home population and resistance in the face of overwhelming odds. It also comments, somewhat unfairly:

"The Americans listened impassively to the anguished messages as two thousand Czechs were slaughtered." It was of course the Soviet leadership who had prevented the American forces from engaging, so surely it was they who must take the blame for this.

As I pondered this I re-reviewed the account of Colonel Perkins of SOE, who with OSS members was one of the first of the western allies on the scene. He was not convinced of the effectiveness of the home resistance, and even at the time saw a process of myth-making underway. However, my attention was drawn to one of his more positive throwaway comments:

"Our chaps in particular did very well..." he says, referring to the SOE trained parachutists.

"...the so-called Prague rising was the work of a handful of men led by Nechanský."

#

By 9th May Prague was back in Czech hands. Having played their part in the liberation of Prague, the men of FOURSQUARE may have enjoyed a brief celebration. But the first Russian forces would have started to appear in the city quickly. The members of FOURSQUARE, like those of CHROME, and MORTAR were not officially in Prague and the Soviet forces could not know that they had ever been there. Nechanský would have sent them back to the US army bases where they officially still were, and to craft their cover stories carefully; they were to say nothing.

I reached for another note I'd found in my grandfather's files. Written in English, it was accompanied by a picture of him, his face full and youthful.

I read it carefully.

"Herewith I testify that Cadet Officer Bednář Jaroslav is attached to Czechoslovak Ministry of National Defense."

The note was signed by Karel Paleček and asked for safe passage through allied occupied territory. These were his credentials to help him and his team filter back through the allied troops after the completion of their mission, as he had told me they did. I reviewed a photo I had taken of another note from the British intelligence services that now seemed to be pertinent, in particular in its perjorative tone. It's dated May 11, two days after the Red Army had entered Prague.

"Have received vague message from captain of FOURSQUARE that aircraft now returned to Italy and Panter and party went UK. Can you confirm?"

My grandfather's photo album contains several shots of FOURSQUARE in Paris on their way back to England, standing in front of the Eiffel Tower and other famous monuments with playful smirks all around.

There were many reasons to keep the actions of FOURSQUARE secret. Jaroslav Bublík had done his duty selflessly, successfully and without strong official cover. What he had done could never be known: no guilt, no praise, no mention at all. He would have to take it with him to his grave. But in the end, he didn't need to be the good soldier any longer. I was pleased that he felt able to tell me the truth of it.

EPILOGUE

As my efforts were drawing to a close, my sister told me a story from long ago. When visiting our grandparents, she had been party to a playful - but prickly - exchange initiated by my grandfather.

"Do you remember when you wanted to divorce me?"

My grandmother had quickly dismissed this but somewhat alarmed, my sister inquired into what he meant. He explained that, a year or two after his second exile to England began, he had been approached by one of his old friends and was contemplating an invitation to go out to the Middle East, "…to organise a new uprising."

A group of his old colleagues were to base themselves there, and seek to overthrow the Communist regime in his homeland. My grandmother's response to this had been interesting on two levels. She had said that if he did so she would divorce him, but how she said it was of interest.

"I couldn't stand him being involved in another uprising."

My sister had then asked my grandfather about the nature of the first one.

"It was to liberate our country," he had said.

"From the Germans?"

"Yes," came the simple response.

#

I found a story about Václav Knotek that tallied with my sister's story. After the War, he was initially promoted to staff captain in the home army but, with Communist suspicion against him growing, he was put in the reserves and placed on a list of suspected British agents. When the coup came, the new government quickly found evidence of him working with the police on a counter action to the coup, allegedly with the support of President Beneš. Knotek, like my grandfather, found exile to Great Britain arriving just weeks after the coup in March 1948. But the story then gets very strange. He apparently took on a British alias and returned to Czechoslovakia undercover, to organise an espionage ring to overthrow the Czechoslovak regime. His features had been surgically altered to such an extent that, when he was captured soon after his arrival, his identity could not be definitively proven. On capture, he swallowed a cyanide tablet and successfully took his own life. He was buried in a wooden casket, in the same common grave as the parachutists who died on Resslova Street. The communist police then went after the other members of CHROME, including Knotek's other ex-VRÚ teammate Jan Štursa, who was given eight years' hard labour in the uranium mines.

Jaromír Nechanský was accused of treason in 1950. Allegedly forced to sign a false confession, he was executed. The received wisdom in what I read was that this was a show trial in every sense and that he was innocent of all charges. However, I could now see that, regardless of the way the trials were conducted, the accusations themselves were credible. And from what I had now learned, nothing at all to be ashamed of. My mind wandered back to the story of Čestmír Šikola's arrest and imprisonment. Communist interest in his study of the chemistry of explosives now took on a different angle too. These men had spent the previous ten years fighting for the independence of their country. It would be understandable if they had wished to continue that fight.

#

"When they came back to England, they had a place that belonged to a Czech, or something. He let it to them," Píška's voice asserted. I knew that this would have been one of the buildings used by the government in exile in the immediate aftermath of the war. "I think that was in Central London near a department store: Selfridges. Somewhere near Oxford Street?"

"We went to see them there. Only once. Then the Czech needed it for something so they had to go."

#

After his escape to England from Berlin my grandfather initially had a difficult time establishing himself. Refugees with central European accents were regarded at best with suspicion in England in the aftermath of the War. He found a job as a factory hand, but he was restless. He was still a young man in his prime and had a new life to build. After deciding against taking part in a new uprising, he applied for a job as a cable room technician for the Post Office in London, a role for which his skills were very well suited. Initially his application was rejected by a suspicious civil servant, perhaps understandably, given the tensions in these early days of the Cold War.

#

I thought again about the 'Slánský' show trials in 1952, when the Jewish members of the Czechoslovak government were purged. I was still confused as to why my grandfather had described one of those executed - his old tent-mate Vlado Clementis - as his friend, when Clementis had been part of the Communist conspiracy against Beneš. As the Soviets turned on the Communist Czechs, Klement Gottwald - in fear of his own life - led accusations that the defendants were 'bourgeois nationalists,' involved in a Zionist conspiracy to overthrow the state. There is no doubt that as foreign minister immediately after the coup, Clementis had provided military support to the newly formed state of Israel and had strong links with the government there. When my grandfather was considering supporting a second uprising just a short time before – from a base in the Middle East - was Clementis his patron? Or Slánský himself?

#

"Where did they live after that?" I heard Píška inquiring, seeking to jog his memory.

"In Wanstead, in Essex."

I heard some mumbled affirmations before the next words. "He always made gardens..."

"...beautiful gardens." Mrs Píška said definitively, with a tone of wonder.

"Yes, with rockeries and fountains," I added.

I smiled at a memory of my grandfather's creations. Even when his house in Lincolnshire was completed, he couldn't stop

332

remodelling his garden or adding unnecessary building extensions. My Mum once told me how as a girl she had watched as he mixed the mortar for building his latest work, fascinated by the process and his obvious expertise.

"Where did you learn to do that, Dad?" she asked innocently. His reported response was terse and full of self-amusement.

"Germans taught me."

#

He protested vehemently about his civil service job rejection. After consultation between the Post Office and the British intelligence services, he received an apology and a job offer. They had been informed that his conduct in the war had in fact been exemplary and if anything commended him for the role. Ironically, and unbeknownst to them, he did still have some contact with the communist intelligence services in his homeland. They were calling him at his home in Wanstead on occasion - late at night - to warn him away from any engagement with his old colleagues; to remind him that they hadn't forgotten him or his family and knew perfectly well where they were. At some point in this period, disillusioned with what became of his country and seeking to move on with his life, he threw away his war cross and his other medals. They only provided evidence of the actions he had taken, and reminded him of the futility of them.

#

"We went to see them there. After that we saw them in Brentwood – near Shenfield."

I strained my ears to hear Píška's words above the increasing hiss of the tape.

"They called their house 'Domov'." I heard a chuckle as I was reminded of the hand carved sign on the front door of his final home in Lincolnshire.

#

In the late 1960s, Czechoslovak perseverance, principles and passive resistance now had a chance to chime with broader social change across the world, as the post-war generation came to maturity and sought to sweep away the more suffocating elements of the old world. In Czechoslovakia, this manifested itself as a challenge to the Communist regime. Alexander Dubček was elected First Secretary of the country at the very start of the year, replacing the hardline Antonín Novotný. Dubček substituted his predecessors' policies with more liberal ones, loosening censorship and initiating the 'Prague Spring' of democratic reforms. Encouraged by these developments, my grandfather decided it was finally safe for him to go back to Banov and see his brothers, sisters and all his family in Moravia.

That summer, with my grandmother and Uncle Martin, he drove his caravan across Europe, covering much of the same journey that he had taken in 1939. Banov had not forgotten him. His large extended family and the whole village – more than a thousand people - came to see the return of their exiled son and local hero. A traditional Moravian marching band belted out Czech folk tunes as he arrived and carried on intermittently into the night. As the night wore on the slivovic flowed, and my then teenage uncle became increasingly baffled by its effect and the growing, garbled Czech babble around him. A steady procession of the people of Banov came in to see the inside of the caravan; a curious museum exhibit. It was a momentous night for Banov and a pivotal trip for my grandfather. But the thawing in the Cold War was regrettably brief. Just days after they left to return to England at the end of August, Dubček was ousted, as the Soviet Union and other countries of the Warsaw Pact invaded to suppress his reforms. At this point, my grandfather became resigned to the fact that his estrangement from his homeland was permanent.

#

"…and the one in Lincolnshire is called 'Domov now too."

I heard a laugh. "Is it?"

"Why did they go there?" Mrs Píška interjected.

"They used to go caravanning…"

"Yes.."

"…and my granddad was looking for somewhere to retire and build a house. They went to this little village called Chapel St Leonards and he saw that there was a plot of land."

"Yes."

"So he bought the land, and he built the house. He did the whole thing himself - It took him two years and…"

The tape lurched to a stretched halt. I felt a passing surge of grief as I realised it was time to leave the Píška's to their silence once again.

#

My grandfather was a perennial fish out of water and his thick accent and stubbornly persistent Czechness always marked him out. Despite this, he found his niche. He spent his working life at the headquarters of the Post Office in London, eventually becoming the head of the East European section there. Known to his colleagues as 'Jerry' Bublík, he was an active member of the post office chess team. Like many men of his generation, he struggled to readjust to a civilian life after the drama and tragedy of the War. But by the time I came to know him, when time and experience had mellowed and readjusted him, he had become comfortable with his life and role. In his later years, he followed political developments closely and always had his nose in a book or a newspaper. And he held court as our family patriarch, with a firm hand, a strong moral code and a dry sense of humour.

#

By the late 1980s, the 'Iron Curtain' had begun to collapse and this was felt within Czechoslovakia as the 'Velvet Revolution.' Emboldened by developments, on June 18 1989, the remaining parachutists and associated soldiers in Czechoslovakia met at the Church of St Cyril and Methodius, forty-seven years to the day after the deaths of their seven colleagues there. While there, they all took the time to sign a postcard and send it to their old colleague Bublík.

It says simply, "A greeting from an act of remembrance in Resslova Street." There are about thirty signatures, scribbled with flourish in black and blue biro. Some names are clear: Karel Paleček, Rudolf Krzák and Václav Modrák. At the very bottom is that of FOURSQUARE's Karel Hubl, the only other member of his team at that point still alive.

Five months later, on the 50th anniversary of the Nazi crackdown on Prague students, in which the young student Jan Opletal had died and become a martyr for the cause of an independent Czechoslovakia, a demonstration was held. That demonstration was itself met with a violent crackdown, serving to strengthen the population's resolve still further. After more mass protests from the Prague populace and a general strike, the Communist government resigned. The playwright Václav Havel was elected President on December 29 of that year.

On June 18, 1990, the last twelve surviving parachutists in Czechoslovakia – including Šikola and Klemeš - met again at the Church and were this time personally greeted by President Havel.

Another postcard found its way to my grandfather, a 'Greeting from surviving parachutists.'

Just a week later, he had a chance to meet his old colleagues face to face. Sixty-four soldiers flew to England for the fiftieth anniversary of their arrival in the north west of England in 1940. Šikola's memoirs recollect how he met with many of his old colleagues, including his friend Jarda Bublík with whom he had served in France and trained in England. Jiří Louda was one of the visitors on that occasion too. He found himself in Chester Cathedral for part of the commemoration and went to take his seat next to another old soldier he didn't recognise.

'I'm Louda. Can I sit here?" he asked.

'Don't be silly,' came the reply, after a quick glance back. 'I'm Bublík. Sit down."

"I didn't recognise him as he had put on a bit of weight," Louda had commented when sharing the story with me. "He was quite lean when I knew him."

#

In the latter documents of my grandfather's files is another of particular note. Dated the May 22 1991, it is issued by the Czechoslovak Ministry of Defence. Helpfully, when I came across it in the file, it was accompanied by a translation my grandfather had produced himself.

"As a partial expression of political and military rehabilitation of Czechoslovak former paratroopers for their resistance, to promote Sergeant Aspirant Jaroslav Bublík, born 14th December 1914, to Lieutenant Colonel, retired."

At this time, the government recognised the promotions he had received in the latter part of the war and had even promoted him from his final rank of Major. He was free of the fear of retribution. The government was even openly referring to him as a paratrooper. His colleagues - those men who had spent the post-war years ostracised, in prison and in exile – received similar belated recognition for their actions and dedicated service. I wondered whether this was too little, too late. But I remember that he was very pleased at this recognition. I saw his pride and contentment when he explained it to me. He was amused that it even entitled him to a small additional pension.

"I ended up lieutenant colonel – and I was not even professional soldier. I didn't do too bad," he said with a smile.

He even planned to go to Resslova Street for the commemorations that year. But just a few weeks after he received the letter, he had a heart attack, the first of the succession of physical shocks that would come in his remaining years. After the event, a final postcard came. Only ten signatures this time, and a personal message from Modrák: "Jarouš, we are thinking of you and sending our greetings to you and your wife and family. We are sorry you could not come."

#

He corresponded with Louda and Novák in those final years. Rather than reminiscing they shared knowledge about the fate of their old colleagues and continued cynicism about the legacy of communism in their home country.

"I heard that they made me a full colonel, but no one remembered to tell me," my grandfather quipped to Novák in one of their last notes. The communications also chart the gradual decline of their health. His final letter to Novák finished sombrely.

"....I have forgotten everything by now. My memory is like a riddle and I speak Czech as a foreigner. When I was in hospital I couldn't quickly recall my date of birth and my address. They asked me for the name of the queen then, but I couldn't recall it either. Regards to you all, Jarda."

#

Emerging from prison in 1951, Jiří Louda worked in government approved jobs such as forestry and working as a librarian. But all the while he busied himself with his hobby of studying and designing coats of arms. As the years passed, he began to publish books on heraldry, some of which were much acclaimed. Following Louda's own rehabilitation and promotion, and in preparation for the peaceful separation of the Czech Republic and Slovakia into two separate states, President Havel knew exactly who to go to for a standard for the new country. Louda produced one of his finest designs, a coat of arms surrounded by the leaves of the linden tree, proclaiming the national motto: "Pravda Vítězí" - Truth Prevails. And so it continued to do, as the layers of Communist subterfuge and misinformation gradually peeled away in the years that followed. In 2003, the death of Jan Masaryk was once again reviewed by the Prague police who this time concluded that he had, of course, been murdered.

#

A final recollection. I'm fourteen or fifteen years old, at my grandfather's house, and listening to his advice and stories. I remember what I was like then: almost entirely ignorant of religion and politics but seeking to build my own philosophy and world view. Reflecting on the story of how he got expelled from school for speaking out against the Catholic Church, I asked a simple question.

"Do you believe in God?"

He nodded.

"Yes."

I took this information in before I asked my next logical question.

"But if God exists, how come so many horrible things happen in the world?"

He responded with a calm, almost guilty look back. I felt as if he'd almost been expecting this question at some point or perhaps that he was just intimately familiar with it. The answer, when it came, was oblique and accompanied by a shrug that indicated that it wasn't complete.

"Think about ants…"

I took a mental step back and did my best to do this.

"Ants have very ordered society." He pinched his thumb and forefinger together as he spoke. "Each ant has its individual role. But all of them are building away, working together."

I had the picture in my head.

"Then someone – some person – comes along and maybe without even knowing, kicks anthill over...everything is destroyed. It is chaos."

I nodded.

"Ant doesn't know why. Ant doesn't understand."

I pondered this hard. I still think about it today. My small clump of grey cells occasionally gets tied up thinking about it, just as it did then.

"And then what does ant do?"

I raised my eyebrows in expectation.

"Ant builds it all back over again."

ACKNOWLEDGEMENTS

I would like to thank a number of people for their support in researching and telling this story over a large expanse of time. Neil Rees provided excellent knowledge, contacts and information on the VRÚ in Hockliffe and the movements of the government in exile just at a point where I thought my information sources were running dry, and helped with translation and identification of personnel and locations in photographs too. Jana Garnsworthy provided very practical, efficient and accurate translation services and her support was key to unlocking my understanding of the parachute missions in the latter stages of the war. I would also like to thank my cousin Ivana Průšová, for her assistance with translation of key documents in the period before I had the services of Jana. Others who provided invaluable support and feedback were David Bridge, Josh Samton, Adrian Thomas, Ed Rothery, Alex Beatty, Jacqueline Ward, Thomas Zanon Larcher, Kara Bearfield and Lee Bearfield who all read various drafts of the manuscript and gave me invaluable, honest feedback and encouragement.

This book could not of course have been written without the active support of several people who are no longer with us: Jiří Louda, František 'Frank' Kaplan, Alois Píška and Evelyn Píška MBE. I am indebted to them for being generous with their time and support and open about their experiences living through some of the most momentous and tragic events in history. My respect and admiration for them has only grown as I have completed the final stages of this book and understood their stories in their full context, and I hope that they, and my grandparents, would have felt that I have done their stories some justice.

Finally, I would like to thank my wife Nicola who has shown nothing but patience and support to me, despite the significant time and effort I have put into the endeavour of writing this book, and the distraction it has often been over many, many years.

SUPPORTING INFORMATION

Key intelligence relationships in Czechoslovak government in exile circa 1940-1945

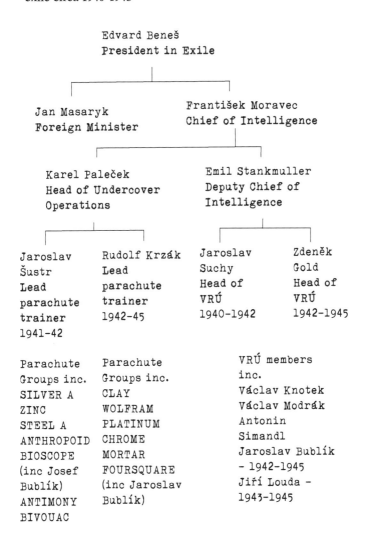

Edvard Beneš
President in Exile

Jan Masaryk
Foreign Minister

František Moravec
Chief of Intelligence

Karel Paleček
Head of Undercover
Operations

Emil Stankmuller
Deputy Chief of
Intelligence

Jaroslav
Šustr
Lead
parachute
trainer
1941-42

Rudolf Krzák
Lead
parachute
trainer
1942-45

Jaroslav
Suchy
Head of
VRÚ
1940-1942

Zdeněk
Gold
Head of
VRÚ
1942-1945

Parachute
Groups inc.
SILVER A
ZINC
STEEL A
ANTHROPOID
BIOSCOPE
(inc Josef
Bublík)
ANTIMONY
BIVOUAC

Parachute
Groups inc.
CLAY
WOLFRAM
PLATINUM
CHROME
MORTAR
FOURSQUARE
(inc Jaroslav
Bublík)

VRÚ members
inc.
Václav Knotek
Václav Modrák
Antonin
Simandl
Jaroslav Bublík
- 1942-1945
Jiří Louda -
1943-1945

Key posts in Czechoslovak post-war government, and inter-relationships with the Czechoslovak Communist Party: 1945-48

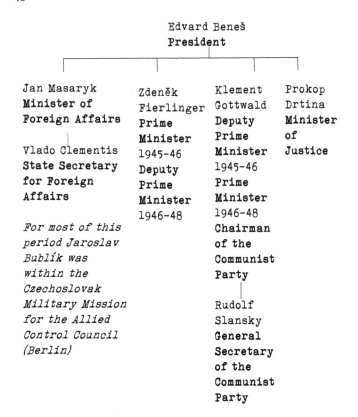

Edvard Beneš
President

Jan Masaryk	Zdeněk	Klement	Prokop
Minister of	Fierlinger	Gottwald	Drtina
Foreign Affairs	**Prime**	Deputy	**Minister**
	Minister	**Prime**	**of**
Vlado Clementis	1945–46	**Minister**	Justice
State Secretary	Deputy	1945–46	
for Foreign	**Prime**	Prime	
Affairs	**Minister**	Minister	
	1946–48	1946–48	
For most of this		**Chairman**	
period Jaroslav		**of the**	
Bublík was		**Communist**	
within the		**Party**	
Czechoslovak			
Military Mission		Rudolf	
for the Allied		Slansky	
Control Council		**General**	
(Berlin)		**Secretary**	
		of the	
		Communist	
		Party	

Key Organisations

Obrana Národa (ON) - Defense of the Nation

Czech resistance organization that opposed Nazi rule in the Protectorate of Bohemia and Moravia during the Second World War. The group was founded by General Josef Bílý in April 1939. The commanders were all former military officers, and the teams were recruited mostly from former soldiers and organizations such as Sokol (the Czech Gymnastics Association), Orel (a Catholic athletics organization).

Office of Strategic Services (OSS)

The Office of Strategic Services (OSS) was a wartime intelligence agency of the United States during World War II, and a predecessor to the Central Intelligence Agency (CIA). It was formed under the Model of the British Special Operations Executive, to coordinate espionage activities behind enemy lines. Like SOE it was also engaged with the use of propaganda and subversion.

Vojenská Rádiová Ústredna (VRÚ) – Headquarters of the Central Wireless Exchange of the Czechoslovak Forces

The VRÚ was established in Dulwich, London by František Moravec at the start of World War 2. Over time stations were also established in Warsaw, Paris, Belgrade, Bucharest, Geneva, Istanbul, Moscow, Tehran and Jerusalem. The VRÚ moved to Woldingham, Surrey in 1940 and finally to Hockliffe, Bedfordshire where it remained until the end of the war. The VRÚ's role was to maintain the exile governments communications with all parties but in particular with the home resistance organisation and with agents that were dropped behind enemy lines.

Rada Tří (R3) - Council of Three

The R3 was a guerrilla organisation put together by former members of the Czechoslovakian army - Vojtěch Luža, Josef Robotka and Karel Steiner-Veselý. It was set up to assist the armies of the United States and the Soviet Union in liberating Czechoslovakia. In practice it worked closely with Red Army partisan units and Soviet forces.

Special Operations Executive (SOE)

Variously known as the "Baker Street Irregulars" (after the location of its London headquarters), "Churchill's Secret Army" or the "Ministry of Ungentlemanly Warfare," the SOE was set up by the British Government in 1940. Its purpose was to conduct espionage, sabotage and reconnaissance in occupied Europe. It was a highly secret organisation and operated with a high degree of autonomy supporting all of the local resistance movements in occupied Europe.

Secret Intelligence Service (SIS)

The Secret Intelligence Service (SIS), commonly known as MI6, is the foreign intelligence service of the government of the United Kingdom, tasked mainly with the collection and analysis of overseas intelligence in support of the UK's national security.

The name "MI6" (meaning Military Intelligence, Section 6) originated as a flag of convenience during World War II, when SIS was known by many names. Its existence was not formally acknowledged until1994. During the Second World War it gained influence through its control of codebreaking and the knowledge that this brought.

Ústřední Vedení Odboje Domácího (ÚVOD) – Central Leadership of the Home Resistance

ÚVOD served as the link between Edvard Beneš and the Protectorate. It sought to be a shadow government until Czechoslovakia's liberation from Nazi occupation. It was an umbrella organisation for various other resistance organisations including ON and was mostly formed from former officers of the disbanded Czechoslovak Army. ÚVOD professed allegiance to the democratic ideals of past-Czechoslovak president Tomáš Masaryk and sought the establishment of a socialist republic. ÚVOD made use of its own secret radio stations for the transmission of intelligence and military reports to the exiled government via the VRÚ.

BIOGRAPHICAL SKETCHES

In reality many, many more people played an active part in the story told than those mentioned by name. Although in this account I have sought to minimise the number of people introduced to the minimum necessary to convey the story, there are still a large number of individuals described. These biographical sketches are to assist the reader in maintaining a grasp of the overall story and as a quick aide memoire as to who's who.

Government in Exile and Intelligence forces

Edvard Beneš

President of Czechoslovakia from 1935 to 1938 and again from 1945 to 1948 and leader of the Czechoslovak government in exile, based in London during World War II.

Prokop Drtina

Czech lawyer, member of the Czechoslovak government in exile during World War II and Czechoslovak Minister of Justice from 1945-1948.

Sergěj Ingr

Defence Minister of the Czechoslovak government in exile in London during World War II. Commander-in-Chief of Czechoslovak Army from 1944–1945.

Jan Masaryk

Son of Tomáš Garrigue-Masaryk. Czechoslovak ambassador to the United Kingdom 1925-1938. Foreign Minister in Czechoslovak government in exile during World War II and Foreign Minister of Czechoslovakia from 1940 to 1948.

František Moravec

Fought with the Czech Legion in Russia in World War I. Chief of Czechoslovak military intelligence from 1937-39 and as part of the Czechoslovak government in exile during World War II.

Karel Paleček

Veteran of the Czech legion in World War I like his boss František Moravec. Worked in military intelligence between the wars. Upon exile to Great Britain was in put charge of the ciphering group before taking on a role in training parachutists which continued after World War II.

Emil Stankmuller

František Moravec's deputy chief of military intelligence during World War II and one of the eleven men who arrived with him in London in March of 1939.

Jaroslav Šustr

Pre-war Czechoslovak army officer who fled to France via Yugoslavia to avoid Gestapo persecution. After the fall of France, and his arrival in Great Britain, was appointed to oversee training of parachutists for despatch to the homeland. In March 1943 he was transferred to work for General Miroslav in the regular military and from June 1944 was Czechoslovak military attaché in China.

Rudolf Krzák

Appointed by Karel Paleček to take over training of parachutists in 1943. Trained the second wave of parachutists including the final batch of missions in April/May 1945 which included operations CHROME, MORTAR and FOURSQUARE.

Czechoslovak Politicians and Government

Tomáš Garrigue-Masaryk

Founder and first President of Czechoslovakia he was a politician, sociologist and philosopher. Masaryk gained independence for a Czechoslovak republic with the help of the Allied powers at the end of World War I. He was from the town of Hodonín and a Moravian Slovak by birth.

Alois Eliáš

During WWI he was an officer of the Czechoslovak Legion in Russia and France and subsequently held military and governmental posts. Following the invasion of Bohemia and Moravia by Germany he took a role in the Protectorate government. In this role he closely cooperated with the underground group 'defence of the nation' and maintained secret contact with Edvard Beneš who he recognised as the legitimate President.

Emil Hácha

A lawyer by profession, Hácha became the third President of Czechoslovakia following the Munich agreement and Beneš exile. In March 1939, following the German invasion of Bohemia and Moravia he became state President, with little or no authority, until the end of the war.

Emanuel Moravec

A career army officer with service in the First World War, Emanuel Moravec was a proponent of democracy during the 1930s and warned about the expansionist plans of Germany under Adolf Hitler. He appealed for armed action rather than capitulation to German demands for the Sudetenland. However, after the German occupation of Czechoslovakia, he became an enthusiastic collaborator and fascist serving as the Minister of Education of the Protectorate of Bohemia and Moravia between 1942 and 1945. He committed suicide at the end of World War II.

First wave of Parachutists 1941-Summer 1942

Alfréd Bartoš

Pre-war cavalry lieutenant who fought in the battle for France as an Intelligence Officer. As an infantry officer in exile in Great Britian he volunteered for special missions in his homeland, where he led operation SILVER A – the most critical and arguably most successful of all parachute missions in Bohemia and Moravia during World War II.

Josef Bublík

Law student who escaped from his native Moravia, with his cousin Jaroslav, and joined the Czechoslovak Forces in France in 1940. After arriving in England, following the French defeat by Germany, he volunteered for parachute missions and was parachuted into the Protectorate as part of the sabotage mission, Operation BIOSCOP.

Karel Čurda

A soldier before the outbreak of war, Čurda left for France through Poland after the occupation. In June 1939. He joined the Czechoslovak Army Abroad but did not see action on the front. In Britain he volunteered for missions behind enemy lines and, following training, he was assigned to operation OUTDISTANCE to sabotage the Škoda works in Pilsen.

Oldřich Dvořák

Born in Moravia, to a railwayman, Dvořák's father moved the family frequently. After education in Slovakia, the family returned to Moravia on the establishment of the Slovak state in 1939. At the start of 1940 Dvořák escaped via the Balkans and the Lebanon to join Czechoslovak forces in France. He did not see action in France, and found exile in England in July of 1940. Dvořák was selected for a solo parachute mission, STEEL A, which was dropped in April 1942 to add resilience to the communications network SILVER A and bring supplies requested by that group.

Jozef Gabčik

Trained as a blacksmith and locksmith before the war in his native Slovakia. Served as an NCO in the Czechoslovak army from 1934–1937. Following escape from his country, he took part in the war in France war and was awarded for his bravery. He was amongst the very first men to volunteer for assignments in the occupied territory and was assigned to Operation ANTHROPOID.

Viliam Gerik

Viliam Gerik was apprenticed as a radio mechanic in his native Slovakia before the war. He via Yugoslavia, and Beirut in November 1939 for France. In France he took part in the battle against Germans forces. After exile to Britain he was selected for secret parachute missions. Gerik was airdropped into the homeland as a radio operator of ZINC, under its leader Oldřich Pechal. The mission was intended to be the development of an underground network in Moravia but it encountered difficulties from the start and was unsuccessful.

Jan Hrubý

A Moravian who joined the Border Guard Battalion of the Czechoslovakian army in Trebisov before the war, Hrubý fled to Hungary through Slovakia and headed to Yugoslavia, Greece, Turkey, and fought in the Battle of France. On arrival in England he was selected for parachute missions and was a team mate of Josef Bublík's in the sabotage mission Operation BIOSCOPE.

Ivan Kolařík

A medical student before the war, his studies were curtailed after the closure of the universities in Bohemia and Moravia. He left his country for France via Slovakia and the Balkans and served with the 8th Company of the 1st Infantry Regiment in battles against the Germans in France. Following the fall of France he was evacuated to Britain on the ship Rod-el-Farouk and volunteered for special missions in the Protectorate. Was parachuted back as the radio operator of the mission OUTDISTANCE to sabotage the Škoda works in Pilsen.

Jan Kubiš

An NCO in his native Moravia before the war, he left via Poland in 1939 to join the Czechoslovak forces in France. He was awarded the French War Cross for his conduct there. After arrival in England he volunteered for parachute missions to his homeland, and replaced Karel Svoboda as a member of ANTHROPOID following Svoboda's injury in training.

Arnošt Mikš

Mikš was apprenticed as a stone mason before undertaking his military service from 1936 to1938, where he was discharged as a sergeant. After the occupation of Czechoslovakia he went to France via the Balkans. Fought in France as 2nd in command of the Machine Gun Platoon. After exile to England was selected for special missions and after training was placed with operation ZINC to build an intelligence network in Moravia.

Adolf Opálka

Opálka graduated from the Hranice military academy as a lieutenant in 1938 and then in July left his country for France through Poland. He then participated in battles on the French front as part of exile forces. Upon arrival in Britain Opálka volunteered for missions behind enemy lines and was sent to Bohemia as the leader of OUTDISTANCE, a mission to sabotage the armaments production being undertaken at the Škoda works in Pilsen. He was Alfréd Bartoš' second in command of all parachutists dropped from Britain at the time of the Heydrich assassination.

Jiří Potůček

Pre-war shoe sales executive. Joined the Czechoslovak Army in 1940 where he was placed with the communications unit. Volunteered for special missions on arrival in England and was sent into the Protectorate as radio operator for the vital communications mission, operation SILVER A, responsible for its transmitter 'Libuše'.

Oldřich Pechal

Graduated as an infantry lieutenant before the occupation of Czechoslovakia after which he left his country for France via Poland where he served with two different regiments in the battle for France. He volunteered for special Missions in the homeland and was made commander of operation ZINC with the objective of building an intelligence network in Moravia

Vladimír Škacha

Apprenticed as a mason and worked as a builder's assistant before the war, he found exile via Poland in 1939. He fought in the front line in France before exile to Great Britain. Following special agent training he was made a member of operation SILVER B.

Josef Valčík

A pre-war shoe salesman in his native Moravia, he went into exile via the Balkans following his military service. When in England he volunteered to be deployed behind enemy lines and was made second in command of operation SILVER A, the mission to re-stablish communications with the German undercover agent A-54.

Czechoslovak Military Radio Centre, known in Czech as 'Vojenská radiová ústředna – the VRÚ.

Jaroslav Bublík

Imprisoned in a labour camp in Kiel before the war, he escaped and arrived back in his hometown of Banov Moravia at the end of 1939. Went into exile with his cousin Josef, via the Balkans, in early 1940. Joined the French forces via the foreign legion in the Lebanon and subsequently fought in the battle for France. Upon arrival in England was one of the very first soldiers recruited for parachute missions, but was not initially parachuted, instead being given a role training radio operators for subsequent missions. From late 1942 officially became a member of the VRÚ, maintaining radio contact with underground agents in the Protectorate. Leader of operation FOURSQUARE, which was one of the final flurry of missions planned for 1945.

Zdeněk Gold

Head of the Government in Exile's radio communications centre - the VRÚ - who also oversaw training of parachutists in the art of clandestine communications.

Jiří Louda

Born in Kutna Hora, in Bohemia. He arrived in France via Poland. Despite volunteering for parachute missions on arrival in England he was unable to undertake a parachute mission due to a knee injury sustained in parachute training. Became a member of the VRÚ for the duration of the war.

Václav Modrák

From Louny in Bohemia, he was apprenticed as an electrician at the local power plant and then began his military service in 1929 in the Air Force. Subsequently spent several years as a radio operator for a commercial airline. He was recruited to intelligence work in Prague by Colonel Balabán and sent to England via Poland in 1939 to bolster Paleček's nascent radio centre. He was a core member of the VRÚ throughout the war, before being selected to lead operation MORAR in 1945.

Miroslav Novák

He fought in the battle for France following his exile. Upon arrival in England was one of the very first soldiers recruited for parachute missions but, like Jaroslav Bublík, was not initially parachuted, instead being given a role training radio operators for subsequent missions. Subsequently became a member of the VRÚ, with a specialism in tuning communications equipment into the right frequencies to maintain radio contact with underground agents in the Protectorate.

Václav Knotek

Born in Prostejov, Moravia, Knotek trained as a teacher before being drafted into the army in 1931 where he served as a signaller. He returned to teaching until the war, also becoming a local Sokol leader. After the occupation he became active in the underground, and found exile to France via the Balkans. On assignment to the VRÚ he quickly became a core member and the expert at devising codes. He also held the records of parachutists for validation of credentials and messages once agents were dropped. Was made leader of Operation CHROME in 1945, with the objective of maintaining robust communications between Prague and the exiled leadership.

Antonín Simandl

Stalwart of the VRÚ and its specialist in radio technology. Built a variety of radio transmitters and receivers and made a number of innovations, including developing the ability to easily change frequency for the best transmission.

Jan Štursa

VRÚ wireless operator alongside Jaroslav Bublík at the VRÚ. Was assigned as the radio operator of operation CHROMIUM under Václav Knotek in 1945.

Second Wave of Parachutists – Autumn 1942-1945.

Antonín Bartoš

Born in Lanzhot, southern Moravia, the son of a railway worker, he started work in the postal service. Undertook national service in 1932 in the border patrol but was not accepted for officer training. Mobilised again in 1938, he decided to go into exile after his country was taken by Germany and after leaving through the Balkans he fought in the Battle of France. On arrival in the UK he excelled in the infantry and in 1942 he volunteered for special missions, being selected to lead operation CLAY.

Pavel Hromek

Born in Prušánky, in Moravia, Hromek was an artillery officer who trained at the Hranice military academy before the war. Initially an infantry man he volunteered for intelligence work, and was eventually dispatched in a single person supply mission, BAUXITE, in March 1945.

Lubomír Jasínek

Born in Tomáš Masaryk's hometown of Hodonín, Jasínek became engaged with 'Defense of the Nation' and made several attempts to escape his country until finally making a successful exist via Slovakia, through the Balkans. After the defeat of France he made his way to England where he joined the infantry. Battalion. He volunteered for special duties and undertook extensive radio training before being dispatched as the radio operator of ANTIMONY in the immediate aftermath of the Heydrich Assassination.

Jaroslav Klemeš

Born to Czech parents in 1922 in Čadca in Slovakia his family returned to its Moravia roots after the declaration of an independent Slovak state. In January 1940 Klemeš crossed via the Balkans to the Lebanon and then to France where he served as a signaller. After the defeat of France he went to Great Britain where he volunteered for special missions and undertook training from as early as 1942. Eventually dropped in February 1945 as one of two radio operators in operation PLATINUM.

Jaromír Nechanský

Czechoslovak army captain. Captain of Operation PLATINUM, which served as a vital link from the Protectorate to outside support from the UK SOE and the US OSS in the final days of world war two. Played a pivotal role in organising disparate forces in the Prague uprising, despite having the bare minimum of combatants, material and weapons at his disposal.

Čestmír Šikola

Born in Mala Skala Šikola left his homeland at the start of 1940 and found his war to France where he took part in the Battle of France as a signaller. On arrival in England he volunteered for special duties and undertook intensive training with a small elite group of signallers. He was eventually dispatched to his homeland as the radio operator of Operation CLAY establishing effective communications between the exile government and the resistance in Moravia.

Karel Svoboda

A pre-war draftsman, he joined the Czechoslovak forces in France after finding via Poland in June 1939. He was assigned to the Communications Company of the 2nd Infantry Regiment there. Volunteered for special missions on arrival in England and was selected as one of the original two members of operation ANTHROPOID however did not undertake the mission following his injury in a practice parachute jump. His family were killed by the Gestapo for providing support to the members of BIVOUAC. Was parachuted into Moravia in 1944 as a member of operation WOLFRAM.

Stanislav Srazil

Born in Pahranov near Pardubice, the son of a shoe maker, Srazil worked as a waiter before the war and managed to escape from his occupied homeland via Poland in 1939, after two previous unsuccessful attempts. Excelled in the army in the UK and volunteered for special training including sabotage. Was dispatched as part of operation ANTIMONY in 1942.

František Závorka

Born in Příbram, the son of a station master who relocated to Slovakia Zavroka took up legal studies at the University of Prague In 1931 but his studies were curtailed began basic military service. By the time of the occupation was an artillery lieutenant and made his way to France via the Balkans and Middle Est in early 1940. Didn't see active service in France but on arrival in England volunteered for special duties and was leader of the parachute group ANTIMONY which was despatched in 1942 to rebuild connections with the underground in the aftermath of the purges following the assassination of Heydrich.

Czechoslovak Home Resistance

Josef Balabán

A member of the Czechoslovak Legion in Russia in World War I, he held a variety of senior military posts between the wars. Following the dissolution of the Czechoslovak military establishment in 1939 he became a key actor in the work of the underground group 'defense of the nation'. In this role, became known as one of the 'Three Kings' along with Mašín and Moravek.

Marie Moravcová - 'Auntie Marie'

Born Marie Krčilová in Prague-Žižkov she married Alois Moravec in 1918. She was a volunteer member of the Czechoslovak Red Cross before the war and post Munich she helped people displaced from the borderlands. After the occupation of the rest of Bohemia and Moravia by the Nazis she began to work for the Prague resistance. Known as 'Aunt Marie' her house began the receiving point for parachutists arriving from Great Britain.

Vlastimil 'Ata' Moravec

Auntie Marie's eldest son Ata was an active member of the Prague underground in the early years of the war. He acted as a courier carrying information between Prague and the transmitter 'Lubuse' in Pardubice and accompanied Josef Valčík on a mission to retrieve dropped parachute equipment from Křivoklát Forest.

Václav Moravek

Václav Moravek was an army officer before the disestablishment of the Czechoslovak military by Germany in 1939. After failing to escape Czechoslovakia via Poland he established contact with Josef

Balabán and Josef Mašín who along with him came to be known as the 'Three Kings' in their work in the Czechoslovak underground. Became the key contact between the 'Defence of the nation' in Prague and the Government in Exile, in particular enabling the flow of information between the German agent A-54.

Josef Mašín

Josef Mašín was a veteran of the Czechoslovak Legion in Russia who served with the 1st Artillery Regiment between the first and second world wars. After the occupation he created an intelligence group, as part of 'Defense of the Nation.' Became known as one of the 'Three Kings' along with Balabán and Moravek.

Ladislav Vaněk - 'Jindra'

Ladislav Vaněk was born in Olomouc and before the Second World War was a high school teacher of chemistry and a local Sokol leader. He founded and led the underground 'Jindra' organisation which provided refuge and support to the parachutists that arrived in the Protectorate from Great Britain prior to the assassination of Heydrich.

Jan Zelenska - 'Uncle Hajský'

Key member of the Sokol resistance organization Jindra, with the code name 'Hajský' (after the village of Háj u Duchcova, where he was staying at the time of the Munich declaration). Oversaw the housing of newly arrived parachutists in and around Prague in the period immediately before the Heydrich Assassination

Czechoslovak Forces

Ján Golian

Born in the present day Hungary, the son of Slovaks from Šurany he studied at the Military Academy in Hranice and by the time of Munich was a staff officer in Trenčín on the Moravian/Slovakian border In January 1944 he was appointed chief of staff of the Slovak Ground Forces in Banská Bystrica, where he gathered a group of influential anti-nazi oriented officers sustaining contact with the Czechoslovak Government in Exile in London. He was the supreme military leader of the uprising from April 27, 1944 (while the uprising was still in preparation) until the arrival of Division General Rudolf Viest on October 7, 1944.

František 'Frank' Kaplan

Kaplan was the son of a Czecholovak diplomat. After the German takeover of Czechoslovakia he went to Marseille via Istanbul and Beirut, and he joined the army there in March 1940. He was assigned to serve as a radio operator in the telegraph battalion but did not take part in combat on the front. Kaplan went to England with the Czech forces and in 1944-1945 he took part in the siege of Dunkirk.

'General Miroslav' - Bedrich Neumann

Bedrich Neumann was a Czechoslovak general, and an early supporter of the home resistance organisation 'defense of the nation'. An infantry commander in the Battle of France, he was exiled to England and was appointed Chief of staff for the construction of the Czech military in 1943. He was promoted to the rank of division general in 1944 and held the post of Chief of staff until the end of hostilities. During his work in exile he went by the codename 'Bohus Miroslav.'

Alois Píška

Alois Píška was born in Bánov, Moravia. After the occupation of Bohemia he left his country through Slovakia, and the Balkans to Beirut in Lebanon. From there he travelled to France where he served with a mortar regiment in the Battle for France in 1940. After France's defeat he lived in the unoccupied part of that country until 1942. Eventually arriving in Britain, he joined the Royal Air Force and served with the 310th Czechoslovak fighter squadron.

Rudolf Viest

Rudolf Viest was a Slovak military leader, member of the Czechoslovak Government in Exile. He was the only Slovak general during the interwar period. After going into exile Viest led forces in the Battle for France. He returned to Slovakia from Great Britain in October 1944 to take official command of the Slovak uprising, and commanded the 1st Czechoslovak army during the Slovak National Uprising.

German Military and Politicians

Karl Hermann Frank

A bookbinder by profession, he was one of the leading members of the Sudeten-German party from 1933. In 1939, he was appointed State Secretary of the Reich Protector for the Protectorate of Bohemia and Moravia and later Reich's State Minister and Police General. He planned and oversaw actions against the Czech population such as the actions against university students in 1939 and executions under martial law.

Konstantin Von Neurath

German diplomat who served as Foreign Minister of Germany between 1932 and 1938. Was replaced by the more fervent Nazi Joachim von Ribbentrop in 1938. Von Neurath served as 'Protector' of Bohemia and Moravia between 1939 and 1943 though his authority was only nominal after the arrival of Heydrich is 1941.

Reinhard Heydrich

Heydrich joined the Nazi party after being dismissed in disgrace from the German Navy. Rose to become number two to Heninrich Himmler in the SS and Chief of both the Reich Main Security Office and the Gestapo. Became acting Reich-Protector of Bohemia and Moravia from 1941 until his death a year later. In this role he instigated a brutal regime in the Protectorate to drive compliance of the population to the Nazi war effort while he planned for a longer term strategy of murder and exile of ethnic Slavs to 'Germanise' the area. In January 1942 he chaired the

Wannsee Conference which formalised plans for the 'Final Solution to the Jewish Question'—the deportation and genocide of all Jews in German-occupied Europe.

Kurt Daluege

Prussian army veteran and leader in the SS. Following Reinhard Heydrich's assassination in 1942, he served as Deputy Protector for the Protectorate of Bohemia and Moravia. Daluege directed the German measures of retribution for the assassination.

Oskar Fleischer

A member of the Abwehr – German military intelligence - before World War II. After the occupation of Czechoslovakia he became chief investigator of the Prague Gestapo during German Occupation. He was commander of the Gestapo team, commissioned to capture the 'Three Kings' – Balabán, Mašín and Moravek.

PARACHUTE MISSIONS

Selection of Czechoslovak Government in Exile/SOE joint parachute operations 1941-1945

ANTIMONY

Team members: Lieutenant František Závorka, Sergeant Stanislav Srazil, Lance Corporal Lubomír Jasínek.

Drop date: October 24,1942.

Drop Location: Pardubice, Bohemia.

Mission: Re-establish communications with underground networks in the Protectorate and determine the fate of SILVER A.

ANTHROPOID

Team members: Sergeant Jozef Gabčík, Sergeant Jan Kubiš.

Drop date: December 29, 1941.

Drop location: Nehvizdy, Bohemia (near Prague).

Mission: The assassination of Acting Reich Protector Reinhard Heydrich.

BAUXITE

Team members: Captain Pavel Hromek.

Drop date: March 22, 1945.

Drop Location: 7km North East of Velké Meziříčí, Western Moravia.

Mission: Provision of replacement equipment to PLATINUM, and to place himself at the disposal of the local commander (Captain Nechanský). On dropping was instructed by Nechanský to proceed to Prague to support the uprising.

BIOSCOPE

Team members: Sergeant Bohuslav Kouba, Sergeant Josef Bublík, Sergeant Jan Hrubý.

Drop date: April 28, 1942.

Drop location: North West of Křivoklát, Central Bohemia.

Mission: Sabotage of two targets in Moravia: The power station at Brno and the railway bridge at Přerov.

BIVOUAC

Team members: Sergeant František Popíšil, Sergeant Jindřich Čoupek, Corporal Libor Zapletal.

Drop date: April 28, 1942.

Drop location: North west of Křivoklát, central Bohemia.

Mission: Sabotage of two targets in Moravia: The transformer station at Vsetín, near Zlín and sabotage of the railway bridge at Hranice.

CHROME

Team members: Captain Václav Knotek, Lieutenant Jan Štursa, Lieutenant Karel Tichý.

Drop date: Files indicate unsuccessful drop on May 4, 1945.

Drop location: Peřimov (near Jilemnice) – East Bohemia.

Mission: 'Special political tasks' set by President Beneš: Establishing direct contact with the remaining members of UVOD and ON (National Defence) in Prague and the setting up of a representative leadership of the Bohemian and Moravian resistance.

CHURCHMAN

Team members: Captain Vladimír Hanuš, Lieutenant Ladislav Vyskočil, Sergeant Jaroslav Krsek, Sergeant Alois Hladík.

Drop date: Files indicate unsuccessful drop on May 4, 1945. Cancelled on May 7.

Drop location: Near Kladno.

Mission: Providing support to PLATINUM and its leader Captain Nechanský at the time of the Prague uprising

CLAY

Team members: Captain Antonín Bartoš, Lieutenant Čestmír Šikola, Lieutentant Jiří Štokman.

Drop date: April 12, 1944.

Drop Location: Příluky, Moravia.

Mission: Building an intelligence and communication network in Moravia.

FOURSQUARE

Team members: Lieutenant Jaroslav Bublík, Corporal Karel Hubl, Corporal Josef Krist, Corporal Josef Špinka.

Drop date: Files indicate unsuccessful drop on May 4, 1945.

Drop location: Outside Pilsen, South West Bohemia.

Mission: Mission report says only that is was for provision of supplies and to support 'organisation'.

OUTDISTANCE

Team members: Lieutenant Adolf Opálka, Sergeant Karel Čurda, Corporal Ivan Kolařík.

Drop date: March 28, 1942.

Drop Location: Telč, Moravia.

Mission: Planning and supporting the bombing of the Škoda works at Pilsen.

MORTAR

Team members: Lieutenant Václav Modrák, Sergeant Alois Horáček, Sergeant Jan Sekerka.

Drop date: Files indicate unsuccessful drop on May 4, 1945.

Drop location: Peřimov (near Jilemnice) – East Bohemia.

Mission: To set up new radio communications between London and Košice, general intelligence work, aircraft navigation and the receipt of weapons.

PLATINUM

Team members: Captain Jaromír Nechanský, Sergeant-Major Alois Vyhňák, Sergeant-Major Jaroslav Pešán, Sergeant Jaroslav Klemeš.

Drop date: February 16, 1945.

Drop location: Nasavrky, Eastern Bohemia.

Mission: To organise reception of stores and agents and eventually top prepare landing grounds for the reception of aircraft.

ROTHMAN

Team members: Captain Klement Hlásenský, Lieutenant Oswald Peroutka, Corporal Vladimír Ruml, Corporal Antonín Stolarik.

Drop date: Cancelled at the start of May.

Mission: To bring supplies, train local resistance and support Captain Nechanský in the uprising.

SILVER A

Team members: Lieutenant Alfréd Bartoš, Sergeant Josef Valčík, Corporal Jiří Potůček.

Drop date: December 29, 1942.

Driop location: Near Poděbrady, Bohemia.

Mission: Setting up an intelligence network and communications capability to link the exile government with the underground in the Protectorate. Key to this was establishing contact with the critical agent A-54.

SILVER B

Team members: Sergeant Vladimír Škacha, Sergeant Jan Zemek.

Drop date: December 29, 1941.

Drop location: Telč, Moravia.

Mission: Delivery of a transmitter to the underground and arranging supply drops.

STEEL

Team members: Lance-Corporal Oldřich Dvořák.

Drop date: April 28, 1942.

Mission: To bolster communications capability by adding Dvořák to the network and also supply of key equipment: a transmitter for the Czech underground; spare crystals, cyanide tablets and supplies for SILVER A.

TIN

Team members: Sergeant Ludvic Cupal, Sergeant Jaroslav Švarc.

Drop date: April 30, 1942.

Mission: To assassinate the Protectorate Minister of Education and Propaganda, Emanuel Moravec.

WOLFRAM

Team members: Captain Josef Otisk, Sergeant Řezníček, Sergeant Karel Svoboda, Sergeant Josef Bierski, Sergeant Josef Černota, Sergeant Robert Matula.

Drop date: September 13, 1944.

Drop location: Intended point was Grúň on the Slovakian-Moravia border.

Mission: Organisation and establishment of partisan groups in north-north-east Moravia.

ZINC

Team members: Lieutenant Oldřich Pechal, Sergeant Arnošt Mikš, Corporal Viliam Gerik.

Drop date: March 28, 1942.

Drop location: Gbely, Slovakia.

Mission: To bolster the capability of SILVER A and expand intelligence gathering and organisation into Moravia.

PRIMARY SOURCES AND BIBLIOGRAPHY

Primary Sources

Public Records Office, London

HS4/2 Policy, planning and organisation of SOE activities; proposed Czechoslovak uprising

HS4/4 Policy and planning: SIS/SOE joint effort to obtain Czech codes

HS 4/22 Air dropping operations - Mola di Bari: results and reports.

HS 4/39 SILVER A and B: to re-establish communications between UK and Protectorate; ANTHROPOID: liquidation of Heydrich; PERCENTAGE: communications operation

HS 4/46 FOURSQUARE; operation cancelled

HS 4/50 SHALE; RADIUM; IRIDIUM; BRONZE; TIN; INTRANSITIVE; BIOSCOPE; BIVOUAC; STEEL A; STEEL/OUTDISTANCE; ZINC

HS 4/51 NUREMBURG/CHEQUEBOOK: liaison mission OSS; Colonel Perkins

HS 4/52 Reports on parties dropped to CSR 1944-45: WOLFRAM, BAUXITE, PLATINIUM, TUNGSTEN, GLUCINIUM, MANGANESE, CARBON, CLAY, CHALK, SULPHUR

HS 4/54 Slovak rising; WINDPROOF; PLATINUM

HS 4/55 Slovak rising

HS 4/56 Slovak rising: SOE supplies; Czech broadcasting

Personal Records

Significant parts of the content of this book are taken from records of conversations with several first hand witnesses to the events described in particular Jaroslav Bublík, Marjorie Bublík, Jiří Louda, Alois Píška and Evelyn Píška. The conversations with Jaroslav Bublík are based on notes taken in two discussions circa winter 1998/9. Conversations with Jiří Louda occurred between January and March 2004. The conversation with Alois and Evelyn Píška is based on an audio recording taken at their house in Southsea, Hampshire on April 31, 2005. Research has been supported by a substantial archive of private documentation and photographs held by the author. All photographs and documents reproduced here are from the private collection and photograph albums of Jaroslav Bublík, unless specifically referenced in the following notes. Every effort has been made to seek copyright permission for the reproduction of images. Any omissions are entirely unintentional and can be corrected on request.

Select Bibliography

Albright, Madeleine, Prague Winter, A Personal Story of Remembrance and War, 1937-1948, 2012

Allen, Stuart, Commando Country, Glasgow 2007

Beneš, Dr Edvard, From Munich to New War and New Victory, London 1954.

Burian, M. Knizek, Aleš, Rajlich Jiří, and Stehli Edvard, Assassination: Operation ANTHROPOID, 1941-1942, Prague, 2002.

Burgess, Alan, Seven Men at Daybreak, London 1960.

Churchill, Winston, S. The Second World War, Volume V, Closing the Ring, London 1952.

Churchill, Winston, S. The Second World War, Volume VI, Triumph and Tragedy, London 1953.

Čvančara, Jaroslav, Akce Attentat, Prague 1991.

Douglas, R.M, Orderly and Humane: The Expulsion of the Germans after the Second World War, 2012.

Ivanov, Miroslav, Target: Heydrich New York 1972.

Jelinek, Zdeněk, Operace SILVER A, Kolin 1984.

Judge, Sean M. Slovakia 1944: The Forgotten Uprising: Wright Flyer Paper No. 34, 2008.

Korbel, Josef, The Communist Subversion of Czechoslovakia, 1938-1948: The Failure of Coexistence, Princeton 1959.

Kunc, R., Bartoš, A., CLAY-Eva volá Londýn.

Lockhart, Sir Robert Bruce, Comes the Reckoning, London 1947.

MacDonald, Callum, The Killing of SS Obergruppenfuhrer Reinhard Heydrich, London 1989.

Mamatey, Victor S., and Luza, Radomir (Eds), A History of the Czechoslovak Republic 1918-1948, Princeton 1973.

Masaryk, Jan, Speaking to my Country, 2011.

Moravec, Gen František, Master of Spies, New York 1975.

Ramsay, William, G. (Ed), After the Battle Number 24, 1979.

Rees, Neil, The Czech Connection: The Czechoslovak Government in Exile in London and Buckinghamshire, Chesham 2005.

Reichl, Martin. Cesty Osudu [Paths of Destiny], Cheb 2004.

Ripka, Hubert, Czechoslovakia Enslaved: The Story of the Communist Coup d'Etat 1950.

Popisil, J and Šikola, Radista skupiny Clay Eva vzpomíná (undated book with no stated publisher – published circa 1990-1992)

Jiří Solc, Ve Sluzbach Prezident, Vysehrad 1994

Táborský, Edward, President Edvard Beneš: Between East and West 1938-1948, Stanford 1981.

Ullman, Walter, The United States in Prague 1945-1948 1978.

Alexander von Plato et al, Hitler's Slaves: Life Stories of Forced Labourers in Nazi-Occupied Europe, New York 2008

Wiener, Jan, The Assassination of Heydrich, New York 1969.

White, Lewis M., On all fronts – Czechoslovakia in World War II, Part 1, New York 1991.

White, Lewis M., On all fronts – Czechoslovakia in World War II, Part 2, New York 1995.

White, Lewis M., On all fronts – Czechoslovakia in World War II, Part 3, New York 2000.

HOME:

p. 7	The attribution of the quote to Bismarck is apocryphal, though referenced by many including Albright.
pp.7-9	Descriptions of the motivation behind the creation of the Czechoslovak state and the context of the birth of the country are informed by Albright.
pp. 12-19	The description of the evolving political situation between the wars is informed by Moravec, MacDonald and Mamatey & Luza.

EXILE:

p. 27	The refusal of Moravec's superiors to heed his advice about the impending German invasion of Czechoslovakia is described in Moravec, pp. 139-141.
p. 27	"there comes a time in the life of every man…", Moravec, p. 144.
p. 28	"I found myself suddenly swept by black thoughts…", Moravec, p. 146.
p. 29	An overview of the German use of Czech forced labour throughout World War II is provided in Alexander von Plato et al, pp.47-59.
p. 29	Details of Jaroslav Bublík's forced labour posting are provided in Richard Ditting Rendsburg letter, F71191: 'Unterlagen und Auskünfte Über Angehörige der Vereinten

Nationen' ('Documents and information about members of the United Nations') dated October 26 1946 and available from the Arolsen Archives: International Center on Nazi Persecution.

p. 31   "Last September, The Franco-British proposals…" Beneš, p. 65.

p. 32   Details of the setting up of intelligence operations are provided in Moravec pp.152-153.

p. 35   "There will be a war…", from Václav Modrák's account 'Radio Contact', White [Part 3], p. 133.

p. 36   "We have declared through the lips of Edvard Beneš…", from the transcript of Jan Masaryk's BBC Radio broadcast of September 8th, 1939 in Masaryk.

p. 38   "Today on the 28th of October we are meeting once more…", from the transcript of Jan Masaryk's BBC Radio broadcast of October 28th, 1939 in Masaryk.

p. 39   The use of the nickname 'Kah-Hah' for Karl Herman Frank is described in Wiener, p. 21.

pp. 49-50 The descriptions of Modrak's arrival at Rosendale Road and his discussion with Moravec are described in his account 'Radio Contact', White [Part 3], p. 134.

FRANCE:

p. 54   There are various accounts of the poor
               equipment provided to the Czechoslovak
               volunteers by the French including the accounts
               of Souček's and Němec in White [Part 1], p. 53
               and p.85 respectively. Reference is also made to
               this is MacDonald p.86.

pp. 54-55   The method of radio working described, as it
               was in place at the time of Modrák's arrival is
               described in his account in 'Radio Contact',
               White [Part 3], p. 136-7.

p. 56   Václav Moravek's motto: "I believe in God and
               my pistols…", is taken from Burian et al, p. 52.

p. 56   The details of Václav Moravek's heroism are
               from Wiener pp. 24-25.

p. 58   "Soon our lads too will fight…", from the
               transcript of Jan Masaryk's BBC Radio broadcast
               of May 1st, 1940 in Masaryk.

p. 58   Jánošík was a legendary Slovakian highwayman,
               similar in many respects to the English folk hero
               Robin Hood. His name was often invoked in
               Slovakia as a symbol of Slovakian resistance to
               oppression.

p. 59   A description of the difficulty of the soldiers
               retreat is provided in Souček's account in White
               [Part 1], p. 53.

ENGLAND:

pp. 66-67   The description of the troops encountering the British fleet at Gibraltar is informed by the speech by Major Kašpar on 9th July 2000 at Cholmondeley Park, during the 60th anniversary of the arrival of Czechoslovak forces there. A transcript of the speech was provided to the author by Colonel František Kaplan soon after the event.

p. 68   The note from Beneš that the Czechs are providing information that the Poles, Dutch and French can't match is quoted in MacDonald, p.75.

p. 71   An account of the rebellion including the naming of Schwarz and Vroc as its leaders is provided in Jaroslav Nemec's account in his chapter, 'The Crisis in the Czechoslovak Army in England in the Second Half of 1940': From the Diary and Recollections of a Participant.', White [Part 3], pp. 83-94.

COUNTER OFFENSIVE:

p. 76   A detailed description of 'Funny Neuk' is proved in 'The Secret Wireless War 1939-1945, Geoffrey Pigeon (Whaddon).

p. 85   "I do not see why the Czechs should not be placed on the same footing…", Lockhart p.115

p. 85   Details of the exile's communication equipment, including the designs of Simandl are included in

Practical Wireless magazine, January 2002 pp. 41–43.

p. 85   "Contact is a magic word...", from Václav Modrák's account 'Radio Contact', White, Part 3, p. 134.

p. 86   "Along with these came memories of those back home..." from Václav Modrák's account 'Radio Contact', White, Part 3, p. 141.

p. 87   Details of Emil Stankmuller's visit to Leamington are included in MacDonald, pp. 88.

pp. 95-96   "The selection would not be easy...", Moravec, pp. 198-9.

pp. 88-89   There are several notable inaccuracies and omissions in František Moravec's account of the planning and execution of Anthropoid in Moravec, pp 194-211. For example, Moravec fails to mention that Karel Svoboda was originally selected for the mission instead of Jan Kubiš and his account implies that the mission was dropped only weeks before the assassination, rather than months. Although written as his first-hand account he describes some events which were only known after the war. He also claims that the detailed mission planning was undertaken in the UK whereas the accounts in Ivanov imply that the plan was formulated in Prague with the assistance of Jindra - this being one of the reasons for the delay in carrying out the mission. The discrepancies are noted in a letter between Jaroslav Bublík and Miroslav Novák that is held by the author.

p. 102   "Long live Czechoslovakia…", Burian et al, p26.

pp. 102-103   "The blood of the students of Prague…", from the transcript of Jan Masaryk's BBC Radio broadcast of October 1st, 1941 in Masaryk.

p. 104   "The radio and newspapers have told you…". Ivanov, pp. 43-4.

p. 106   Details of Moravek's replacement transmitter being detected are provided in Ivanov, p. 91.

PROPHECIES:

Much of the story of Silver A in this chapter is informed by Jelinek, Ivanov and to a lesser extent Burgess.

p. 109   "disaster…", Ivanov, p. 50.

p. 109   "I had joined the resistance…", Ivanov, p. 49.

pp. 111-112   A description of how Silver A settled into routine communications is included in Ivanov, pp. 64-66.

p. 115   The communications from Alfréd Bartoš paraphrased on pp.98-9 is from Public Records Office file 4/39, and in particular the communication CMcVG/374, February 23, 1942.

p. 115   "It is therefore impossible to commit…", Ivanov, p. 92.

p. 116   The commitment created with the RAF for the Škoda raid is described in MacDonald, p. 152.

THE RETURN:

pp. 126-128   Details of the parachutist commando training are described in Allan, pp. 180-184 and in various SOE files in the collection of the Public Records Office.

p. 134   An account of the trainees signing Karel Čapek's book for their trainer Lieutenant Ernest Van Maurik, is provided in Allen, p 182. Allen notes that ten men signed the book which is held in the Imperial War Museum Department of Documents, Misc 2734. The author corresponded with Stuart Allan who confirmed that Josef Bublík was one of that cadre of recruits.

p. 128   "America is at war...", from the transcript of Jan Masaryk's BBC Radio broadcast of December 25th, 1941 in Masaryk.

pp. 133-134   Regarding the parachutists views of their likelihood of survival, František Moravec states that the men of Anthropoid were made fully aware of their fate: "I added that the greater probability was that they would be killed at the place of action.", Moravec, p. 200. However with reference to Silver A, a member of the underground reported a contradictory position: "Certainly they had volunteered; but not for a hopeless mission...But in fact they had been told in London that the end [of the war] was near.", Ivanov p. 80.

p. 140   Details of the family of Karel Svoboda supporting BIVOUAC, and their ultimate fate are provided in Jelinek.

p. 141   "Judging by the preparations…", is from Public Records Office file HS 4/35, title 'daily broadcast of world broadcasts Part 1, No 1409, 27th May.

THE SIEGE:

p. 144   Dvořák's nickname of 'the Gypsy' is mentioned in Ivanov.

p. 144   The account of how Josef Bublík's landlady found his gun is included in Ivanov, p. 101

p. 146   "Is he dead?", Ivanov, p.186.

pp. 146-147   "An attempt on the life of acting-Reichsprotektor SS Obergruppefuhrer Heydrich…", Ivanov, pp. 206-7

p. 150   "I can see that you and your friends are absolutely determined…", MacDonald, p. 180.

p.154   "Extreme Measures…" MacDonald, p184.

pp. 154-156   An overview of the Nazi's reprisals for the assassination of Heydrich is provided in MacDonald p.184185

p.158   Vaněk's plans to evacuate the parachutist are described in his account in Ivanov, pp. 224-5 p.169   'Ležáky was levelled. I am the only one left.', is from Václav Modrák's account 'Radio Contact' in White, Part 3, p. 139.

p.169   Notes of discussions between Roy Tink and Neil Rees –29th October 2004 (Copy held by the author).

p.170   As regards the secrecy of the mission at the time of its execution Public Records Office file 4/39 make clear how SOE involvement was not widely communicated even in the wider British intelligence services.

AFTERMATH:

pp. 180-181   The story of ANTIMONY's capture is from 'Radio Contact' in White, Part 3, p. 141.

p. 184   "I am making this declaration...", from the transcript of Jan Masaryk's BBC Radio broadcast of October 19th 1942 in Masaryk.

pp. 187-189   The quotations from Eduard Kukan and Major Kašpar are based on transcripts provided to the author by Colonel František Kaplan soon after the event.

THE SECOND PHASE:

p. 194   "…listening, writing, smoking and sweating…", is from Václav Modrák's account 'Radio Contact' in White, Part 3, p. 143.

p. 195   "pull chestnuts from the fire [of war in Europe]" is from SOE file HS4/4. Many of the notes in this file expand on the theme that the exiles were interested only in intelligence and not military action.

pp. 195-196   Communications regarding the behaviour of ANTIMONY, capture of its radio and the concerns of British intelligence are described in Public Records HS 4/2 and HS 4/39.

p. 196   "completely lost confidence in the good faith of the Czech Intelligence Service.", is from Public Records Office file HS4/4, C/3098 27th April 1942.

pp. 198-199   The details of Moravec's visit to discuss independence of Czech codes is provided in a public records office file HS 4/4, in particular the note MZ/CZ/4260, 22nd June 1943.

pp. 200-201   A detailed description of Beneš attitude to the United States including his visit to see President Roosevelt is included in Taborsky pp. 115-133 and further useful description is provided in Beneš, pp.167-196

p.209   "Usually the Czechs are an extremely logical people…", is from the letter in the Public

	Records Office files HS4/2, MP/CZ/4350 dated 17th July 1943.
pp. 211-212	Captain Šustr's visit to British Intelligence is described in Public Records Office file HS4/4, MY/873, dated 30th November 1943.
pp. 213-215	Beneš gives his own detailed account of the Moscow 'Christmas' visit in his memoir, Chapter VII, pp.239-291.
pp. 215-216	"Three weeks before his death…", from the transcript of Jan Masaryk's BBC Radio broadcast of October 19th 1942 in Masaryk.
p. 216	"He never specified to me what that limit was…", Moravec, p. 218
p. 216	The claim that the Czechoslovakian Communist Party was briefing against Moravec is included in Moravec, p. 224.

UPRISINGS:

The Slovak Uprising and the political context in which is occurred are described in Anna Josko's paper, 'The Slovak Resistance Movement' in Mamatey and Luza, pp 362-384. Another key reference for this chapter is Judge, Sean M. Slovakia 1944: The Forgotten Uprising: Wright Flyer Paper No. 34, 2008. Details are also provided in public records office files HS 4/54, HS 4/55 and HS 4/56.

pp. 218-219	Description of the political make-up and alignment to Beneš views is described in Mamatey, p. 355-6.

p. 221	"Sir, you can count me in now, save you coming back in three days' time.", Šikola, pp.23-4.
p. 222	Details of Clay's drop are provided in HS4/52, Kunc and Popisil.
p. 224	"Slovak political matters might be solved in accordance with the interests of the USSR.", Táborský p.177.
pp. 225-226	The description of the day to day goings on at the VRÚ was recounted to the author by Jiri Louda.
pp. 227-233	Details of WOLFRAM, and Karel Svoboda's capture and torture throughout Chapter 12 is taken from the operation report for WOLFRAM in Public Records Office file 4/52.
pp. 233-234	The story of the 'percentages agreement' is covered in detail in Churchill, Volume VI, p. 198.
p. 234	Modrák's account of how he temporarily went blind is from 'Radio Contact', White, Part 3, p. 141.
p. 235	"geography left only Soviet forces to do it", Mamatey, p. 381
p. 235	"The Czechoslovak Army command announces herewith that…", Mamatey, p. 382.
p. 236	"When I regained my breath, I did not mince my words.", Moravec, p.229.
p. 237	"Have I not said that the 'lords' in London…", Kunc, p.171.

p. 238	'Molotov asks you not to insist on the dismissal of the Subcarpathian Ukrainian volunteers…', Táborský, p.184.
p. 239	'Enrolment of our citizens into the Red Army must be stopped at once…', Táborský, p.184.

THE MISSION:

The extensive quotations and excerpts concerning Operation Foursquare are all from Public Records Office file 4/46.

pp. 245-246	The description of the Gestapo attempt to capture Antonín Bartoš is taken from the operation report for CLAY in Public Records Office file 4/52.
pp. 260-262	Details of the dropping of PLATINUM taken from the operation report for it in Public Records Office file 4/52.
p. 271	FOURSQUARE is reported as being 'finally cancelled' in a cipher message to London on 11th May 1945, in Public Records Office file 4/46. This decision is subsequently documented in Reichl, Military records in the Czech military archive and in a personal copy of Jaroslav Bublík 's mission report, held by the author.
p. 272	"Calling all allied armies…", Dickerson p.128.
p. 272	The rapturous reception of the US 16th Armoured Division entering Pilsen on the 6th of May is described in Dickersen pp.104-105.
pp. 272-273	The Pilsen uprising is described is detail in Dickerson pp. 97-99.

pp. 270   Details of General Dwight D Eisenhower's decision to send the US Third Army into Czechoslovakia are covered in Dickerson p. 86 and extensively in Ullman pp.7-16.

p. 272   "This is Pilsen, the free Pilsen calling…", Dickerson p. 106.

p. 273   General Antonov's expectation that US forces hold back from Prague is detailed in Dickerson p. 133.

p. 274   'Feel most strongly in view of continued fighting in the area that should continue…", Public Records Office file 4/46, 'Top secret memo for Punch', dated 7th May 1945.

p. 274   Details of Beneš arrival in Prague on May 16th amid rapturous appreciation and celebration are provided in Mamatey p. 392.

p. 277-278   Let us remember their exemplary and successful effort…", from Václav Modrák's account 'Radio Contact', White, Part 3, pp. 145-6.

THE COUP:

p. 288   Disagreements over the trial of war criminals are described in Luza, p. 335 and Mamatey, p. 421

pp. 288-290   The story of Čestmír Šikola's encounter with Čurda and Gerik is based on the account given in Šikola pp. 81-6

p. 290   The picture of Gerik and Curda referred to is shown in Čvančara, p 121.

p. 291	The picture of Gerik referred to is shown in Čvančara, p 121.
p. 292	The execution of Karl Herman Frank was filmed and the video is freely available from various internet sources.
p. 292	The description of the physical and mental state of Karel Svoboda, when found after the war is taken from the operation report for WOLFRAM in Public Records Office file 4/52.
p. 297	Hubert Ripka's visit to Beneš at the time of the resignation of the pro-democracy ministers and the assurances he felt he received are described in Ripka. p. 257-8
p. 299	An account of Jan Masaryk's actions as the Foreign Ministry was taken over is provided in Ullman p.162
pp. 301	"One felt the impression, at once sorrowful and painful..." Ripka, p. 302.
pp. 302-303	The story of František Moravec's journey into exile is told in Moravec, pp. 239-40.
p. 303-304	"For a long time I believed that...", Táborský, p. 240
p. 308	Václav Modrák's dismissal from the army in 1950 in described in his summary biography in White, Part 3, p. 326. The others accounts of reprisals are from Popisil and Burian.

FOURSQUARE:

p. 313   'make the Russians negotiate in equal terms.', Ullman p.13

pp. 313-314   Evidence of the OSS landing in Banská Bystrica are dropping supplies in September 1944 is in William J Millers account 'Unforgettable days of the Slovak National Uprising' in White, Part 3, pp. 207-218.

p. 315   Pavel Hromek's claim that he used the wrong signalling ciphers by mistake is mentioned in the summing up in the operation report for BAUXITE in Public Records Office file 4/52.

p. 316   The quotation regarding Chrome is a translated excerpt from a Czech language newspaper, provided to the author by Jiří Louda in 2005. The newspaper name and date are not contained on the clipping. The photograph of FOURSQUARE is from the same newspaper. It is assumed that it was published in Bohemia circa 2004. The author is keen to know where it came from as part of continuing research and understand more about its provenance.

p. 317   'We consider leader Foursquare very reliable' is from Public Records office file HS 4/46, memo no 1986, 23rd April 1945.

p. 319   The note from OSS indicating that FOURSQUARE would stay with US forces after mission cancellation is from Public Records office file HS 4/46, memo no F$, serial number 285, May 4, 1945.

p. 320   The proposed exchange between 'Zeman' and 'Tauber' beginning "Do you have Bohemian Kolaches?"…is described in Public Records office file HS 4/46, in a note from Captain Panter numbered M3/133, dated April 23, 1945.

p. 321   Majewski's offer of surrender to the US Army is described in Dickerson p. 95.

p. 323   Details of the US 16th Armoured Division's approach to the Škoda works are provided in Dickerson p.103.

p. 323   The account of Majewski's suicide is from Dickerson, p.115.

p. 323   'buoyant and full of resolve…' Luza, p. 228.

p. 323   An account of how the US military was awaiting a formal request to enter Prague from the Czech National Council is provided in Ullman pp.13-14.

p. 324   Reference to the sending of a small number of OSS troops to Prague is in Dickerson p. 129.

p. 325   Calling all allied armies...", Dickerson, p. 128.

p. 325   "The Americans listened impassively to the anguished messages as two thousand Czechs were slaughtered," Luza p.229.

p. 326   "Our chaps in particular did very well…" is from Colonel Perkins letter to Colonel Boughey

<table>
<tr><td></td><td>(undated) in the Public Records Office file HS 4/51.</td></tr>
<tr><td>p. 327</td><td>"…have received vague message…" is from Public Records Office file HS 4/46 cipher message M3/5607, dated 11th May 1945.</td></tr>
</table>

EPILOGUE:

<table>
<tr><td>p. 330</td><td>The account of Knotek's return to Czechoslovakia after the war is taken from František Ostrý's account: 'Tragic Postscript to the Operation CHROMIUM' in White, Part 2, pp. 253-9</td></tr>
<tr><td>p. 341</td><td>The investigation into Jan Masaryk's death was conducted by the 'Office for the Documentation and the Investigation of the Crimes of Communism.' According to the report from 2003, police indicated that they suspected Jan Masaryk was murdered either by being thrown or pushed out of his window. No perpetrators have been tracked down in relation to the crime but the report indicated that Russian agents of the NKVD were suspected

(https://www.policie.cz/clanek/the-office-for-the-documentation-and-the-investigation-of-the-crimes-of-communism-police-of-the-czech-republic.aspx).</td></tr>
</table>

As is now inevitable much of the primary information above has been supported and understood with help from a range of internet resources. In particular, a key reference was the website www.lib.cas.cz/parasut which includes a comprehensive set of photographs and military records of all members of Czechoslovak parachute groups in World War II and from where much of the biographical detail of the parachutists in the annex is drawn.